Upward, Not Sunwise

Upward, Not Sunwise

Resonant Rupture in Navajo Neo-Pentecostalism

KIMBERLY JENKINS MARSHALL

UNIVERSITY OF NEBRASKA PRESS
LINCOLN AND LONDON

Portions of chapter 2 originally appeared as "'Navajo Reservation
Camp Meeting a Great Success!': The Advent of Diné Pentecostalism
after 1950," in *Ethnohistory* 62, no. 1 (2015), used by permission of
Duke University Press. Portions of chapter 3 originally appeared as
"Soaking Songs versus 'Medicine Man Chant': Musical Resonance
among Diné Oodláni (Navajo 'Believers')," in *The Spirit of Praise:
Music and Worship in Global Pentecostal-Charismatic Christianity*,
edited by Monique M. Ingalls and Among Yong (University Park PA:
Penn State University Press, 2015). Portions of chapter 5 originally
appeared as "Non-Human Agency and Experiential Faith among Diné
Oodláni ('Navajo Believers')," in *Anthropologica* 57, no. 2 (2015), used
by permission of University of Toronto Press.

Library of Congress Cataloging-in-Publication Data
Names: Marshall, Kimberly Jenkins, 1978– author.
Title: Upward, not sunwise: resonant rupture in Navajo
neo-pentecostalism / Kimberly Jenkins Marshall.
Description: Lincoln: University of Nebraska Press, 2016.
Includes bibliographical references and index.
Identifiers: LCCN 2015047851
ISBN 9780803269767 (cloth: alk. paper)
ISBN 9780803288881 (pbk.: alk. paper)
ISBN 9780803294950 (pdf)
Subjects: LCSH: Navajo Indians—Religion.
Pentecostalism—United States.
Classification: LCC E99.N3 M388 2016
DDC 299.7/826—dc23 LC record available
at https://lccn.loc.gov/2015047851

Set in Lyon Text by Rachel Gould.

CONTENTS

ILLUSTRATIONS

ACKNOWLEDGMENTS

There are many people to thank for their assistance in creating this book. First and foremost, I owe a great deal of gratitude to Pastor Wallace Begay and the members of his church community, who consistently welcomed me graciously and patiently shared their thoughts on matters of great personal importance. In particular, I thank Beverly Joe, Eugene Joe, Pastor Alice Norton, Pastor Fred Smith, Elaine Joe, Michelle Joe, Laura Etcitty, Lydell Rafael, Barbara Jack Joe, Grandma Alice Joe, Betty Wagner, Grandma Rosie Lewis, Rita Naargo, and Jimmy Waters. For their openness and for the hugs, handshakes, and smiles I still receive every time I return, I feel quite honestly blessed. Of course, unparalleled thanks go to Pastor Wallace. I am very grateful for the time he took out of his busy schedule, over numerous lunches, phone calls, and cups of coffee to explain to me important aspects of Oodlání history, theology, music, and daily life. *Ahéhee' shi-Pastor.*

I also appreciate the support I received from other members of the Navajo Nation, especially the research assistance of Larry King and the language instruction of Dr. Wesley Thomas, Alice Wagner, and Lorraine Begay Manave. Manave, in particular, has been a constant source of guidance throughout this project, including providing instruction on Navajo orthography (although any errors in spelling are, of course, my own). Finally, I wish to acknowledge the Navajo Nation for allowing me to conduct this work. I have a deep respect for the Navajo mandate to oversee the research conducted within its borders and am particularly grateful to Ronald P. Maldonado and Tamara Billie of the Navajo Nation Office of Historic Preservation for guiding me through the acquisition of proper permissions and reporting.

In conducting this research, I have been very fortunate to have been the beneficiary of financial support. Preliminary research during the summers of 2006 and 2007 was funded through the support of the Jacobs Fund of the Whatcom Museum Society and the David C. Skomp Fund of the Department of Anthropology at Indiana University. Special research funds for supplementary research in Phoenix, Arizona, were provided by a Grant-in-Aid of Doctoral Research by the Graduate School of Indiana University. Primary financial support for this research, however, was provided by a generous grant from the Dolores Zohrab Liebmann Fund.

At the University of Oklahoma (OU), this work was supported by Junior Faculty Fellowships from the College of Arts and Sciences in 2012 and 2014 and by a Junior Faculty Fellowship from the OU Research Council in 2013. Preparation of this manuscript was covered by a Faculty Assistance Program Grant funded by the Department of Anthropology, the OU College of Arts and Sciences, the OU Research Council, and the OU Office of the Provost.

Just as my research would not have been viable without generous financial support, it would not have been intellectually possible without the generous academic support I have received from teachers and colleagues. At Indiana University, I am indebted to Professors Richard Bauman, Daniel Reed, Beverly Stoeltje, and Wesley Thomas, and I am grateful for the calm and confident guidance of Anya Royce and Ruth Stone. Jason Jackson, in particular, has inspired me as a teacher and scholar and has shown me dedicated and unwavering support that I truly appreciate.

At the University of Oklahoma, I am grateful to work in a department and for a college that both stood behind me fully and nurtured my success. In particular, I am indebted to Daniel Swan, who remembered to ask me, "But what have you been *writing* recently?" Thank you to all of my students, but particular thanks go to Susanna Pyatt, Miriam Laytner, and Justin Lund. This work would not have been possible without the logistical support of OU's excellent writing center. Thanks to my writing coach Doc Hudson for getting me through a rough patch. And for reasons both writing-related and not, I owe a huge debt of gratitude to my wonderful WRKD faculty writing group: Dan Emery,

Lisa Foster, Sarah Ellis, Ellen Rubenstein, Ronnie Grinberg, and Andreana Pritchard. In particular, the steadfast and patient support of Erika Robb Larkins has kept me writing.

Thank you to Charlotte Frisbie, who has been overwhelmingly supportive of my work from my very first contact with her, wherein she promptly invited me to come and spend the weekend at her farm. Thanks also go to my "committee-for-life" member Virginia Gorlinski.

At the University of Nebraska Press, I am particularly grateful to Matthew Bokovoy, Joeth Zucco, and Sally Antrobus. Thank you to the anonymous reviewers for their constructive criticism and helpful insights. All of the book's shortcomings are, of course, my own.

I acknowledge the Penn State University Press, the University of Toronto Press, and Duke University Press for allowing the reproduction of short experts of previously published articles and book chapters that appear in the following manuscript.

Finally, I owe enormous thanks to all of my friends and family for their support during this long process. Thank you to Sarah Cluff, Ellen Salter-Pedersen, Lauren Miller-Griffith, Zohra Ismail-Beben, Evelyn Dean-Olmstead, Heidi Bludau, Angela Scharfenberger, Deborah Justice, Elise Anderson, and especially Rebekah Moore. You know why. Thanks to the Knee High families, and to Carol Jacob, Kate Vincent, and Noah Boone. Thanks to Rev. Marci Auld Glass. A special thank you to Cathy and Mark Bingham, Trisha and Gary Bean, and Jen and Brian Hunt. I love you all. My husband, Chris, has accompanied me to many places he would rather not have gone, providing the calm and safe resting place that I often needed. I am thankful for his unyielding support and encouragement. I am especially grateful to him for making it possible for me to be both a mother and a scholar. My sons, Jesse and Spencer, have spent their young lives in the shadow of this project, whether or not they realized it. Just the other day Jesse, six, asked me with surprise, "You're writing a book?" My parents and sister have been consistently supportive of my studies, over the course of the past decade, in more ways than I can even begin to enumerate. It is from them that I first learned to have joy in music, curiosity about the world, and wonder at the divine. For their confidence in me, I am forever grateful.

...

Proceeds from the sale of this book will be donated to the Navajo Nation Museum.

NOTE ON TRANSCRIPTIONS

In general, verbatim transcriptions have been presented in this book as block text. Place holders ("like" or "you know") have occasionally been deleted in order to support clarity of speaker intention. Ellipses are used to indicate the omission of a portion of the transcription without altering the meaning.

Occasionally I felt that the intention of the speaker was better communicated in an ethnopoetic setting of the text. Following Hymes 1981 and Tedlock 1983, this approach attempts to set text using lines, verses, and stanzas in such a way as to capture some of the beautiful artistry that constitutes much of the Navajo neo-Pentecostal verbal and musical repertoire.

In particular, I have used this approach in transcribing public oratory, such as the sermons of Pastor Wallace Begay (see chapter 4). These lines of public oratory are set in such a way as to highlight the underlying parallelism often present in these texts. I have also used an ethnopoetic setting to highlight parallelism when recounting private conversations from a few individual interviews (see chapter 2).

I also closely analyze a few carefully chosen texts. The first text consists of the lyrics and translation of the Navajo-language song *Háálá Ayóo Diyin* (table 1, chapter 3). Since this song was composed in Western verse-chorus form, I have set the transcription this way and used standard Navajo orthography to represent the original Navajo text.

The other main text discussed is a sermon by Pastor Wallace on the dangers of country music (table 2, chapter 4). In this text I have adopted certain ethnopoetic conventions for clarity and emphasis. Sentences are broken at distinguishable pauses and are grouped into numbered paragraphs by topic. Navajo-language text is presented in italics, and the English translation is notated by braces, thus { }. For this text I adopted a two-column system to present side by side the mixed Navajo/English text as it was delivered and a fully English translation, so that the translation can be read directly along with the original. This method of transcription allows for ease of comprehension for those with no knowledge of Navajo while preserving the original text for those interested in neo-Pentecostal use of Navajo code-switching. In order to capture some of the sense of the performative moment, I use square brackets to indicate stage directions (e.g., [mimes drinking it]) as well as to indicate how something was delivered (e.g., [mimicking, high voice]). I also use angle brackets to indicate audience responses (e.g., <shouts of approval>). Finally, I have attempted to reflect some of the verbal artistry of Pastor Wallace in this transcription by using a line-ending dash (—) to indicate a strident vocal cadence he adopted for emphasis at the end of each indicated line in this sermon.

Through these techniques I hope I have succeeded in conveying some sense of the beautiful ethnopoetics of Navajo neo-Pentecostal expressive culture.

Skinwalker Stories

In the gathering dark of the small church kitchen, and while the raucous praise music of the tent revival thumps away outside, Ma Beverly tells me about the night that she was attacked by a skinwalker. "I was sleeping in my living room," she says, "and I saw a figure come to our screen door. I saw all the makeup that he was wearing . . . painted all the way down to his toes. I saw what he had put on. And it was going to do away with me."

Skinwalkers are terrifying apparitions, nefarious Navajo shapechangers who can curse and harm those who cross them. The stories tell about individuals who, through practicing unspeakable deeds on their loved ones and the dead, gain the power to take on animal form and travel at lightning speed across the dark desert. Even hearing stories about skinwalkers can invoke irrational fear, which we both felt. "What did you do?" I ask Ma Beverly breathlessly.

"Well, I got up," she says. "I kind of yelled out, 'Hey' . . . I couldn't even speak, you know. I was so shocked." She pauses. "And then I called my son, Wallace. And then right there he said, 'Let's pray!' He started praying for me . . . prayed over me with Psalms 91.

"And as he started saying the verse, I felt something just peeling off of me." She motions pulling something like spider webs off her arms. "And I saw something coming off of me, and it was like a little bug . . . little bug like a beetle. It ran down from me and then it went down to the ground. I saw it. It had rough skin . . . like a horned toad. I saw that little bug that this person would have used to attack me. When Wallace prayed it just ran down, and into the ground."

"Why did he attack you?" I ask.

"Because I turned away from . . . the religion."

"The Traditional Way?"

"Yes."

Beverly Joe is Navajo and part of an influential and growing religious movement of neo-Pentecostalism among Native Americans. Among Navajos (*Diné*), this movement is known as the *Oodlání* (believers) movement.[1] It is characterized by Navajo control, evangelical Christian theology, and charismatic (spirit-filled) worship. The *Oodlání* movement has been growing exponentially on the Navajo Nation over the past six decades, now claiming the allegiance of up to 60,000 Navajos—around 20 percent of the Navajo population.[2] In the summer months, the tent revivals of the neo-Pentecostal Oodlání movement have become ubiquitous across the Navajo Nation, located in the high desert Southwest of Arizona and New Mexico. Ma Beverly's son, Wallace Begay, pastors one of the many small, independently operating, and Navajo-run Oodlání churches. Pastor Wallace has no degree or formal ordination from any outside organization. His authority is based on nothing but the strength of his "anointing" in the Holy Spirit. Like other Oodlání pastors, he preaches and leads worship in the Navajo language to a congregation that includes his own extended family, and like his mother, he has "turned away from" Navajo traditionalism.

Turning away from traditionalism is fundamental to Oodlání neo-Pentecostalism. Just like pastors in the growing neo-Pentecostal movement in Africa, Latin America, and East Asia, Oodlání preach the biblical literalism of evangelical Christianity and practice the spiritual gifts of the Pentecostal revival: speaking in tongues, dancing in the spirit, and faith healing. Those who convert become "born again"; that is, they leave behind them a "life of sin" and enter into a new state as a "child of God." Traditional religion is reinterpreted as flirtation with dangerous and inherently negative powers. Oodlání refuse to participate in the healing ceremonials of their relatives.

Given the rupture that Ma Beverly and Pastor Wallace have established with Navajo traditionalism, Ma Beverly's skinwalker tale may seem like a paradox. Some have argued that the persistence of beliefs about skinwalkers and witches among Navajo converts is evidence that the conversions are "soft": that Navajos cannot really be Christian if they continue to believe in skinwalkers. If they believe in skinwalkers, they must surely return to traditional practices in times of crisis. If they believe in skinwalkers, then surely their Christian life is a thin (and perhaps syncretic) veneer over a deeper continuity with timeless Navajo culture.[3]

In this book I use ethnographic data from field research with Oodlání believers to complicate the idea that their conversions are soft or inauthentic. If conversion is understood as the remaking of reality structures, the way Ma Beverly understands reality is fundamentally different from the religious worlds of her ancestors.[4] Ma Beverly believes in skinwalkers and believes she was attacked by one. But she says she is not afraid of them anymore because she believes that her attacker was thwarted by the Christian God's superior protecting power under which she lives. In fact, the man she believes tried to witch her had a heart attack and ended up in the hospital. "God's power," she said, "overpowered his powers . . . and to this day he doesn't go against Christians again."[5] Regardless of the trappings of cultural continuity that remain, Oodlání faith is fundamentally not based upon continuity but upon rupture.

The tension between continuity and rupture, inherent in globalizing religions, is the central topic of this book. In some senses, Native American adoption of Christianity has always involved some degree of cultural rupture. Indeed, forcible or coerced Christian conversion was one of the primary tools of the assimilative policies that typified U.S. relations with Native people for more than two centuries. Agents of Christianity (both churches and missionaries) have been intimately involved with the political, economic, religious, and social aspects of what has amounted to a sustained effort toward Native American cultural genocide.[6] In the American Southwest, Christian agents have participated in assimilative programs by colluding with the colonial slave trade, utilizing forced labor in missions, and dispossessing Native people of land—disrupting communities in service of a Euro-American individualistic agricultural ideal.[7]

Christian collusion in Native American cultural genocide gained its most toxic form in the Christian-run boarding schools that commonly operated across the United States and Canada in the nineteenth and twentieth centuries. In these boarding schools, modeled on the Carlisle Indian Industrial School of General Richard Pratt, Native children were separated from their families, forced to have their hair cut and to dress like Euro-American children, kept on a military schedule, and punished for speaking their own languages.[8] These children were taught not only reading and writing but also industrial or domestic skills.[9] Their presence was required at weekly chapel services and Bible studies. Christian-run boarding schools on the Navajo Nation operated until the 1950s without secular alternatives and were instrumental in promoting alienation from ancestral teachings and language, a disjunction that in turn provoked the contemporary economic and social challenges characterizing life on the Navajo Reservation.[10]

However, to focus too completely on this important history of violence against Native people would miss the very real agency some Native Americans have exercised through the medium of the Christian faith. By focusing on the ways that Christianity has been *practiced* by Native Christians, we can begin to see the ways in which Native Christians (both past and present) have used Christianity as a tool to assert and maintain cultural stability. Rather than taking the perspectives of the missionaries (typically the authors of archival accounts) at face value, historians and ethnographers alike have been attending to Native perspectives on the mission encounter, with the aim of discovering "what native people *made of* the Christian tradition" (McNally 2000b, 835). These accounts tend to emphasize how Native people have used Christian forms such as hymn singing (McElwain 1990; McNally 2000a; Lassiter et al. 2002), funerary practices (Kan 1999), interactional symbols (Schultz 1999), and language (Kidwell 1997; Nevins 2010) to preserve long-held values, community identities, languages, and kinship structures.[11] The figure of the native pastor has been of particular interest to recent historians (Lewis 2003; Tarango 2014), as a way of examining how Native control of Christian churches allowed for an emphasis on aspects of the Christian message that empowered Native cultures, languages, and epistemologies. And Andrea Smith's book about Native Americans and the Christian Right (2008) argues that contemporary Natives have used adaptable strategies of rearticulation to forge alliances with diverse Christian actors in order to advance Native causes such as sovereignty.

Without overlooking the hegemonic structures that limited the free choice of individual Natives, these studies have used the many voices of actual Native Christians (past and present) to highlight the development of a Native American theology (Kidwell et al. 2001).[12] This theology, based in Native worldviews and lifeways, tends to preserve an "ethos of religious relativism" (McNally 2000b, 847) that sees different approaches to the sacred as equally valid. Sometimes called an "all roads are good" model of ecumenicalism, relativism in situations of Native control promotes a sense of fluidity between religious traditions (particularly as they are performed, rather than confessed). An "all roads are good" approach assumes that all religious paths are based upon "the experiences of worthy elders and ancestors" and "all derive ultimately from the power of the Creator" (Jackson 2004, 192).[13] What all this emphasis on Native agency assumes is that when Natives are in control, the vitriolic condemnation of the old ways that characterized the colonial approach to missionization will be toned down or even replaced with ecumenical respect.[14]

The recent wave of neo-Pentecostalism among Native Americans, however, complicates an equation that draws simple parallels between outsiders (promoting rupture) and insiders (promoting continuity). The Oodláni movement is a stark example of this complexity. Although Oodláni churches are (by definition) Navajo-led, Oodláni pastors do not "tone down" their opposition to traditional spirituality. In fact, they take the spiritual reality of traditionalist cosmology so seriously that their opposition goes beyond the modernist dismissal of rational Protestantism into all-out spiritual warfare. In contrast to Anglo missionaries who taught assimilation in boarding school and dismissed traditional lifeways as "superstitious nonsense," Oodláni believe quite literally in the power of the traditional ways. They believe in skinwalkers. Or, as Ma Beverly put it, "The word that they do is real too." However, instead of mapping continuity with these powers, Oodláni turn this cultural continuity on its head.[15]

Which brings us back to the questions raised by Ma Beverly's skinwalker story. In telling a skinwalker story, Ma Beverly was practicing a kind of cultural continuity: she believes she was visited by a skinwalker, and she talks about it in a traditionally recognizable way. She believes skinwalkers exist. But she believes that they get their power (to change shape, to speed across the desert night, to curse those who cross them) from the Devil, a figure entirely foreign to traditional Navajo cosmology. Can this really be viewed as cultural continuity?

Against Culture?

The ability of Pentecostalism to work simultaneously with and against local cultures as it globalizes has been described by Joel Robbins as one of the "paradoxes" of its vigorous spread (Robbins 2003b). The complicated nexus of continuity and rupture has emerged as one of the central themes in the growing field of the anthropology of Christianity (Lampe 2010). Formulating a theoretical framework that respects both the observable cultural continuities (Amster 2009; Chua 2012) and the rupture that converts intend (Meyer 1998; Engelke 2010) has become a central concern of this growing subfield, particularly when discussing global Pentecostalism.

Some scholars, for example, tend to emphasize the ways in which neo-Pentecostal converts emphasize rupture with traditional culture (Corten 1997; Daswani 2013). In Native North America, Kirk Dombrowski has been the strongest voice for this perspective, arguing that Tlingit and Haida converts actually constitute themselves "against culture" (2001). He explains ambivalence toward traditional ways as a reaction to the continuing colonialism expressed in the unfair and unequal distribution of resources legislated by the Alaska Native Claims Settlement Act of 1971 (Dombrowski 2001, 181). He argues that Pentecostalism is appealing to marginal community members precisely because of their marginality. Thus, argues Dombrowski, the appeal of joining the Pentecostal movement for those not benefiting in traditional cultural participation is in the way Pentecostal theology positions itself above culture. Pentecostals adopt a worldview in which, according to Dombrowski, "being Native American has no significance" (Dombrowski 2001, 15). Anyone, no matter culture or past, has the same opportunity to "become saved," so marginality or affluence is irrelevant. Dombrowski states, "This dramatic denial of Culture per se—not just particular cultures—has special appeal to people whose particular culture has become an unbearable, unavoidable, undifferentiable burden" (Dombrowski 2001, 15).

In contrast, other scholars have questioned the totality of this abandonment, particularly since Pentecostal churches (especially neo-Pentecostal churches) are usually run entirely by indigenous actors. Rather than replicating a Western form of colonization, these scholars argue, the indigenous control of neo-Pentecostalism makes it eminently adaptable to the local culture. It thus represents a sort of indigenous appropriation that is about continuity and empowerment (Bastian 1993; Kiernan 1994; DiBernardi 1999; Manning 1980; Smith 2008). In Native North America scholars have emphasized the continuity of indigenously controlled neo-Pentecostal churches, viewing Pentecostal converts as continuing to value their traditional culture. This cultural continuity is expressed by regarding the natural world through a shamanic lens (Laugrand and Oosten 2009), or through the continued use of traditional sacred speech idioms in Independent Christian contexts (Nevins 2010). Continuity is also expressed, as highlighted by Clinton Westman, in the ways that Northern Cree Pentecostal converts promote traditional subsistence patterns and collectively organize (as Native Christians) for continued land use and subsistence hunting rights (Westman 2010a). He astutely asks, "Can a Cree-led congregation, meeting in Cree, in which elders counsel and heal their kinfolk, in which membership supports maintenance of ties between kinfolk and hunting partners, be 'against' Cree culture?" (Westman 2010b, 7).

Among Navajos the tension between the cultural continuity and cultural rupture of Navajo Christian converts has been a longstanding debate as well. Most scholars, understandably invested in demonstrating the continuity of Navajo culture over time, have pointed out the many ways in which Christianity is incorporated by converts to access new modes of wealth or supernatural power but in very Navajo ways (Blanchard 1977; Shepardson 1982; Aberle 1982 and 1991).[16] In Gladys Reichard's 1949 study of Navajo Christianity, she relates that a missionary "astounded" her by observing that "he did not know a single Navajo who 'truly understands Christianity'"(66). And as William Hodge summarized in his 1969 study of Navajo Pentecostalism, "I seriously doubt that these people had a comprehensive understanding of either conventional Christianity or Pentecostalism. Or, it may be that an understanding was there, but was rejected, and only those elements which could be fitted into a traditional conceptual framework were accepted" (89). These quotes highlight the degree to which scholars have remained skeptical that any real rupture accompanied Navajo participation in Christianity.[17]

On the other hand, this argument for underlying continuity is complicated by other authors who observe the contemporary conflicts between Navajo Pentecostals and Diné traditionalists. In her survey of the contemporary Navajo religious landscape, Charlotte J. Frisbie makes it quite clear that Navajo-led, independently operating "evangelical Protestants" (the group I have identified as Oodláni) presently pose "the strongest challenge to the future of traditional religion" because of their belief that "traditional religion and its paraphernalia are the work of the Devil and thus, are in need of active destruction" (Frisbie 1992, 492). Other current ethnographic work among Navajos supports the "disruptive" presence of this religious movement, particularly in projects of language and cultural revitalization based in traditional Diné philosophies (see, for example, House 2002, 74).

I aim to clarify the complicated nexus of continuity and rupture on the Navajo religious landscape through the introduction of a new theoretical framework to explain the appeal of neo-Pentecostal conversion: resonant rupture. Drawing on a careful consideration of the complexities of cultural identification practiced by one particular Navajo-led neo-Pentecostal congregation in northwest New Mexico, I encourage looking beyond theologies and doctrines to see how continuity and rupture are navigated by Oodláni in performance. Resonant rupture respects the dramatic change wrapped into the Pauline model of born-again conversion (Robbins 2010), but it also explains the exponential growth of neo-Pentecostalism (above and beyond other forms of Christianity) through the way that neo-Pentecostalism can capitalize on the portable ambiguity of expressive forms.

Expressive Forms

There is a grand circular staircase at the entrance to the new humanities wing of San Juan College in Farmington, New Mexico, a town near the border of the Navajo Nation. One day I entered the building with a Navajo friend who was a professor there. I ascended the staircase, only to realize that she was no longer beside me. Without thinking about it, she had headed left up the stairs and I had headed right. When I caught up with her she teased me. "You know Diné go sunwise, right?"[18]

The cardinal directions—east, south, west, and north—orient Diné life. These four directions (sometimes with the addition of zenith and nadir) are symbolically linked to Navajo mythology, philosophy, pedagogy, and ceremonial practice. According to Diné educator Wilson Aronilth, "Our prayers, songs and values are interwoven with the four directions" (Aronilth 1994, 96). The Spirit of Dawn resides in the east, encouraging *Nitsáhákees*—the discipline of thinking and mental strength. Blue Twilight Spirit resides in the south, encouraging *Nahatá*—the discipline of learning and planning. Yellow Evening Spirit resides in the west, encouraging *Iiná*—the discipline of social growth and identity for life. And Folding Darkness Spirit resides in the north, encouraging *Siihasin*—the discipline of awareness and reflection (Aronilth 1994, 96). This symbolism of the four directions anchors Diné homes through the four *hogan* (house) pillars (Aronilth 1994, 107). It also anchors Diné in their homeland, through the spiritual geography of the four sacred mountains: *Sisnaajiní* (Blanca Peak) in the east, *Tsoodził* (Mount Taylor) in the

MAP 1. Navajo Nation. Erin Greb Cartography.

south, *Dook'o'oosłííd* (San Francisco Peaks) in the west, and *Dibé Nitsaa* (Hesperus Mountain) in the north (Iverson 2002, 8–11). *"This is how they were placed for us,"* says Navajo poet Luci Tapahonso (1997, 39).

The cardinal directions orient not just Navajo geography but philosophy and spirituality as well. Sometimes called the *T'áá shá bik'ehgo na'nitin,* or sunwise path teachings, this movement through the four parts of the day (starting with dawn), through the four seasons (starting with spring), and through human life (from birth to old age) is seen a life principle, established by the Holy People, and guiding Diné people (Werito 2014, 27–28). It is a symbolic conceptualization of the "main stalk" of Diné philosophy, *Sa'ąh Naagháí Bik'eh Hózhǫǫn* (Farella 1984; Aronilth 1994, 96). Even contemporary Diné Philosophy of Learning (DPL), which is core to the curriculum at Diné College, is structured around this directional progression: *nitsáhákees* (thinking), *nahat'á* (planning), *iiná* (living), and *siihasin* (assuring).[19]

The Diné cardinal direction orientation is more than philosophy and ceremony. This "sunwise" path is part of the everyday aesthetics of generations of Diné. Cardinal directions guide the placement of homes, movement of people around space, and even the aesthetics of everyday objects, such as the tying of knots (Reichard 1963, 165–66) or how one ascends a staircase. Circular movement from east to north is a fundamental aesthetic orientation for Diné, operating at a subconscious level of "felt" rightness or, when violated, wrongness.

The felt attachment to aesthetic form is key to understanding how culture, all culture, continues through generations. The smell of grandma's fresh-baked cookies adds a meaningful quality to the practice that we replicate even when store-bought cookies are much more convenient. We sing the lullabies of our mothers to our own babies, in part because of the emotional connections they contain. Feelingful connections to aesthetic forms are those that rely on our nonliteral minds: our sensations, feelings, and emotional associations.[20]

In part, the feelingful connections we make between cultural practices and emotions lie in a layered history of experiencing them together. And when new cultural practices become tied to broader experience, they can come to be felt as an authentic part of collective identity. According to David Samuels (2004), feelingful connections allow us to understand culture as the dynamic product of cultural actors rather than the scripted and fixed repetition of "tradition." Samuels argues that anthropologists and others tend to favor a "transparent" type of indexicality: the idea that Apacheness is made up of distinctly Apache language, foodways, and dress. The celebration of these forms, then, becomes linked to ideas about authentic Apache identity. He argues, however, that non-Native forms (such as basketball or country music) can also be seen as "sites for the play of deeply felt expressions of Apache identity" because of their long association with the social history of the community (Samuels 2004, 7). Samuels argues that identity is often tied to perceived or *felt* indexicality, related to history: "This layering of people, places, events, and music is the thickening of experience, the knowledge of what it means and how it feels to be from San Carlos" (Samuels 2004, 39). So basketball and country music are felt to be authentically "Apache" cultural practices, not because they are unique to that culture but because their historical expression in local contexts has invested them with a *feelingful* connection to local identity.

Feelingful connections can be hard to pinpoint and examine since they are often subconscious and intuitive, but they are fundamental to the collective systems of valuation that we call aesthetics. Aesthetics are collective notions of quality based on feelingful (rather than rational) criteria. As Boas noted nearly a century ago, the "emotional attachment to customary forms" helps to explain why aesthetic forms tend to be stable over time (Boas 1955, 149).[21]

But the feelingful attachment to form does more than explain the tendency of artistic expressions to remain stable. This emotional attachment also helps to explain the general stability of cultures, a connection that was not lost on Boas. "The mind" he says, "becomes so thoroughly adjusted . . . to certain types of association between sense impressions and definite activities, that a resistance to change appears as the most natural mental attitude; if for no other reason, because it requires the effort of unlearning and relearning" (Boas 1955, 148-49). This does not mean that cultures cannot or do not change, only that individuals tend to be more comfortable with the familiar; whether in art, language, tools, or culture more broadly.

The connection between emotional attachment to form and cultural stability is particularly relevant given the current anthropological conviction that cultures do not reproduce themselves but are the collective accumulation of millions of tiny decisions made by millions of acting and choosing individuals over time.[22] Aesthetics are an important factor in this configuration of culture, because they are the emotionally laden learned values that guide a feeling of "rightness" in what one does (Handelman 2007, 197), inform a sense of being "at home" in the body (Sheets-

Johnstone 2000, 360–61), and provide the groundwork for the cultural "common sense" of innumerable everyday actions: even the making of bread, the arranging of flowers, and the way we walk (Royce 2011).[23]

One of the ways that anthropologists have studied aesthetic systems is through bounded performance events. From Milton Singer's Indian temple festivals (1972) to Clifford Geertz's Balinese cockfights (1973), cultural practices that are overtly artistic offer "a view of the world in which our ordinary understanding of who and why we are is brought to a heightened consciousness" (Royce 2004, 1). That is why I focus on Oodlání tent revivals as a space of "heightened" performances (Bauman 1975). Because they gather people together in a lit space in the desert night to sing praise songs, hear preaching, get healed, and dance in the spirit, tent revivals are events that reveal important Oodlání cultural values.

But aesthetic forms do more than reflect cultural values. They also serve as important sites of cultural contestation and change. Expressive culture carries with it a certain level of ambiguity that allows for the play of multiple meanings. This is what Samuels calls the "punning" quality of artistic culture, and is why, he says, expressive culture is able to operate simultaneously as a system of cultural continuity and change (Samuels 2004, 13). Using "intertextual" resources, performers can quote, parody, play with, or invert preexisting aesthetic forms in the creation of something new (Bauman 2004; Nevins 2010). Because expressive forms are based in practice, individual performers may use them as a way of gaining control of the social situation and actually enacting social change (Bauman 1975, 305). When Ma Beverly explains the efficacy of skinwalker curses as derived from the power of the Devil, she is actively transcribing the meaning of these curses and denying their continuity. This does not simply change the meaning of aesthetic forms; it actively rejects a prior "false" meaning. This is a type of directed culture change I call rupture, and it is facilitated by the ambiguous, creative, and feelingful nature of expressive forms.

In spite of the importance of expressive forms as sites for the negotiation and construction of collective culture and identity, attention to expressive practice has been largely overlooked in the literature discussing Pentecostal rupture (Meyer 1998; Daswani 2013; Robbins 2007). This book is based on the idea that the ambiguity of expressive forms and the ability of performers to communicate conflicting meanings through them makes expressive forms the ideal foci for understanding how Oodlání reconcile multiple and contested subjectivities. By examining cultural practices with heightened aesthetic values (rituals, poetic language, singing, dancing, healing), we can uncover the ways that affective attachment to artistic forms can provide a type of deeply felt continuity even in the face of dramatic cultural rupture.

Eugene Joe likes to tell stories about his dad, who was a well-known and respected singer (medicine man) before becoming a well-known and respected Oodlání teacher. When I asked Mr. Joe whether Oodlání still valued the cardinal directions, he shared one of these stories with me:

> My dad told me there were six directions, in humanity. It does not go with, you know, the traditional [four directions]. He says, "Man lives up and down. That's his direction. You're gonna go to hell or you're gonna go to heaven. You're gonna go to the right or you wanna go to the left? Or do you want to go forward or you want to go backward?" See, every direction is a symbol, isn't it? For us to understand where we're at. Which direction we're gonna take. My father said, "There's only one direction to God—that's up. Not forward, upward." (E. Joe 2008)

According to Mr. Joe, the meanings attached to the cultural symbols of the cardinal directions have changed for Oodlání. No longer does east symbolize dawn, beginnings, or the residence of Rock Crystal girl and boy at the heart of Blanca Peak. For Mr. Joe, a dedicated Oodlání, those are symbolic attachments created by humans. The real importance of directionality, for Mr. Joe, is the orientation to zenith and nadir: heaven above or hell below. For him, it is the way this orientation toward heaven dictates daily actions and morality that is primary.

So why continue to explain theology in terms of Diné cardinal orientation? Why did Mr. Joe's father pass on this teaching to him, in these cardinal terms, in the first place? The use of continuous expressive practices such as these in Oodláni contexts suggests that feelingful attachment to expressive form persists, but that the inherent ambiguity of these forms allows for the attachment of drastically different meanings. This is a property I call resonant rupture.

Resonant Rupture

In this book I explain how Pentecostal rupture is neither wholly assimilative nor wholly traditional but is a type of rupture enriched by "feelingfully" familiar aesthetic forms. Because of their feelingful connection to the past, these expressive forms (skinwalker stories, cardinal direction symbols) can suggest a type of cultural continuity. But in actuality they operate more like nonhumorous puns.[24] Their apparent similarity actually masks fundamental denial of similarity happening at the level of asserted meaning. Because this is a kind of rupture amplified by cultural relevance, I argue that it represents a type of resonant rupture.

Resonance is an acoustical principle that explains how certain vibrations amplify other vibrations but without assuming identical frequencies. Resonating chambers (such as the hollow body of a guitar or violin) amplify the sound of a plucked or bowed string. The resonant frequencies of a wine glass and the voice of an opera singer are the physical properties that explain the singer's ability to shatter the object. And brass instruments produce sound based upon the alignment between the harmonic overtone series (a mathematical arrangement of related soundwaves) and the vibrations of the column of air inside the horn.[25] When "resonant peaks" are achieved, the instrument produces a clear, well-focused, rich, and amplified sound (A. Myers 1997, 21).[26] Resonance, in this sense, is also a concept used in vernacular English. When students read about a new cultural practice, they may tell me "that article really resonated with me." The sense of something new amplifying something else is key to both the formal and informal concept of resonance.[27]

Because of the flexibility of the concept of resonance to describe things that are fundamentally different, but enhanced when connected, I find it a rich metaphor to explain the type of cultural rupture that is practiced by Oodlání. In contrast to rational Protestantism, which attempted to weed out "superstition" that constrained the free choice necessary for salvation, neo-Pentecostalism takes seriously Native beliefs about the spiritually populated nature of the invisible world, declaring spiritual warfare on the Devil and demons.[28] And in contrast to the rational Protestantism of Anglo Christian missionaries characteristic of the early twentieth century, the neo-Pentecostalism of the Oodlání movement has been adopted by Navajos at exponentially higher rates because of the way it resonates with traditional culture, even in the face of dramatic denial of this continuity.

Resonant rupture is particularly evident in expressive forms, such as those explored in the present work. Because of the feelingful attachment to form (discussed earlier), a certain conservatism of form exists even when materials or meanings change. As Boas observed, when artists break with the past, through innovation or by using new materials, they often retain traditional forms. The more plastic (flexible) the new materials, the better the substitutions work (Boas 1955, 150). The ambiguity of expressive forms makes them a particularly adaptable "material" for breaking with the past while capitalizing on continuity of form. Like a pun, their meaning can point "in multiple directions at once" (Samuels 2004, 8), allowing individual actors to argue for or "assert" (Nevins 2010, 29) a particular interpretation of meaning.[29] Specific "points of resonance" are isolatable expressive forms that carry with them a feelingful tie to the past, but that when examined closely reveal a very obvious change of underlying meanings.[30]

Resonant rupture also explains the growth of neo-Pentecostalism in a way that does not rely simply on materialist explanations for conversion. Without doubt, the material conditions of life on the Navajo Reservation are largely deplorable and a direct consequence of centuries of settler colonialism in which Christianity has taken part. Poverty is ubiquitous: in 2007 the unemployment rate on the Navajo Nation was 50.52 percent, per capita income was $7,121, and more than 36 percent of Navajo people lived below the poverty level (Navajo Nation 2010, 70). Additionally, rates of substance abuse are high, a factor that may have contributed to a 1996–98 suicide rate nearly twice the national average (Navajo Nation 2010, 7). Rates of domestic abuse are high above the national average as well. Tellingly, according to an Indian Health Service 2002–3 report, in the Navajo region more than 10 percent of total yearly Navajo deaths were attributed to "unintentional injuries," the highest reported cause of death among Navajos (Indian Health Service 2003, 54). According to the same report, Navajos die of diabetes at more than twice the national average (2003, 63), die of alcohol at 6.6 times the national average (2003, 62), and die of "Injury and Poisoning" (a category that includes "motor vehicle accidents, other accident, suicide, homicide, injury undetermined whether accidentally or purposely inflicted, and injury resulting from operations of war") at 4.5 times the national average (2003, 56).[31]

These statistics suggest the basic outline of a life that, for many Navajos, has strong overtones of sorrow and crisis. It therefore follows that the primary model by which anthropologists have explained dramatic religious change among indigenous people is by relying on theories of deprivation (Mooney 1896), relative deprivation (Aberle 1991), or more recently on a dramatic change of material and social conditions—positive or negative (Harkin 2004, xxx). However, as Susan Harding has pointed out, the "instrumental" or "materialist" reasons for religious conversion (poverty, alcoholism, violence, conjugal conflict) are at best partial explanations, given that no direct cause-and-effect relationship can be established (Harding 2000, 36). Many Navajos living in identical circumstances seek answers elsewhere: in traditionalism, in Native American nationalism, in the Native American Church, or less positive avenues such as substance abuse. A central driving concern of this book is how and why, given similar material challenges, an increasing number of Navajos choose neo-Pentecostalism over these other options.[32] I argue that much of the appeal of the Oodláni movement, especially in contrast to other forms of Christianity, is found in the resonant rupture of neo-Pentecostalism.

Resonant rupture is a concept that relies upon "taking seriously" member meanings (such as dramatic conversion), and yet also recognizing the way that these meanings have connotations imbued through local historicity (Samuels 2004).[33] Points of resonance are "potent" specifically because of their multivocal nature, incorporating aspects of both continuity and the denial of continuity (that is: rupture). Converts will tell you that what they are doing is different, new, and a deliberate project of change. And it is. But resonant rupture allows converts to enact this change in locally meaningful ways.

Mapping the Book

In this book I develop a framework that complicates previous explanations of conversion as simply colonizing or appropriated. I do so by focusing on the way that the ambiguity of expressive forms allows for an inversion of meaning along feelingfully familiar lines: the principle of resonant rupture. Each chapter's theme provides another perspective on the way that resonant rupture works in multiple types of expressive forms. Taken together, these perspectives illustrate the complexity of the culture change situation. In this, I seek to move anthropological discussions away from a "continuity bias" inherent in the concept of culture (Robbins 2003b). By examining several expressive genres (ritual, language, music, dance, and faith healing), I seek to recognize what is familiar and feelingfully meaningful while simultaneously respecting the "projects of change" at the core of what Oodlání understand themselves to be doing.

Chapter 1 sets the stage for this ethnographic analysis by describing Oodlání tent revivals and the research on them that undergirds this discussion. I begin with an in-depth look at a typical Oodlání tent revival. I then discuss in detail the research I conducted into the tent revival movement, both through the relationships I built with community members and through the ethical challenges this research presented.

Chapter 2 begins the main core of the book with a focus on

ritual. Specifically, I discuss how the ritual gathering of the tent revival appeals to Navajos because of its structural and atmospheric similarity to certain traditional Navajo ceremonial gatherings. However, I also illustrate the discontinuity that these meetings introduce by discussing a different, private ritual: that of rupture. Using an ethnographic reading of historical cases of *jish* (Navajo medicine bundle) burning, I argue that the perseverance of this practice even after it was formally outlawed by the Navajo Nation demonstrates the significant discontinuity that Pentecostal conversion represents for converts.

In chapter 3 I argue for the resonance of Navajo linguistic ideologies, demonstrating the ways that the difficulties in creating a "Navajo Hymnody" (body of newly composed Navajo-language religious music) represents continuity in a "performative" view of language. Through a close examination of the song *Háálá Ayóo Diyin* (the only widely-known Oodlání song with original Navajo lyrics), I argue that the popularity of this song rests in its resonant rupture: its ability to capitalize on feelingful connections to past forms while simultaneously changing the meaning communicated by these forms.

Chapter 4 continues to focus on the significance of musical practice by exploring the way resonant rupture operates in Oodlání attitudes toward country western music. Despite the unparalleled popularity of country music on the Navajo Nation, and the sonic similarity between secular country music and Oodlání praise music, Oodlání regularly regard country music as evil. In this chapter I explore the resonant rupture of the concept of "mixing" to show how country music is equated with the music of traditional Navajo ceremonialism and the power of the Devil. Furthermore, I explore the ways that Oodlání musicians reframe experience gained in the secular music realm within the sacred framework of the *anointing*.

Chapter 5 examines the resonant rupture of spirit-filled dancing. This practice contains a resonant belief in the agency of various nonhuman actors. And yet there is also rupture. I demonstrate that while the concept of nonhuman agency resonates in the Oodlání context, a close look at the technique and ethno-aesthetics of "dancing in the spirit" reveals a fundamental change in the nature of these nonhuman actors as well as the rules for interacting with them.

Finally, chapter 6 explores the resonance of faith healing as a performance-based expressive practice. Healing has significant feelingful connections to traditional Navajo life: it is absolutely central to the traditional Navajo ceremonial complex, in which the primary purpose of ceremonial life is to effect healing through the restoration of balance, or *hózhǫ́*. I show that while Oodlání faith healing is feelingfully connected to traditional Navajo religion, it actually holds a fundamentally different (and fundamentally anti-pluralistic) healing etiology. Oodlání understandings of sickness and healing are actually more closely connected to the practice-based theology of global Pentecostalism, a theology where participation is based upon material effects in the world: believers say they are healed. So while the feelingful connections to health concerns provide the veneer of Navajo cultural continuity, this chapter shows that a close examination of Oodlání faith healing reveals significant rupture as well.

In conclusion, I view the expressive culture of Navajo "believers" at tent revivals as a site for exploring the discursive creation of culture change, as facilitated by the ambiguity of expressive forms. The central examples in each chapter provide concrete illustrations through which we can begin to see how the concept of resonant rupture helps explain a movement that relies for its dramatic success on being at once locally relevant and nonlocal, feelingfully similar and meaningfully different, culturally continuous and culturally disruptive.

CHAPTER 1

The Oodlání Movement
Revivals, Research, and Relationships

Lighted white tents dot the evening landscape of Dinétah, Navajoland, in the summer months like scattered lanterns. Music spills out of them from huge PA systems that can be heard across the sparsely populated high desert for miles around. In Navajo, they say: Nibaal niit'ah (they set up a tent) or Nibaal baa ak'ee si'ą́ (a tent is sitting over there), which means that the Oodlání, the "believers" as they call themselves, have gathered for a tent revival. From the outside, it looks and sounds like other tent gatherings across America filled with the faithful who come together inspired by the Pentecostal or Holiness movements. Standing outside the tent, you can hear the evangelist shouting through the amplified sound system with strident vocal rhythms made famous by TV evangelists like Oral Roberts. Also familiar might be the constant shouts of affirmation "Amen!" and "Praise Jesus!" from the assembled. Even the music sounds generically American. You can imagine yourself entering a giant tabernacle tent in Kentucky, or Ohio, or Texas, and hearing the same energetic singing:

> *Meeting tonight*
> *Meeting tonight*
> *Meeting at the old camp ground*
> *Meeting tonight*
> *Meeting tonight*
> *Meeting at the old camp ground . . . .*

As you enter the tent, however, you notice that everyone is clapping along to the music, but on beats one and three, rather than on beats two and four. You realize that the pastor is not speaking ecstatically in tongues but rather quite earnestly in Navajo. The people gathered inside the tent range from young babies to elderly women, traditionally dressed and with their long hair tied up in a yarn tsiiyééł. And, most strikingly, it is immedi-

ately obvious that nearly all of the 50 or 150 or 750 people gathered under that tent, including the pastors, evangelists, and musicians, are Navajos.

Tent revivals are the beating heart of the neo-Pentecostal Oodlání movement. They provide the ritual frames under which all of the expressive practices explored in this book take place—poetic language, music, dance, faith healing. Navajo tent revivals are related to the camp meetings of the Second Great Awakening of early nineteenth-century America, in which people gathered outdoors to hear a traveling preacher. In the United States, tent revivals have been one of the hallmarks of the Pentecostal or Holiness movements and today often feature charismatic practice like speaking in tongues (glossolalia), faith healing, and other miraculous occurrences (Sims 1988). In the Navajo context they have been an essential mechanism through which the neo-Pentecostal Oodlání movement has spread and the means by which this fundamentally decentralized faith gains unity.

In this chapter I describe Oodlání tent revivals in ethnographic detail, both structurally and narratively. These descriptions are based upon participant observation during three summer revival seasons (2006, 2007, 2008) as well as in-depth study of a few focused revivals (in 2008 and 2012). In total I observed more than 40 individual Oodlání camp meetings, totaling more than 160 cumulative hours. As part of this research I built relationships with Oodlání community members and navigated ethical challenges associated with working with (and writing about) this Navajo community. In the second part of this chapter I acknowledge the way these personal relationships influenced my research and briefly reflect on the ethical hurdles of conducting ethnographic fieldwork with Native American neo-Pentecostals like the Oodlání.

Going to a Tent Revival

On any evening in summer, Oodiání revivals can be found by following hand-painted signs that indicate turn-offs from any of the main highways on the Navajo Nation. Following the arrow

FIG. 1. Oodláni tent revival. Photo courtesy of Eugene B. Joe.

on the sign will take cars down a bumpy dirt road, past scattered houses and livestock, farther and farther from the highway. Sometimes signs with arrows continue to guide drivers to the land of the people or church hosting the camp meeting. As cars draw close, passengers can often see a large white canopy with an assortment of trucks parked around it. (If it is already dark, they may also be guided, as I was on several occasions, by rolling down the car window and following the music.)

The hosting congregation has been preparing the tent revival for days (and often weeks): praying over the ground, painting and assembling the platform, spreading wood chips, putting up the tent, washing and setting up the folding metal chairs, some borrowed from other area pastors. As cars drive closer to the large white tent, often there are youth from the church acting as "parking attendants," directing drivers to a patch of dirt where they will (ideally) not be blocked in by others.

After parking, attendees often walk past a shade arbor stand where women from the church are selling concessions: $1 for a bottle of water or can of soda, $2 for a hot dog, or $1.50 for some fresh, hot Navajo frybread. New arrivals are free to wander around

FIG. 2. Hand-painted revival sign. Photo by author.

the grounds and in and out of the big tent as they please: no admission is charged, and no gatekeepers stand between attendees and the interior of the tent. Navajo tent revivals typically start officially at 7:00 p.m., but very few people will actually be there before 8:00 p.m., and in the summer the energy does not pick up until after dark, at least another hour later.

The only activity happening at 7:00 p.m. under the tent involves friendly chatting and greetings.[1] People slowly trickle in, go around shaking hands, and find seats. As attendees enter the tent, their initial impression may be of the vast amount of space under the tent. This space extends in all directions, including up, to the incredibly high vaulted canvas ceiling. The rapidly cooling, crisp high-desert air circulates freely in this open-air cathedral. And if it is early, attendees really may get the sense of being in a cathedral as the sun lights up the tent and makes the interior glow with diffuse light.

Tents of this size are typically oval and can be set up with the stage or "platform" along the narrow edge of the oval (as in fig. 4) or along the long edge of the oval. Either way, the stage is

FIG. 3. Oodláni tent and concession brush arbor in the early evening. Photo courtesy of Eugene B. Joe.

FIG. 4. Interior of an Oodláni tent during a revival. Photo courtesy of Eugene B. Joe.

large enough to accommodate both musical groups and chairs for several guest pastors. The stage is flanked on each side by a tower of gigantic speakers, easily eight feet high. At the center is the podium behind which the preacher or evangelist will stand. There is at least one drum set and an electric keyboard as well as multiple monitors, microphone stands, and amplifiers. A rug may be laid down to cover all the various power cords and sound cables running from the platform into a small mixing board off to the side of the platform. At the very front of the platform are two sets of stairs or (more commonly) ramps, one on each side, to accommodate the flow of people past the healing evangelist. Directly in front of this may be a small table or tables with anointing oil, tissues, and a basket or bucket used during the service to collect offerings.

As people enter the tent, many make their way to the front, rub anointing oil on their hands, and kneel at the edge of the platform in private (and often tearful) prayer.[2] In this pre-service time the "house" musicians from the hosting church gather, tuning up or playing around on their instruments. Sometimes recorded Christian music is played softly through the public address system.

As attendees turn from the podium, they cross a large open area where the dirt has often been covered with wood chips or straw. This area is completely empty, save for one of the massive tent poles, but later in the evening, when the energy builds, this area will be alive with the energetic dancing of those who have been "filled with the spirit."

Beyond this cleared dancing area are rows and rows of metal folding chairs, reaching almost the entire span of the tent. Chairs are organized in large blocks around a few aisles: typically one down the center and one on either side. If one has arrived early, most of these chairs will be empty, but people will be milling around, greeting visitors or chatting with friends. If you know people, going over to them and greeting them with a handshake is expected polite behavior.

At some point (usually before 7:30) the host pastor will stand behind the podium and "open" the service with a prayer. This prayer is usually a long-form invocation, lasting upwards of ten minutes. After the prayer may be a formal welcome from the hosting pastor. These welcome announcements typically indicate the inclusive nature of the tent meeting and are rather conversational in tone. As Pastor Wallace summed up in one of his welcome announcements:

> We got everybody under the tent here. We got Baptists here, Methodists... it don't matter if you're Assembly of God, Church of God... Salvation Army. We welcome you. We got Mormons... yea we got Mormons here with us tonight. Pretty soon they're gonna be dancin' under the tent with us.
>
> Seems like camp meeting just unifies everybody.[3]

After welcoming guests, the host pastor typically begins singing, initiating a standardized ritual structure generalized by one Anglo pastor as "an hour of singing, an hour of testifying, and an hour of preaching."[4] Oodlání themselves might eschew this strict organizational formulation, claiming (like the southern Indiana Pentecostals in the work of folklorist Elaine Lawless) that the Holy Spirit is ultimately in control of what happens when. However, while Oodlání acknowledge that "'anything' can happen at any time in a church service" (Lawless 1988a, 59), they also recognize that in general there is an order in which events at a revival typically occur.[5]

Signaling the beginning of the singing (or "praise and worship") portion of the revival, the pastor typically leads a session of group singing. The songs are not usually hymns and therefore encourage the participation of all through open-ended praise songs full of repetition and internal intensification. As among the Pentecostals that Jeff Titon observed in Appalachia, "The group stands and the pastor leads the chorus. There is no need for hymn-books. Reading from a hymn-book would diminish the enthusiasm" (Titon 1978, 584). Although this singing is designed (through simple praise songs with repetitive or iterative lyrics) to encourage audience participation, the majority of the attendees at this early hour in the revival simply sit and enjoy the music produced by the pastor and a core group of participants, typically from the pastor's church. Although the Holy Spirit may descend at this point in the tent meeting, it is still light outside, people are still trickling in, and the pastor is typically simply aiming to lead praise music, rather than utilizing any of the melodic strategies (discussed later) that would encourage the infilling of the spirit among participants.

After the initial musical set, the pastor begins to act more as an emcee, calling up various visiting congregations and bands to perform for the service. This portion of music making lasts at least an hour, and can go much longer, as the pastor generally strives to include musical contributions from every performing group present. Some of these Navajo gospel groups and musicians have become famous among Oodlání, attracting a dedicated fan base who follow them from revival to revival to hear them play. This "presentational" music making is characterized by organized groups playing fixed-length songs to an attentive but nonparticipatory audience.[6]

The presentational music portion of the revival service is generally followed by an "individual contribution" segment. The host pastor greets visitors and sometimes invites visiting pastors to come up onto the platform to "greet the service." These visiting pastors contribute either a song or a testimony or short sermon, encouraging the assembled. At other times the host pastor asks for individuals to come forward and share their testimony. This portion of the service usually lasts between fifteen minutes and an hour, but again it can go on much longer if the pastor decides to include everyone who may want to speak. It is usually closed by the pastor inviting a musical group to provide music while an offering is taken up. A few central members of the hosting church (sometimes called "ushers") stand on the ground in front of the podium holding baskets or buckets. While the music plays, and in apparently random order, audience members come forward and put money in one of the baskets before returning to their seats.[7]

After the offering is over the host pastor generally transitions the service into the preaching frame (called "bringing the Word"). This is generally considered to be the most important portion of

FIG. 5. Visiting evangelist Negiel Bigpond (Yuchi) prays for healing. Photo courtesy of Eugene B. Joe.

the service to insiders. In no instance did I observe preaching to last less than one hour. Sermons generally follow one of a few patterns common to tent evangelists across America. They can either be loosely structured around main points with biblical evidence or structured by biblical explication and application to the daily lives of listeners.[8] Some seem to have no discernable structure.[9] In general, the end of the sermon increasingly exhorts listeners and builds the collective energy into the next ritual frame: the faith healing or altar call.[10]

In the neo-Pentecostal contexts like Oodlání revivals, this period of the service is not focused on salvation or spirit baptism as much as on ritual healing.[11] Typically, at this point in the revival the darkened sky creates a more intimate space within the lighted tent. Music pours out of the speakers at such high decibels that it becomes aurally enveloping.[12] But if things are done right, and, as they say, the people are "of one accord," the Holy Spirit may descend on the assembled and become manifest through the speaking of tongues, dancing in the spirit, and gifts of healing. Usually healing activities are formalized, such as the formation of a line that files past an evangelist or pas-

FIG. 6. Dancing in the Holy Spirit. Photo courtesy of Eugene B. Joe.

tor who lays hands on believers and prays for healing. At other times, the spirit moves through this portion of the service in an informal manner.

The focus of attention moves from the stage to the extra-large space between the platform and the first row of chairs. Those who have been filled with the Holy Spirit move and dance erratically, sometimes weeping, praying, or speaking in tongues, and are gently guided by relatives into this open space, where they will eventually be "slain" and fall to the ground, unconscious, to be covered with a red cloth while they recover. This portion of the revival can last anywhere from fifteen minutes to several hours, depending on the size of the revival, the mood of the assembled, and the "will of the spirit."

As the healing ritual winds down, the bodies of those who have been "slain in the spirit" eventually occupy much of the clear space in front of the platform, covered with red cloths to maintain their modesty and guarded by ushers from harm by the unaware dancers filled with the spirit. Oodlání revivals end when the energy from this altar call dissipates, generally some-

FIG. 7. Being slain in the spirit. Photo courtesy of Eugene B. Joe.

time around midnight. Occasionally attendees gather for a late-night meal provided by the host church before heading home in the dark, pickup truck lights bouncing over the uneven ground.

Research and Relationships

During the first week in June, if you drive a few miles north of Shiprock, New Mexico, you'll see a large banner marking a small dirt road off the highway that reads: "Welcome to: Intertribal Pentecostal Campmeeting 7:00 p.m."

If you are Navajo, you may have heard about this revival by checking the posted fliers on the announcement board at the Shiprock Trading Post. You may have been invited by a friend or relative. You may be Christian and be supporting your pastor, who was invited to preach here. Or you may have heard the host pastor, Pastor Wallace, announce the revival in Navajo during the "Community Announcements" broadcast over the noon hour on AM 960, KNDN Farmington.[13] You may be coming by to take advantage of the free meal being served. Or you may be coming up to check out the racket you keep hearing from your house late into the night.

If you are Anglo, you might be following the sign down this bumpy dirt road because you are visiting with your church youth group, coming to teach Vacation Bible Study to a group of Navajo children.[14] Or you may

Fig. 8. Revival sign. Photo by author.

be part of a church work team, coming to build a kitchen or bathrooms with running water for this Navajo-led ministry. Or perhaps you are an ethnographer, interested in Navajo tent revivals and looking for a good place to begin your work, as I was in the summer of 2006.

The first time I saw Pastor Wallace singing, I sensed the energy in the room change. The atmosphere became electric, and the fairly passive mood of the audience transformed: people were on their feet, clapping and moving, and before long, dancing

FIG. 9. Pastor Wallace Begay. Photo by author.

erratically "in the spirit." I watched this unassuming middle-aged Navajo man, of medium height and build, long black hair tied back in a pony-tail, and marveled at the charismatic power of his economy of movement, effortless mastery of the rhythmic groove, and skillful additions of unexpected shouts, knee lifts, and praises. Although I had no word for it at the time, I came to know this power surrounding his preaching and singing as what Oodláni call the *anointing* on his ministry.

The majority of the research for this book was conducted over nineteen months with Pastor Wallace's church. During this time

I engaged in participant observation at a variety of activities in the life of church members: weekly church services, dozens of revivals and camp meetings, women's group meetings, holiday parties, and birthday parties. I conducted specially focused, in-depth research on all aspects of planning, logistics, and activities for this church's week-long camp meeting in 2008 and again in 2012. In many ways participant observation involved simply being a participant in the services: I stood when others stood, clapped when others clapped, sang when others sang. I engaged in the process of learning how to act, so that even though I was often the only Anglo in the room, people around me began to "go about their business as usual" when I showed up (Bernard 1994, 137).

Business as usual for Oodlání primarily involved attending church services. On Sunday a morning service (from 10:00 a.m. to around 1:00 p.m.) focused on preaching, and the evening service (from 6:00 p.m. to around 9:00 p.m.) focused on member testimonies. Often there was a meal prepared by, and served to, church members between these two services. Members also met on Wednesday evenings from 7:00 p.m. to around 10:00 p.m. for a service focusing on Bible study. All these services began with a "praise and worship" segment of enthusiastic music making. Church practice was unabashedly charismatic, and when the music was particularly good, members said the Holy Spirit moved among the congregation, causing dancing in the spirit, speaking in tongues, and occasionally members being slain in the spirit.[15] Revivals are also a very important part of this church community, with the church sponsoring several revivals a year, including one usually held the first week in June, which constitutes one of the biggest revivals in the Shiprock area each year.

With a population of around eight thousand, the town of Shiprock (known in Navajo as *Naat'áanii Nez*), is the largest town on the Navajo Nation east of the Chuska Mountains that represent the border between Arizona and New Mexico. Practically, this means around six fast food restaurants and a handful of stoplights. The town is large enough to support its own high school, a grocery store, a campus of Diné College, and a rather large new medical center. Shiprock, named in English for a dramatic rock

MAP 2. Shiprock region. Erin Greb Cartography.

formation nearby, provides a point of centering for many of the smaller, isolated Navajo communities in northern New Mexico and southern Utah. But Shiprock is also itself is a border community, located around fifteen miles from the eastern border of the Navajo Nation and about thirty miles from the large off-reservation town of Farmington, New Mexico.[16]

A few miles north of town, down a long dirt road that is passable in *nearly* all seasons of the year, is Pastor Wallace's church. This church was founded and originally pastored by a different and unrelated Navajo family: they still attend the church, and it is located on their land.[17] In 2007 the main church building was decades old and not originally intended for regular use. It was not built on a foundation, and folding chairs were arranged on packed dirt floor, covered with old carpets. Exposed log beams held up a ceiling that leaked when rain came, and the church was cooled by a window-unit swamp cooler in the summer and heated by a few space heaters in the winter. The building had no running water for the kitchen and no indoor restroom facilities. In the final months of my fieldwork in 2008, an Anglo mission team helped to connect running water to the church kitchen. During 2009 the congregation was able to raise the funds and mobilize networks to build a new church building next to the old one. In 2013 they were finally able to install the plumbing for indoor restrooms.

Family affiliation remains central to membership in Oodláni churches, and part of the success of the movement can be attributed to the way it has capitalized on kin networks rather than isolating individuals from them. Navajo society is organized into more than sixty distinct clans (Kluckhohn and Leighton 1946, 111).[18] Since Navajo society is matrilineal, the most important clan affiliations are traced through the mother's side.[19] Pastor Wallace's maternal relatives provided important support for his ministry. His sisters and female maternal cousins were the primary workers laboring to prepare meals and raise money for the church. But it was his mother, Mrs. Beverly Joe, who most steadfastly supported Pastor Wallace's ministry. "My son, he's the pastor here," she told me. "We as a family have to be here and support him" (B. Joe 2008).

One of the primary ways in which Mrs. Joe supported her son's ministry was through managing the church kitchen. Feeding the entire church community on a regular basis required a massive marshaling of resources, labor, and knowledge, conducted for the majority of my fieldwork in a small kitchen with dirt floor, no running water, and no heating or cooling. In addition to the main gathering room, where services were held, the church kitchen also became my school room as I learned about Oodláni life. Helping out in the kitchen under the watchful tutelage of Mrs. Joe (whom I quickly began to think of as Ma Beverly for her warm and nurturing demeanor), became one of the primary ways I participated in Oodláni life.[20] Other means of participation may have been less gender-typed or yielded better insight into theology or history, but kitchen work was an easy way for me to do something practical to help out in a socially appropriate way.

FIG. 10. Mrs. Beverly Joe. Photo by author.

I spent many hours in the church kitchen doing whatever tasks were necessary to feed the church community. I spent so much time in the kitchen during my fieldwork that Ma Beverly made sure I went through the training to obtain a Navajo Nation food handler's permit. I chopped vegetables, washed dishes, and became a slow but competent maker of frybread. I showed up on time, tried

FIG. 11. Women of the church kitchen. Photo courtesy of Eugene B. Joe.

to be helpful, and followed Ma Beverly's instructions. I listened to the melodic Navajo conversation going on among the women around me; I got to know them and joke with them. They called me *Shideezhí* (little sister), and I ate many meals with them, but only after we served the church.[21]

Kitchen work involved a lot of waiting: mostly for the service or activity to finish so that we could serve the people, and in those hours of waiting Ma Beverly would tell me stories about her life, her beliefs, and her convictions. In these quiet moments, in the dawn glimmer and the deep night, as we waited to pass out bologna sandwiches or mutton stew, Ma Beverly taught me something of what it meant to be Oodlání.

In addition to participant observation in church services and the church kitchen, my instruction in Oodlání life was significantly enriched by dozens of ethnographic interviews. Over lunch at the Shiprock Kentucky Fried Chicken or Furr's Cafeteria in Farmington, the members of Pastor Wallace's church community shared their lives and faith with me in conversations that often lasted hours. Later, as our rapport grew, many of the church families invited me to conduct interviews over a meal in their own homes (on these occasions, I brought the KFC dinner with me). Tears are not uncommon in Oodláni church services (one of their nicknames in Navajo is *Dimoí Dachaa'í*, "Christians who cry"), and in these more intimate interviews I often shared in these tears as I learned reasons behind them. I came away deeply moved by the sense of helplessness, tragedy, and stinging personal loss that drives some Navajos (particularly women) to seek "strength in the Lord," as they would say.

Although I learned many things from the members of Pastor Wallace's church community, one man undertook my tutelage more fully than most. Eugene B. Joe is a Shiprock native who is deeply passionate about preserving the history of Shiprock, serving as one of the founders of the Shiprock Historical Society. In one of our first interviews, I drove him all around town so that he could point out historical landmarks: the dilapidated old building that used to be the Bureau of Indian Affairs hospital, the land (now a BIA housing development) that used to support fields of watermelon and fruit trees, the place where the old drive-in movie theatre once stood, and the location of the old trading post, where he used to sit on the porch, sipping a soda, listening to his grandpa chat in Navajo with friends. Mr. Joe was deeply committed to making sure I understood the vibrant history of Shiprock, especially its Christian history, and the important role that his own family plays in this history. His father was a *hataałii* (medicine man), who was healed and exorcized of demons by healing evangelist A. A. Allen and became one of Allen's early advocates in the Shiprock area (B. Joe 2008).[22] After this life transformation, Mr. Joe Sr. became one of the first secular sand-painting artists, transforming traditional sacred art into a folk art form that brought him, and later his son Eugene, a significant presence on the fine art market.[23] Eugene Joe's artistic sense is unparalleled, and I am particularly grateful for his beautiful photography and permission to include many of his photographs in this work.

The final major piece of my research involved the close translation of recorded events from Navajo into English. Because Oodláni operate in an inter-generational setting where the oldest

FIG. 12. Mr. Eugene B. Joe. Photo by author.

generation may not understand English and the youngest generation may not understand Navajo, nearly everything I observed happened in a bilingual context. I still felt that the meanings gained from a close attention to targeted Navajo speech events could yield important insights about Oodláni life. For this work I significantly benefited from the help of Larry King, a Navajo elder. Mr. King began as a classmate in Navajo language at San

Juan College but quickly became an invaluable consultant, not only for his knowledge of Navajo but also for his reflective, philosophical insights. He possesses not only Navajo fluency but also the rare and developing skill of Navajo literacy (it was this skill that he was working to improve in our shared Advanced Navajo class). Despite six semesters of study of the Navajo language at Diné College, Indiana University, and San Juan College, my own proficiency in this very difficult language never allowed for the dynamic fluency necessary for translating the important speech events (sermons, testimonies, speeches) that I had recorded. Mr. King's contribution to my research included not only literal translation of these recordings but also hours of conversations about the poetic meanings, contexts of use, and connotations of Oodlání word choice. He provides a much-needed non-Christian Navajo perspective on my research.

Ethnographic fieldwork is, if nothing else, an exercise in getting to know people. Objectivity is certainly something ethnographers should strive for if we continue to aim to tell the stories of others, not simply the reflections of ourselves. But ultimately the ability to tell a story that rings true for the people living it rests in the strength of the long-term relationships we build with individuals. Our descriptions reflect our own biases and theirs as well. And while responsibility for errors rests firmly with me, and the perspectives of many more individuals inform my work, I am forever grateful for the opportunity to get to know these four individuals. *Shi'pastor* Wallace, *Shimá* Beverly, *Shizhé'é* Eugene, and *Shicheii* Larry: *Ahé'héé*.

The Ethical Challenges of Research with Oodlání

It is often joked that Navajos are so overstudied by anthropologists that we have become part of the traditional Navajo family unit. This is not the case among Oodlání. Though several important studies have incorporated the Oodlání movement into their analysis, I am (to my knowledge) the only scholar ever to conduct ethnographic fieldwork solely with the Navajo neo-Pentecostal community.[24] I approached my research this way in an attempt to tell their story from their perspective, not the way they are so commonly (mis-)represented by others, including other Navajos. My approach yields the contribution of an important broadening to the understanding of the Navajo religious landscape. But it is not without significant ethical challenges and obstacles. In this section I briefly outline three of the major ethical hurdles to conducting ethnographic fieldwork with Native American neo-Pentecostals like the Oodlání. These include issues surrounding the colonial and confrontational history of Christianity, the identity politics of traditionalism, and the resulting difficulties of conducting research in ethical and respectful ways.

THE COLONIAL AND CONFRONTATIONAL HISTORY OF CHRISTIANITY

There is no doubt that the Christian religion has played a role in the assimilative practices of settler-colonialism that have destabilized traditional Navajo lifeways over the past 150 years. And even though the Oodlání movement is not directly tied to these Christian agents, Oodlání continue to promote Navajo cultural fragmentation through confrontational denouncement of traditional lifeways. Given these loudly anti-traditional attitudes set against a backdrop of structural settler-colonialism, some might question the ethics of even giving voice to Oodlání perspectives. While acknowledging the broader historical and cultural context within which Navajo Christianity currently operates, I continue to insist on the anthropological first principle of religious relativism, even when (and perhaps especially when) confronted with fire-and-brimstone Christianity.

Christianity has always accompanied efforts by outsiders to destabilize the sovereignty of the Diné (Navajos). Spanish Franciscans, the vanguard of Spanish imperialism, first attempted to convert Diné to Catholicism in the seventeenth to nineteenth centuries. American agents became interested in controlling the movement and actions of the Diné after the 1848 Treaty of Guadalupe Hidalgo put large portions of the Southwest, including the Diné homeland, under U.S. control. Christianity became one prong of a multipronged effort to induce Diné assimilation. Teaching Navajos Christianity was one of the rationales by which the United States justified the forced removal to *Hwéeldí* (Fort

Sumner), a removal that was facilitated by a scorched-earth military campaign against Diné families and involved a forced march of hundreds of miles. Christianity was also implicated in the mandatory education that was a condition of the treaty releasing the Diné from the brutal conditions of Hwéeldí in 1869. In this treaty Diné leaders conceded to allow the establishment of Christian-run boarding schools on their land.[25] Operating without local secular alternative until the 1950s (Iverson 2002, 124), these schools were blatantly assimilationist in intent, as noted in the introduction. Children were isolated from their families, required to wear Anglo clothing and hairstyles, and often punished for speaking the Diné language (Szasz and Ryan 1988).[26] While simultaneously being taught a Western way of thinking and believing, students growing up away from their families for most of the year were also unable to participate in the ceremonial lives of their families. Most were unable to experience the cultural instruction present in coming-of-age ceremonies such as the girls' *kinaaldá*. So while it may be inaccurate to regard Diné culture as ever existing as a totally stable and bounded entity, it is undeniable that Christian-run boarding schools contributed to the fragmentation of Navajo traditional lifeways.

The Oodlání relationship to this colonial Christian history is not direct. Christianity is not a monolithic entity, and the Anglo traveling charismatic tent evangelists of the 1950s who planted the seeds that would become the Oodlání movement had very different intentions than Christians who had come before. The most important orientation that differentiated the charismatic tent evangelists from other Christians is that they focused on communicating a "spirit-filled" theology.[27] These charismatic Anglo evangelists never intended to establish a permanent mission presence among Navajos, nor were they interested in providing services (educational, healthcare, or otherwise) to Diné families. Rather, these evangelists were part of a movement in the United States sometimes referred to as the "healing revival" of the 1950s, as I elaborate in the following chapter. Once Navajos got their own tents and began their own ministries (something well established by the 1960s), the Oodlání movement had begun.

Because of its roots in the healing revival, the Oodlání movement is a distinct development among Navajos, separate from the denominational churches that had come before. This distinction is preserved most clearly in the way Oodlání refer to the various forms of Christianity. While non-Christian Navajos may refer to all Christians as *Dimoi* (Sunday-ers), and in fact may see them as a rather unified group, when viewed from within the distinctions are more pronounced. Oodlání refer to Catholics as *Éé'nishoodii* (long robes) and mainline Protestant groups (such as Methodists or Christian Reformed) as *Éé'ádaałts'ííaí* (short robes).[28] These two groups are seen by Oodlání as those most involved in missionary projects like boarding schools and hospitals, and are typically run by Anglos.[29] Oodlání further distance themselves from denominational Pentecostalism (such as the Assemblies of God), preferring to refer to themselves not as Pentecostal but as Oodlání (believers).[30] Regardless of the name on their church sign, Oodlání are by definition Navajos.[31] They never ran boarding schools, nor did the traveling charismatic evangelists from whom they adopted their version of Christianity.

However, what Oodlání lack in colonial history they make up for in confrontational theology. Anti-traditionalism is a bedrock Oodlání principle, and traditional ceremonialism is regarded by Oodlání as (at best) idolatry and (at worst) demonically driven witchcraft. Oodlání are taught (by *Navajo* pastors) to speak out boldly against traditional practices, and contemporary gatherings of Diné (fairs, fleamarkets, festivals) are almost certain to contain a Navajo from the Oodlání movement loudly denouncing Navajo traditional spirituality. Oodlání are vocal in criticizing language revitalization programs or Diné college classes with traditional or sacred content (House 2002, 74–75). Perhaps even more offensive in the Navajo cultural context is the fact that Oodlání often directly confront family members over faith, as I explore later. Anecdotal evidence suggests that every contemporary Navajo extended family has at least one Oodlání member intent on convincing relatives that they need to convert or else they are bound for hell.

While many American families may contain a similar hetero-religiosity, one should not underestimate how very controversial this kind of evangelization is from a Diné point of view. The Diné philosophy of proper behavior is grounded in the principle of *t'áá hó'ajít'éego t'éíyá* (it's up to him or her). According to this principle, all individuals have both the responsibility and the freedom to make up their own mind, and it is therefore inconsiderate to try to influence the thoughts of another.[32] Direct confrontation (especially between family members) is consequently considered highly impolite and offensive. The regularity with which stories about these kinds of conflicts with Oodlání family members are shared suggests that Oodlání do regularly act as a force for cultural fragmentation and change.

Given the role of Oodlání in perpetuating processes of cultural fragmentation begun by settler-colonialism, creating an ethnography that serves to give further voice to these perspectives so unabashedly offensive to the majority of Navajos is somewhat controversial. These are very emotionally charged debates, emplaced within structures of colonial hegemony. I personally do not advocate neo-Pentecostalism or any other religious faith.[33] However, this ethnography rests on the axiomatic anthropological principle of religious relativism. Relativism holds that cultures need to be judged not by ethnocentric standards but from within.[34] Religious relativism advocates a scholarly position that presents the viewpoints of believers with empathy and an eye toward understanding their own perspectives on why they do what they do, rather than judging religious attitudes as objectively good or bad. This is a precarious empathetic neutrality to maintain in the face of fire-and-brimstone Christianity.[35] It is a particularly difficult kind of positioning to maintain when Native-led cultural revitalization movements become the target of Native-led neo-Pentecostal ire, as they so often are.[36] However, I forge ahead in the hope that empathetic understanding of Oodlání culture can produce worthwhile reconciliation between these two currents in Navajo life that outright dismissal, rooted in legitimate offense, could not.

IDENTITY POLITICS OF TRADITIONALISM

A second major hurdle to conducting ethnography among Oodlání rests in the politics of identity among Navajos. Let me be clear: many Navajos regard Oodlání as not really Navajos. For instance, Thomas Csordas discovered the controversial nature of including Navajo Christians in research on Navajo healing systems when one project staff member commented, "I thought this was a Navajo healing project, but these interviews are all with Christians" (Csordas 2004, 4).[37] Oodlání, on the other hand, regard themselves as Navajo in all areas of life other than religion. Both of these sentiments are based upon contingent constructions of what it means to be Navajo.

Navajos who criticize Oodlání as not "authentically" Navajo perpetuate an idea of Navajo culture as monolithic and reified. Because of the associations between Christianity and boarding school, many Navajos feel that those who convert to Christianity are betraying their tradition or roots, and are simply "selling out," or capitulating to Anglo assimilation. The old insult about the "apple" (red on the outside, white on the inside) is occasionally leveled at Oodlání by other tribal members as well. As Samuels would say, it is a definition of Navajoness rooted in "transparent" indexicality: Navajos speak the Navajo language, eat Navajo food, listen to Navajo music, and dress in Navajo ways (2004, 7). Scholars have perpetuated this one-dimensional understanding of Navajo culture through the standard use of the singular to refer to this culture group (that is, "The Navajo think/believe/act/etc."). In part to counter this trend, I always refer to Navajos in the plural.[38] The truth is that there are more than 300,000 Navajos (Donovan 2011), and they like many different kinds of music, food, and dress. So any sweeping statements about Navajo people as a whole are generalities that homogenize the heterogeneity of contemporary Navajo lives.

Another factor regarding Oodlání identity politics is that some narratives of Navajoness are privileged over others by certain powerful actors on the Navajo landscape.[39] This is not always a bad thing. In highlighting the way that certain aspects of "tradition" are emphasized over others, I do not wish to use my "discursive authority" as a scholar to undermine the good work done by cultural revitalization movements.[40] The Navajo Nation has a strong cultural revitalization movement, fostered and shaped by an increasing number of critical Diné scholars. Although they have been trained in different areas of expertise, these scholars often find orienting commonality using the traditional philosophical grounding of *Sa'ąh Naaghái Bik'eh Hózhǫǫn* (SNBH), translated loosely as "one's journey of striving to live a long and harmonious life" (Cajete 2014, ix). Variously referred to as the "corn-pollen path" (L. Lee 2014a, 5), or the "sun-wise path teachings" (Werito 2014, 27), the philosophy of SNBH is a traditional Diné philosophy experienced through the four directions (starting with east), the four seasons (starting with spring), the four parts of the day (beginning with dawn), the four stages of life (starting with birth), and the four primary points of the landscape (the four sacred mountains).[41] SNBH is critical to the Blessingway, the ceremony that forms the backbone of all curative Diné ceremonies (L. Lee 2014a, 6).[42] And it has become the bedrock principle of Diné cultural revitalization programs.

According to Diné scholar Larry Emerson, SNBH is multifaceted: it is a pedagogy (way of learning), an epistemology (way of knowing), and an ontology (statement about what exists in the world; Emerson 2014, 61). As a pedagogy, it has helped Diné College faculty lead the way in establishing SNBH teachings as the core of their educational mission. Since the 1980s they have operationalized SNBH through the Diné Philosophy of Learning (DPL). This pedagogical philosophy emphasizes four learning processes: *nitsáhákees* (thinking), *nahat'á* (planning), *iiná* (living), and *siihasin* (assuring). As an epistemology and ontology, it is a critical call to rethink the categories of value communicated by the Western settler-colonial order, providing a new framework that values the maintenance of kin (*k'é*) networks of reciprocity, including the natural world. SNBH also provides a Diné-based framework for research that emphasizes community responsibility (L. Lee 2014b, 181), the value of Diné oral history (Denetdale 2007; 2014), and a critically informed recognition of the ways that settler-colonial realities have shaped contemporary difficulties with cultural and language revitalization (T. Lee 2014, 158).

While I celebrate the strong work of cultural revitalization spearheaded by critical Diné scholars, this ethnography focuses on a Navajo community that is rendered marginal by privileging DPL and SNBH. Minority voices also exist on the Navajo Nation, and one of those minority voices is that of the Oodlání. Although Oodlání are Navajo, they reject the idea that the fundamental essence of Navajoness is rooted in SNBH. They do not speak for all Navajos, but they present a contrasting narrative of Navajoness, and it is this perspective that I examine in what follows.

If the cultural revitalization movement relies on a monolithic framework for what it means to be Diné, this same erroneously monolithic framework is used by Oodlání when isolating themselves from "traditional religion." As already mentioned, Oodlání regard themselves as Navajo in all areas other than religion. Navajo language, dress, food, and culture are all celebrated by Oodlání, but religion is parceled out and rejected. This orienting framework not only artificially constructs traditional ethics/ philosophy/ceremony/spirituality as a "religion"; it also falsely presumes that aspects of Diné culture are separable and interchangeable and not holistically interrelated.

When Oodlání claim they have kept Navajo culture but abandoned Navajo religion, they are presuming that Navajo traditional religion and Christianity are parallel systems. Oodlání may think in terms of religious dualism (Christian vs. traditional), but in fact the category of religion is itself foreign to traditional Diné concepts of spirituality. As I explore in more depth in chapter 1, Navajos have traditionally regarded things that might be classified as "religious" under a more holistic concept that might be thought of as the total Navajo way of life. It is the holistic system that includes ethics of behavior, kinship and relatedness, mythology, cosmology, spirituality, ecology, and philosophy as well as the overt ritual of healing ceremonials. Many Diné would argue that the maintenance of *hózhǫ́* (balance, beauty, or harmony) is both the philosophical root of all ceremonial activity and also forms the core of what it means to be Diné. Oodlání instead regard selected aspects of traditional Navajo life (ceremonies, paraphernalia, deities, singers) as constituting a "religion," one that they have rejected in favor of a different religion: charismatic Christianity. Thus both Diné cultural revitalizationists and Oodlání neo-Pentecostals participate in creating what Milne has called the "ideology of traditionalism" (2011, 513) that tends to homogenize artificially the vibrant diversity of Diné culture, both past and present.

ETHICS OF RESEARCH

Given the colonial associations of Christianity and the contested position of Oodlání as authentically Diné, conducting research with this community in ethically respectful ways proved challenging. Anthropological research has historically been a colonial process, drawn from the impetus to "collect" information about "others" in order to explain them to "us." Neither the product nor, crucially, the process has historically benefited the populations with whom anthropologists work. Indigenous scholars since the 1990s have led the charge in reorienting the colonial research process so that the benefits of research do not simply move in one direction. As influential Maori scholar Linda Tuhiwai Smith has stated, "Research can no longer be conducted with indigenous communities as if their views did not count and their lives did not matter" (Smith 1999, 9). Following Smith, Navajo scholars such as Jennifer Nez Denetdale, Wilson Aronilth, and Lloyd Lee have outlined several ways in which researchers working with Navajos can conduct their work respectfully by supporting projects that foster sovereignty, that are oriented through a Navajo philosophy of knowledge, and that further agendas of cultural revitalization. My challenge has been in orienting my research ethically among a minority community of Navajos (the neo-Pentecostals) who are actively opposed to these underlying philosophies of cultural and political revitalization.

According to Smith, indigenous research agendas should privilege healing, decolonization, transformation, and mobilization of the community with the ultimate goal of supporting projects of sovereignty (Smith 1999, 117). In the Navajo context specifically, Denetdale calls for research that helps Navajos document "the continuing significance of clan relationships, a sense of community with the land, and the importance of pastoralism [which] are connected through a philosophy that stresses the continual search for *hózhǫ́*, the path to harmony and Old Age" (Denetdale 2007, 31). Some of these goals directly counter the evangelistic goals and values of the specific Navajo community within which I worked, because of their particular Christian convictions. Oodlání are perfectly willing to support projects of Navajo sovereignty—but not if they are grounded in the fundamental orienting concepts of the traditional philosophy of *hózhǫ́*. The ethical conundrum here highlights the ways in which indigenous communities are not composed of monolithic actors. For the Oodlání with whom I worked, a research philosophy that took their voices seriously would hear the ways in which they subscribed to a new philosophy that privileged church over clan and "holiness" over *hózhǫ́*.

Another priority of indigenously driven research agendas is to destabilize the exclusively Western frameworks of knowledge that traditionally frame the research enterprise, particularly in anthropology. As Denetdale has pointed out, these frameworks of knowledge continue to "sustain colonialist discourses and serve to perpetuate ideas of dominance, hierarchy, and asymmetry" (Denetdale 2007, 6). For instance, in this book I spend a lot of time comparing traditional Diné and neo-Pentecostal "religions" although (as already mentioned) the category of "religion" is itself a Western framework overlaid on a holistic and all-encompassing philosophy of life. The difficulty I face, of course, is that Oodlání themselves (through boarding school and exposure to other hegemonic institutions) have adopted a Western framework for explaining the world around them. My options, then, are to perpetuate the Western frameworks that Oodlání espouse or to engage in a full-scale deconstruction of their incorrect assumptions. Given these stakes, I feel that the worst possible choice would be to perpetuate a tradition of outsiders telling Navajos how to think. As a result, I have attempted to present Oodlání perspectives without much corrective or critical deconstruction, even when these perspectives perpetuate a Western framework of knowledge.

In other areas I have had more success aligning my work with indigenous research agendas. Overall, says Smith, ethical research with indigenous communities should attend to processes (methodology and method) over product. "Processes," she says, "are expected to be respectful, to enable people, to heal and to educate" (Smith 1999, 128). I attempted to conduct this kind of research in three major ways. These included securing fully informed research clearance at many levels, respecting the importance of returning what I learned with good reporting practices, and finding creative ways to give back to the community through reciprocal projects.

Informed by Denetdale, I view consent as an ever-ongoing process. I received formal clearance to conduct ethnographic research from the Navajo Nation Office for Historic Preservation, obtaining an ethnographic research permit before beginning my study. Since that initial approval I have kept in regular contact with the NNOHP, renewing my permit three times, receiving pre-publication approval of every manuscript I intend to publish or present, and submitting to the NNOHP three copies of all manuscripts I have published or presented, including the present work. The Navajo Nation requires local sponsorship of research as well, which I obtained from Pastor Wallace Begay as well as from other formal leadership of his church. Pastor Wallace never chose to announce my purposes formally in a church service. So I worked throughout my research to make sure as many people as possible knew what I was doing in the community. Again, since membership (apart from a dedicated core) is fairly fluid among Oodlání, I view this declaration of my purposes as an ongoing process.

Another ongoing process I adopted in order to maintain an ethical position is that of consistent reporting. As noted, the Navajo Nation OHP receives copies of everything I publish or present. But key members of Pastor Wallace's congregation (particularly

FIG. 13. Author presenting Pastor Wallace with her beginner's attempt at a Navajo rug. Photo courtesy of Eugene B. Joe.

those whose voices are present in the document) obtain copies of my work as well. Every person in Pastor Wallace's church with whom I conducted an interview between 2006 and 2008 received a hard copy of a full transcription of their interview. Several central members of Pastor Wallace's congregation received copies of my dissertation, and I undertook a special research trip during 2012 specifically to receive feedback from the broader Oodlání community on this document. Every article I have published on this community has first been circulated for feedback, a process I intend to continue. While my analysis of situations may not always be the same as theirs, I believe that a respectful research process encourages an ongoing dialogue where community actors have a right to see what is being written about them and to respond to this writing.[43]

The final way I attempted to approach my research ethically was by adopting a process-based attitude of constant and creative reciprocity. To the extent possible, without advocating neo-Pentecostalism as a missionary or specifically working against projects of cultural revitalization (both of which would have contradicted my personal convictions), I have attempted to think of creative ways to help the church community with whom I was working. In addition to kitchen work, I put to use the video documentation I made of camp meetings for the benefit of the community. Drawing from more than forty hours of video footage on several cameras, I created two two-hour highlights videos of the 2008 and 2012 camp meetings and distributed more than two hundred free copies of these videos among the community. I also used my computer skills for the benefit of the community by assisting Pastor Wallace in developing a church website. I continue to maintain contact with Pastor Wallace, acting promptly on his requests to send photos or update his website. My reciprocity with him is a process, and I conduct myself so that he continues to view me as someone within his network of resources. My research thus benefited some Navajos, although clearly not all Navajos. But given the heterogeneity of indigenous communities, isn't this always the case?

CHAPTER 2

Under the Tent

The Resonant Rupture of Ritual

Follow the bumpy dirt road that winds past decades-old double-wide trailers and eventually, on the horizon, you will see a massive white tent the size of a small building. If it is night, the tent may be lit up from the inside like a giant paper lantern. But even before the sun goes down, it will be surrounded by concentric circles of large pickup trucks, groups of children running around playing, and some type of shade-arbor concession stand selling shaved ice and frybread. The aural presence of the tent will be immediately noticeable: before you even leave your car you will be able to hear the thumping of the drum set, the extremely amplified electric guitars, and the energetic singing of a pastor or evangelist, usually in a mix of English and Navajo. Later in the night, the singing may be mixed with tearful testimonies or declarative preaching, but one thing is for sure: once Oodlání (Navajo neo-Pentecostals) get going at a tent revival, they won't quit until the early morning hours.

Some scholars of Navajo contemporary religion have attributed the success of the Oodlání movement (in various guises) to the mechanism of tent evangelism (Blanchard 1977, 210; Dolaghan and Scates 1978, 65; Frisbie 1987, 206). Most have attributed this success to the tent's portability: any Navajos who have translated for Anglo evangelists under a tent and feel so inspired can, with relatively little overhead, get their own tents and begin their own ministries.[1] More important for our purposes, the tent represents a kind of continuity with preexisting Navajo ritual forms. In contrast to the somber, formal, and Sunday-morning nature of ritual within denominational Christian mission churches, the tent revival ritual frame fits more naturally onto the Navajo social and environmental landscape. Like traditional ceremonial gatherings, tent revivals are sporadically focused on ritual action but otherwise are dynamic all-day, all-night gatherings. People come and go as interest moves them, children run around and play, and the mood is joyful and celebratory. According to this perspective, it is the continuity of the ritual form that fuels the spread of neo-Pentecostalism (over other forms of Christianity) among Navajos.

In this chapter, I take a closer look at Oodlání rituals, both public and private. On the one hand, my research supports the conclusions of previous scholars that Oodlání tent revivals act, in limited ways, as "rituals of continuity," mapping aesthetic continuity with previous ritual practice. This continuity is particularly evident in the public aspects of certain traditional ceremonials and in select ritual actions like offerings and prayer. Ritual continuity is important to note, given the recent emphasis of many scholars on the importance of practice over "belief" in Native Christian contexts. Scholar Michael D. McNally points out that we are too quick to follow missionaries into assuming that ritual action simply reflects underlying meaning (McNally 2000b, 849), and therefore to overlook the ways in which Native converts have used the slippage between form and meaning to wield Christian expressive forms (such as hymn singing) in ways that preserve traditional values such as "land and community" (McNally 2000b, 852).

However, I maintain that tent revivals use this performative slippage to do more than foster cultural continuity. Rather, I contrast these rituals of continuity with other kinds of rituals, also present within the Oodlání ritual repertoire, that conform to what Joel Robbins has called "rituals of rupture." The most dramatic, controversial, and emotionally charged ritual of rupture in which Oodlání engage is the destruction of traditional Navajo medicine bundles (*jish*). While outlawed by the Navajo Nation after a well-publicized case in the late 1960s, the rupture-filled practice of *jish* burning continues to be practiced by many Oodlání in private.

Resonant rupture is present in both of these ritual frames, public and private. While the public ritual of the tent revival may appear to have aesthetic continuity with certain traditional ritual frames, the underlying meaning of tent revivals actually lies in their embodiment of cultural rupture. In the inverse manner, while the private ritual of *jish* burning may seem to be the ultimate rupture-filled act, I argue that by destroying *jish* (rather than simply abandoning it), Oodláni continue to treat these bundles as enlivened presences. Understanding why they do so, and whether they really are practicing rupture, requires us to take a closer look at the Oodláni animating principle of the "anointing." In both of these ritual frames, public and private, form and meaning are shown to be portable, ambiguous, and discursively created. Oodláni rituals are not simply acts of continuity or discontinuity. Rather, they entail a type of resonant rupture where affective ties bridge the deep chasm created by the denial of continuity.

Ritual Continuity

If we are to understand the tension between continuity and rupture that the Oodláni movement navigates, then it becomes critically important to examine how Oodláni rituals (such as the tent revival) fit into the broader Navajo religious landscape. This focus on religion as "practiced," rather than as "believed" is an important change for understanding how Christianity articulates against previous indigenous practices that typically put more emphasis on *lifeway practiced* rather than on *doctrine believed*. In the past few decades many scholars writing about Native American Christianity have cautioned that we should not take for granted the Western assumption that "religion" is equivalent to a "belief system."[2] Scholars working with communities outside North America agree, noting that defining religion as a belief system lacks cross-cultural validity because it reflects a Protestant theology that ties individual belief to salvation.[3]

Indigenous religions, on the other hand, are generally more holistic: lacking a clear dividing line between sacred and profane (Shorter 2009, 19), providing guidelines for managing relations among humans and between human and other-than-human persons (Shorter 2009, 19, Hallowell 1975), and offering a way of negotiating and passing on knowledge about what is true, helpful, dangerous, or wise.[4] As Kidwell has pointed out, "Typically, elders in almost any Indian community today . . . will deny that their community ever had a religion. Rather, they will argue, their whole cultural and social structure was and still is infused with spirituality that cannot be separated from the rest of the community's life at any point" (Kidwell et al. 2001, 12).[5]

Without doubt, the bounded category of "religion" does not map cleanly onto historical Navajo spiritual life. As Charlotte Frisbie has noted, "there is no word or phrase in the Navajo language that can be translated as 'religion' in the Western European sense of this term" (Frisbie 1987, xxiii). The phrase that has often been used to translate the European concept of religion is *Diné Binahagha'*, more accurately glossed as "moving about ceremonially" (Frisbie 1987, xxiii).[6] As in other Native contexts, the collections of beliefs, myths, rituals, and behaviors that, from a Western perspective, might be grouped together under religion were traditionally seen instead as part of the total Navajo lifeway. Thus *Diné Binahagha'* is only one facet of the sacred organizing principle of *Sa'ah Naaghái Bik'eh Hózhǫ́ǫ́n* (SNBH), a lifeway that included "language, land, cultural knowledge, protocols, trades, and living a distinct sustainable way of life" (L. Lee 2014a, 7) and that might be more generally glossed as "the Navajo Way."[7]

Because the two categories (Oodláni neo-Pentecostalism and "the Navajo Way") are not parallel belief systems, they cannot be directly compared. In part, this difficulty is eased by the fact that in contemporary usage, many Navajos now regard *Diné Binahagha'* as a belief-based system referred to as "traditional religion."[8] This change in view likely is rooted in colonial institutions such as boarding schools, government officials, and mission churches.[9] But another way of gaining clarity when discussing the different orientations (without presuming that they are identical categories) is to focus on practice. Examining ritual practice at tent revivals allows us to see the way in which the governing principles of a holistic Diné lifeway have been "transposed and performed" (McNally 2000b, 850) by Oodláni.

To this end, I follow others who have claimed that the success of the Oodlání movement is attributable in part to the ritual continuity between tent revivals and Navajo ceremonials, particularly in contrast to mission churches. However, rather than assuming (as did missionaries) that ritual behavior could be "read" as a reflection of inner spiritual states, I see the "continuity" attributed to Oodlání tent revivals, and the ritual forms practiced within them (specifically prayer and offerings), as full of performative ambiguity.[10] This ambiguity allows for apparently continuous forms to be read by Oodlání not as ritual continuity but rather as rupture.

RITUALS OF SOLEMNITY, RITUALS OF JOY

To a surprising degree, the lack of success of the Christian churches that evangelized among Navajos between 1880 and 1950 has been attributed to their "foreign" ritual practices. In 1949 Gladys Reichard (an early anthropologist who studied Navajo religion) pointed out that "insignificant custom" was blocking Christian evangelism. Among the most foreign customs, she felt, were the "demands of reverence made by the Church" (1949, 71). Elaborating this idea, she states:

> The Navajo religion is primarily enjoyable; there are but few times when solemnity is required . . . silence is rarely enjoyed because the gods demand it. Ceremonial participation and procedure include good talk, joking, cheerful intercourse and feasting. The Navajo of my acquaintance know few Christians who enjoy their religion—pleasure seems to them a sin. The new religion stresses a long face, suffering, the dead and death, the fear of eternal damnation. (Reichard 1949, 71)

Reichard concludes her article on Navajos and Christianity in the 1940s with the assertion that it seems "hardly fair" to ask Navajos to substitute their joy for Christian solemnity. She further suggests (in her wry and pointed tone) that perhaps Anglo Christians themselves could learn something about "cooperation, sharing, reciprocity, [and] tolerance" from Navajos (Reichard 1949, 71).

Explanations for the rise of evangelistic forms of Christianity after 1950 have built on Reichard's observations. Hodge, in his 1960s study of Navajo Pentecostalism, maintains a skeptical tone, claiming that if Navajos have embraced this form of charismatic Christianity it is "largely due to its manner of presentation" rather than "doctrinal appeal" or "genuine conversion" (Hodge 1964, 90). Blanchard's study of Navajo Nazarenes in the 1970s describes the "defection" of Nazarene church members to Pentecostalism because there was more of a participatory emphasis among Pentecostals (Blanchard 1977, 201).[11] And in their message to churches trying not to lose membership to the growing Oodláni movement of the 1970s, missionary scholars Dolaghan and Scates advise:

> Staid, formal services are not very attractive to the Navajo people. There should be ample time for testimonials and singing. Don't be afraid of "Praise the Lord" and "Amen, brother." Pentecostal people don't have a monopoly on these joyful expressions. Remember that worshipping God should be a joyful experience. People should enjoy going to church. (Dolaghan and Scates 1978, 65)

These writers attest to the fact that the Oodláni movement gained strength among Navajos by providing a type of ritual continuity with previous Navajo ceremonial life. Rather than somber and "reverent" gatherings on Sunday morning, tent revivals provided the "good talk, joking, cheerful intercourse and feasting" to which Reichard refers. This joyful ritual mood has characterized the Oodláni movement from the beginning, and is located in Navajo neo-Pentecostalism's roots in the American healing revival of the 1950s.

Oodláni Tent Revivals and the American Healing Revival

And back then the camp meeting . . .
I went to a lot of camp meetings.
It was a very strong camp meeting, people comin' from all different states.
They bring a bunch of food, and then, they . . .
they really did, you know, get a lot of praising and worshiping.
They weren't scared,
they weren't holding back.

. . . Back then, that's how it was.

And they prayed . . . they prayed all night long.

. . . Back then the anointing was very strong.
People loved one another.
. . . They all cried, hugging each other, crying and praying for each other.

—(A. YAZZIE 2008)

The nostalgic reflections of Amanda Yazzie describe the charismatic Navajo tent revivals of the 1960s and 1970s. The gatherings she described were joyful, full of love and food and people coming from miles around to "praise and worship" together and support one another. These gatherings were dramatically different from Christianity as it had been introduced among Navajos, either by Catholic Jesuits starting in the seventeenth century or by Protestant missionaries starting in the early twentieth century. And the different ritual gathering of the charismatic tent revival had significant effects. Between 1950 and 1977 there was an exponential increase in Christianity among Navajos, and this increase was predominantly within Pentecostal and charismatic churches, most of which were Navajo-led, unaffiliated with an official Pentecostal denomination, and spread through tent revivals.[12]

Without doubt, the informal and spirit-filled ethos of the charismatic tent revivals that arrived after 1950 localized more easily than the previous mission-compound style (Dolaghan and Scates 1978).[13] But revivals among Navajos were themselves part of a broader American movement, identified by some as the "Healing Revival" of the 1950s.[14]

The Healing Revival was a charismatic movement that appealed to disenfranchised 1950s Americans, featuring itinerate faith healers who traveled the country holding large tent meetings during which miraculous events, including faith healing, were reported to occur.[15] Before 1950 Pentecostal Christianity in the United States consisted of what historian David Harrell has called a "confusing patchwork of small [Pentecostal] sects frequently divided by seemingly trivial points of doctrine" (1975,

11), creating a great amount of factionalism. The mood began to change around 1946, with new generations of Pentecostals less interested in doctrine and more interested in the demonstrations of spiritual gifts that began Pentecostalism (Harrell 1975, 19). Into this gap stepped, in 1947, the ministries of two of the major figures of the healing revival: William Branham and Oral Roberts. These two men spearheaded large gatherings of people under tents focusing on the manifestation of miracles, specifically healing, and inspired the ministry of others.[16]

The healing evangelist most influential in bringing Pentecostalism to the Navajos, however, was A. A. Allen. Allen was born in Arkansas in 1911 to alcoholic parents and had an unstable childhood. In 1934 he converted to Pentecostalism and became an Assemblies of God minister (Harrell 1975, 67). Inspired by a 1949 Oral Roberts revival, Allan began a tent ministry. Allen's ministry always focused on the poor, and was an early example of racial integration. He was also "incredibly brash," continuously emphasizing miracles and deliverance from demon possession, even in the face of criticism from the Assemblies of God denomination (Harrell 1975, 68). According to Harrell, "His detractors accused him of creating a carnival atmosphere in his meetings; he generally countered such criticisms with dramatic announcements of new miracles. Allen seemed challenged to heal the hard diseases and frequently reported resurrections of the dead" (Harrell 1975, 69).

After a falling out with the Assemblies of God denomination in 1955, Allen began holding his own "Miracle Revivals" in Phoenix, Arizona, which put him in direct contact with Navajos working in the Phoenix area. These revivals were known for supernatural manifestations, such as the flowing of "miracle oil" from the heads and hands of those attending, and the mark of the cross on Allen's brow (Harrell 1975, 69).

In 1958 Allen was given land in southern Arizona in an area he named Miracle Valley. Throughout the 1960s he used this land (around 1,250 acres) to build a ministerial training center, a printing center for his monthly publication *Miracle Magazine*, and a church that seated around four thousand (Harrell 1975,

196). Navajos who were part of the growing Oodlání movement regularly visited Miracle Valley, and it became a place for Navajo neo-Pentecostals to build networks with other Native and Anglo charismatic believers.[17]

By 1965 charismatic and spirit-filled tent revivals were an established part of the Navajo religious landscape, particularly in the eastern part of the reservation. Many of the best remembered charismatic evangelists ministering under tents in the 1960s were Natives themselves, either Navajo or from a different tribe.[18] Navajo evangelists spoke fluent Navajo, and the "spirit-driven" theology of the Healing Revival justified their leadership. Two of the most influential of these evangelists were David "Boots" Wagner and, later, Jerry Domingo (Domingo 2012).

In addition to Navajo charismatic evangelists, Shiprock area neo-Pentecostals were influenced by the visits of charismatic evangelists from other tribes, many of whom traveled to the Navajo Nation along networks established through visits to Miracle Valley. For example, Samuel Harris (San Carlos Apache) was a regular visitor to Navajo revivals. Connections with other tribes, such as the Blackfeet, were cemented at this time as well (Stewart 2008). Pastor Roger Nomee (Crow) of Lodge Grass, Montana, began making regular visits, and Dr. Negiel Bigpond (Euchee/Yuchi) began traveling from Oklahoma with his gospel band the Flaming Sword in the 1960s.[19] Bigpond's band is still remembered by many as the first time they heard Christian rock, and Navajo Pastor Wallace Begay commented that the sound was "trail-blazing . . . God moved through their music" (Begay 2012).

The 1960s then represent the beginning of a tent-based charismatic revival movement that was Navajo-led, networked with other Native and Anglo evangelists, and was at its core based upon a dramatically different worship style than were the somber Sunday-morning services of the denominational churches that had come before. Drawing on the "brash" and "carnival"-like style of A. A. Allen, Navajo evangelists created tent revivals that included the "outpouring of miracles" through rock music, spirit-filled dancing, dramatic miracle healings, and emotional (often joyful) worship. Or, as Amanda Yazzie put it, "Back then the Holy Spirit begins to move.... People would be all over the place. Jumping, dancing, running, they'd be shouting ... people would be crying with their tears running down" (Yazzie 2008).

THE ENEMY WAY

For many Navajos, the appeal of public rituals like tent revivals is grounded in the way they resonate with (are amplified by) a deep groove of ritual atmosphere in Navajo ceremonial life. By not demanding the "reverent solemnity" of the denominational mission churches, the Oodláni movement capitalized on what Kluckhohn and Leighton observed of Navajo ritual—that it "offers a chance to see and be seen, to talk and to listen" (1946, 228). Nowhere is the social enjoyment of traditional public ritual more evident than in the social facets of certain ceremonials, especially the social dancing of the Enemy Way. Not all Navajo ceremonials that would fall under the category of *Diné Binahagha'* (mentioned earlier) are public events, but one Navajo ceremonial in particular has a major public and social component and is frequently practiced: the Enemy Way ceremony.[20] Like other Navajo ceremonials, this is a curing ritual, and one that specifically cures "ghost sickness" caused when a Navajo comes into contact with the ghost of an outsider. There are several parts to this ceremony, which takes place over three days and nights, and in many ways the ceremony intends to reenact mythological wars (McAllester 1954, 8). By performatively encapsulating the illness within this mytho-ritual frame, the ghost of the enemy can be driven from the patient and slain (McAllester 1954, 8).[21]

Clearly the Pentecostal tent revival is a different ritual with a dramatically different purpose. But at the level of practice, there are some important similarities. First, in addition to the semi-private rituals of the singer, patient, and patient's family, the Enemy Way ceremony has a large public and social component. In his description of Enemy Way ceremonies in the 1950s, David McAllester commented that "the Enemy Way is felt to be a particularly enjoyable ceremony for spectators. Any man may join in a good deal of the singing, and women have been known to do so, too. This is one of the rare occasions in Navaho life on which young men may dance with girls" (McAllester 1954, 8).[22] On each of the three nights of the ceremony a bonfire is lit, and melodically complex dancing songs with a bouncy feel accompany the dancing of couples. Contemporarily known as a Navajo "song and dance" (but referred to in the past as a "Squaw Dance"), this dance begins with girls picking a dancing partner.[23] According to McAllester:

> Couples dance along side by side in a procession which circles around the dance ground. They may be holding hands or have their arms around each other . . . [occasionally] draped in the same blanket. For the most part, the couples simply walk or trot along, but occasionally someone may be seen skipping in a very subdued double bounce, first on one foot and then on the other. (1954, 10)

There are other kinds of singing and dancing that take place during the all-night public and social gathering of the Enemy Way ceremony.[24] But according to McAllester, in the 1950s Enemy Way social dancing was felt to be a particularly enjoyable way to spend an evening in rural Navajo country, and these factors clearly influence the frequency with which these ceremonials were performed (McAllester 1954, 8).

It may seem strange to look for continuity between the social dances of Navajo life and the religious ritual of the tent revival. But as established earlier, those boundaries are more porous than is typically assumed. Both the Enemy Way ceremony and the Oodláni tent revival have sacred and secular aspects, and the two are woven together rather seamlessly. For instance, in the Enemy Way ceremony, it is the "stick" girl (a girl with ceremonial duties in the healing) who begins the dancing by "seizing a youth and dragging him out into the circle" (McAllester 1954, 10). McAllester also notes that these dances were sometimes regarded as helping to bring rain (1954, 13).[25] And the music of the "song and dance," while decidedly less holy than that chanted by the ceremonial practitioner during the curing portions of the ceremony, was still regarded as holy.[26]

The same interweaving exists in Oodláni tent revivals. The preaching and charismatic behaviors of Oodláni at revivals take place in a broader secular atmosphere. At tent revivals people look after babies while their older children run around and play. They purchase and eat concessions: frybread, snow cones, hotdogs, hamburgers, soda. They visit with friends and relatives, and youths engage in cross-gender socialization. In addition to the concession table that raises money for the church by selling food, there are also folding tables set up around the tent where musicians can sell their CDs. Oodlání tent revivals are full of praise, but more to the point, they are also full of joy in family and communal life. As such, they fit into a deep groove of Navajo summer night gatherings that have sustained communities socially and spiritually for generations, their music echoing across the desert dawn as it has for centuries.

RITUAL PRACTICE: PRAYERS

In addition to the way Oodlání tent revivals map a certain kind of continuity with the social atmosphere of public ceremonials, there are certain aspects of traditional healing rituals that also echo into Oodlání practice. The linguistic taxonomy that elicited *Diné Binahagha'* (walking about ceremonially) as "Navajo religion" also identified the following component parts: "*hatáál,* ceremony; *biyee,* offering; *hane',* legend or myth; *sin,* song; *tsodizin,* prayer; and *bee 'ééhózinii,* premonitions" (Werner et al. 1983, 589).[27] I expand on two of these component rituals (prayers and offerings) in order to show the echoes of formal continuity in Oodlání practice. However, as this detailed examination shows, the ambiguity of ritual practice may be used by Oodlání to communicate rupture as much as continuity.

The Navajo word used by Oodlání to describe prayer is *tsodizin* and is the same as the traditional Navajo word for prayer.[28] This linguistic continuity is reflective of a broader performative continuity between certain kinds of Navajo traditional prayer and Christian prayers. Much has been written about Navajo ceremonial prayer.[29] Traditional Navajo ceremonial practitioners use both individual/informal and formal/litany (or "responsive") prayers (Frisbie 1980, 180–87). Litany prayers are common in traditional Navajo healing ceremonies and provide a recitation (call and response) between the patient and the ceremonial practitioner (Frisbie 1987, 19). Gill describes these "highly formulaic" prayers, adding that they are usually performed with the patient sitting "in a ritual position with legs extended, facing east, head slightly bowed, and holding a ritual object" (Gill 1987, 96), and that this prayer "intonement" may take from a few minutes to more than an hour (Gill 1987, 96). Oodláni eschew this kind of verbal call and response as "empty ceremonialism." They avoid call-and-response prayer both from a Protestant Christian standpoint (rejecting the formalism of Catholicism) and as neo-Pentecostal Navajos (rejecting the liturgy of traditional Navajo ceremonialism). Oodláni prayers are more similar to the traditional prayers that are individual or impromptu. Such prayers (also tsodizin) are said "in one's 'own words'" (Frisbie 1987, 117) and express an individual's own thoughts and petitions.[30]

Despite the similarity between Oodláni and traditional impromptu prayers, Oodláni tsodizin have a character all their own that stems from the history of Pentecostalism and healing revivals. There is no emphasis on brevity in Oodláni prayers; the more extended the prayer, the "harder" a person is seen to be praying and the "better" the prayer. Topics covered seem open but tend to elaborate on things Oodláni feel need attention called to them for blessings, from global issues to local concerns. In addition to prayers for "blessings," Maureen Schwarz has pointed out the importance of prayer in Oodláni concepts of healing. Schwarz writes out the testimonies of several Navajo consultants, which stress the power of prayer for healing, even for things as serious as nonfunctioning kidneys or liver disease (Schwarz 2008, 264–69).[31]

There are several significant differences between Oodláni prayers and those of traditional Navajo religion. One is that Oodláni regard prayer as a message: a communication with God. Prayers that are said while one is speaking in tongues (practicing glossolalia) are thought by Oodláni to be particularly pure messages because they are uncorruptable by the Devil, who cannot speak this "heavenly language." According to some traditional Navajo practitioners, however, in the traditional ceremonial complex prayers are more than messages: they are also considered *messengers*. They are beings who know everything, are all-powerful, and can take people on journeys (Gill 1987, 113). As personified actors, these prayers act as intermediaries between humans and the distant Holy People who have removed themselves to the cardinal points.

Another major difference between Oodlání and traditional Navajo conceptions of prayer is in the extent to which they can compel the action of nonhuman actors. For Oodlání, for instance, the source of the power of a prayer always resides in the Christian God, accessed through faith. Oodlání prayers are requests made to an all-powerful and (ideally) sympathetic God. But the efficacy of prayers also lies fully in the hands of God, and unanswered prayers are often explained as the "will of God." In contrast, traditional Navajo prayers are designed to be "compulsive" (Reichard 1966). Gill expands on this point to argue that the prayers of traditional Navajo religion are compulsive not because they are some kind of magical charm but because they seek to remind the *Diyin Diné'é* (Holy People) of the mutually obligating rules of reciprocity "which even the supernaturals are compelled to recognize" (Frisbie 1987, 3). For instance, some ceremonies combine offerings and prayers in order to reaffirm a grandfather-grandchild kinship relationship with the Holy People, assuming all of the attendant reciprocal obligations (Gill 1987, 118).[32] Thus, through the creative act of ritual prayer, the *Diyin Diné'é* may be compelled to act on behalf of humans by reminding them of kinship obligations. It is in the ability to "compel" action that the difference between Oodlání and traditional prayer is clearest. This distinction becomes clearer in a comparative discussion of the ritual practice of giving offerings.

RITUAL PRACTICE: OFFERINGS

Another practice that shows echoes of continuity in Oodlání ritual is the giving of offerings. The Navajo term for offerings (*náá'ii niih*) is used in both contexts and literally means "you go and offer." And while the term *náá'ii niih* continues to be employed by Oodlání to describe the practice of giving an offering, there are dramatic differences in what Oodlání consider an appropriate offering and what offerings are thought to do. Offerings, therefore, become another opportunity for practicing rupture.

In Oodlání contexts offerings are called *béeso naa'ii nííh* (*béeso*, "money"; *náá'ii niih*, "offering") and refer to the fact that Oodlání offerings are monetary. This money is taken up (as a collection) at certain points within the church or revival service, usually by placing a bucket or basket in front of the pulpit and having people come up and put money in the container while music is played. The money is used to pay musicians, visiting evangelists, and sometimes pastors and otherwise to run the ministries. Non-monetary gifts would not typically be referred to by Oodlání as *náá'ii niih*, but rather as "blessings." Monetary offerings are given in Oodlání contexts as an act of devotion and sacrifice to appeal to God, and sometimes to appeal for the blessings of God. Oodlání testify that God can return what is given in blessings "a hundredfold."

In traditional Navajo settings, on the other hand, offerings are usually not monetary but rather can take many different forms of valued natural objects. Particularly common are *ntł'iz* or "hard goods offering" (jewelry, precious stones, etc.) that are used as a gift to the deities in order to "make a connection" (King 2008). One might lay down these goods in order both to initiate and to finalize a prayer. More broadly, traditional offerings are known not as *náá'ii niih* but as *yeel*—which refers not only to the offering but also to the knowledge of what to do with those items. According to my research assistant Larry King, one would say *"Shiyeel hóló̜* (I have a *yeel*), meaning I have a knowledge . . . and traditional paraphernalia to practice" (King 2008).[33]

In significant contrast to the monetary offerings that are given by Oodlání with no certain guarantee of direct benefit, traditional Navajo offerings are made as a way of establishing reciprocal relations with deities to achieve a desired outcome (Reichard 1949, 68). As Aberle explains:

In Navaho religion, man's relationship to supernaturals is fundamentally one of reciprocity. By and large, if one can discover what gift will establish reciprocity with a spiritual being, and supply the gift, the being must respond. Hence supernaturals are angry in Navaho myths when a messenger spirit tells a man seeking help exactly what gift is wanted. (Aberle 1991, 195–96)

Offerings are thus understood as a way of establishing a reciprocal relationship with a supernatural actor.[34] The logic of reciprocity is deeply ingrained in the entire ceremonial system: apprentices and patients make offerings (*yeel*) to the singers, and singers make offerings to the Holy People, in what Frisbie calls a "chain of reciprocity which stretches between the sacred and profane worlds and that includes everyone" (1987. 89). The efficacy of the offerings is grounded in this reciprocal system, because once the gifts are accepted the deities are "compelled to respond" (Frisbie 1987, 89), primarily because they are bound by the reciprocal obligations of traditional Navajo sociality.[35] Thus the reference to *yeel* in the words of a traditional prayer reported by Reichard (1949, 68), suggest a kind of cause-and-effect relationship between offerings and supernatural intervention: "I have made your offering to you / My mind restore for me" (Reichard 1949, 68).

This attitude toward offerings differs rather significantly from the Oodlání perspective, where God's action can be appealed for, but as the all-powerful ruler of the universe God cannot be compelled to any action. As Aberle mentioned of another Christian-derived movement among Navajos, "the peyotist deals with his all-powerful God by beseeching Him in humility. . . . God replies to man's prayers because He is good and merciful and man is helpless and God's child. No compulsions can be laid on God" (Aberle 1991, 196). The Christian God is not bound by the Navajo chain of reciprocity, and while pastors can assure congregations that monetary offerings will increase their blessings "a hundred-fold," there is no guarantee how or when this will happen.

This close examination of both *tsodizin* (prayers) and *náá'ii niih* (offerings) shows that continuity may not be the only (or even most important) orientation communicated in Oodlání rituals like the tent revival. While there are undoubtedly echoes of traditional practice preserved in the language and the affective attachment to form, there seem also to be significant rifts at the level of meaning. These practices resonate, but returning to the primary argument of this chapter, they reflect a resonant type of rupture.

Resonant Rupture

And so, we . . . we are Native, you know? And we have our culture.
But we draw the line when it . . . when it turns into, you know . . . a ceremony.
We draw the line when it . . . when it turns into worshiping, you know, idols and all that.

—(BEGAY 2008B)

On March 7, 1976, in Lower Greasewood, Arizona, a Navajo medicine bundle (called *jish*) was dramatically burned at a Pentecostal revival meeting (Frisbie 1987, 207). This blatant destruction of sacred paraphernalia, and rumors of other similar destructive desecrations, galvanized the Navajo Medicine Men's Association to action. On February 2, 1978, the Navajo Tribal Council passed a resolution (CF-20-78) "to protect religious paraphernalia from desecration and unlawful destruction" (Frisbie 1987, 305). And yet, despite this being explicitly outlawed on the Navajo Nation, some Navajo Christians, especially Oodláni, continue to destroy jish in private.

Christian missionaries have destroyed sacred objects among people they evangelized for centuries, so on the surface this destruction may read as simply another colonial act of outside Christian agents. And indeed, when opening his book with the rumored burning in 1992 of Chilkat dancing regalia among Tlingit and Haida in southeast Alaska, Dombrowski draws direct parallels between these acts of destruction and those of early twentieth-century converts who forced residents to burn village totem poles (2001, 3). However, when these dramatic acts of rupture are conducted and encouraged by Native evangelists and pastors, they represent a complication of the clear distinction between rituals of continuity and rituals of rupture (Robbins 2003b).[36]

Rather than enacting the clear break with the past that may

seem obvious, I argue that jish burning actually represents a type of resonant rupture. The crux of that assertion is this: according to Oodláni discourse, jish that a convert no longer wants cannot simply be given away or abandoned. It must be actively destroyed. This destruction is contingent because jish continue to be regarded by Oodláni as a threat. Jish bundles continue to be endowed with supernatural power.[37] And yet this is not a case of clear continuity either, since the supernatural power of jish is reinterpreted by Oodláni in contrast to the supernatural power of God embodied in the *anointing*.

In this section I continue my exploration of the resonant rupture of Oodláni ritual by unpacking the meaning behind the private rituals of jish burning. This destruction, I may point out, is viewed by non-Oodláni Diné as absolutely offensive, and discussions about jish burning are controversial, provoking reactions of horror and moral outrage.[38] Because of this, and the illegal nature of the act of burning jish, I feel the ethical imperative to highlight that I never saw Pastor Wallace Begay, nor any of the people I have identified by name in this book, engage in any acts of jish destruction. My analysis in this chapter is based on an ethnographically informed reading of historical cases from the 1970s as well as commentary from contemporary collaborators on how jish are regarded and that jish destruction continues to be practiced by some Oodláni in private.

DESTRUCTION OF JISH

Jish, or medicine bundles, are a collection of ritual items such as herbs, rattles, fetishes, whistles, arrowheads, reeds, and pouches of pollen. These items are typically contained in a buckskin bag, also known as jish and used as part of traditional Navajo curing ceremonies (Frisbie 1987, 8–9). For practitioners of Navajo ceremonialism, however, jish are much more than a collection of things. They are sacred objects, regarded as "both a source and a repository of sacred power" (Frisbie 1987, 9). Furthermore, a jish is regarded as a living entity with "feelings and needs" (Frisbie 1987, 9). Jish is meant to be passed from practitioner to practitioner, and part of its power comes from the historical and heritage value of its longevity. Jish bundles can serve as protection to the holder and his or her family. Conversely, improper care, handling, or use will almost certainly bring misfortune (Frisbie 1987, 9). If conversion to Christianity is simply outward accommodation on top of an internal current of continuity, then the burning of jish would be unthinkable.

But the reality is that neo-Pentecostal Navajos have historically destroyed jish bundles and continue to do so. As noted, after the dramatic Lower Greasewood burning in 1976 it was made explicitly illegal to destroy jish. The major fine leveled against a Navajo pastor in 1986 for destroying a jish sent the message to Navajo pastors that the Navajo Nation intended to uphold that law. Effectively, this means that jish destruction now happens behind the scenes. For example, in the more than 150 hours I spent at Navajo tent revivals, I never observed the public destruction of jish. Conversations with church members, however, made clear that area neo-Pentecostal churches still practiced destruction of jish in private, a contemporary fact confirmed by other scholars as well (Csordas 1999, 11; Lewton and Bydone 2000, 494; Schwarz 2008, 263). Because of the ethical and legal challenges to documenting the burning of jish, I use an ethnographically shaped lens to examine two instances of jish burning within the realm of public knowledge. Both of these cases are documented in print in Charlotte Frisbie's well-researched *Navajo Medicine Bundles or Jish: Acquisition, Transmission and Disposition in the Past and Present* (1987).[39]

The first instance recorded in detail by Frisbie is the Lower Greasewood burning of 1976. Frisbie became aware of these events at a special meeting in the Navajo capital of Window Rock held to discuss them. A local delegation reported that a "preacher/ promoter" Brother Freddy, and Collie Yazzie, the church council president (both Navajos), were "brainwashing the People into burning sacred things" (Frisbie 1987, 208). Occurrences such as this galvanized meeting participants to begin to organize as a Medicine Men's Association. It also led to consultations with tribal legal services and the eventual passing of a Navajo tribal council resolution in 1978 outlawing the practice.

Another burning recorded in detail by Frisbie took place in 1986. This burning, publicized by the court case *Edison v. Franklin*, involved the converted daughter of a ceremonial practitioner and the Reverend Scott Franklin, the Navajo pastor of the Indian Bible Church in Flagstaff, Arizona. The converted daughter, without the consent of the other family members, gave the bundle to Reverend Franklin to be burned. When the husband of another daughter, practitioner Dale Edison, went to retrieve the jish, he discovered the destruction and brought suit against Franklin. The code of 1978 was invoked and Franklin was fined (Frisbie 1987, 306). In a later interview Frisbie reports that Franklin felt the destruction of his own jish at his conversion had helped free him from trouble with witchcraft. After all the publicity and the fine (which his church was raising funds to pay), Franklin admitted he would not be destroying any more jish for converts—but he would continue to give people instructions on how to destroy it on their own (Frisbie 1987, 308).

Why the persistence of such destruction? Especially in light of the fact that the Medicine Men's Association publishes detailed instructions, widely available to area churches, on how to give away unwanted bundles? Jish burning persists among Navajo neo-Pentecostals because, from an ontological perspective, it must. For Navajo neo-Pentecostals, just as for Navajo traditionalists, a jish is regarded as a living thing and one that can continue to affect the previous owner and that person's kin. Jish continues to be endowed with power, a stance very much in contrast to the position of rational Protestant missionaries who encouraged converts to put aside past "'superstitions' in the interest of modernization."[40]

That a certain kind of continuity can exist even in the most dramatic rites of rupture attests to the ambiguity of ritual practice. As McNally suggests, practices "have a certain taken-for-granted quality to them," and they are therefore better equipped than discursive thought to "smuggle in all sorts of new (or old) ways of configuring what is real and of value in the world" (McNally 2000b, 852). Reading Jish burning as an act of cultural continuity may seem outrageous, and in fact Whiteley calls the burning of sacred Native paraphernalia "a rather radical form of cultural refiguring" (Whiteley 1992, 50). But the ambiguity of practice is "remarkably capable" of holding these contradictions in tension (McNally 2000b, 857).[41] While the undergirding logic of jish burning preserves the notion that these bundles have power, it is also abundantly clear that jish burning is by no means a practice that attempts to forge continuity with traditional religion. There is ontological discontinuity here as well, and that distinction lies not in the question *that* there is power in jish but rather from where that power derives.

POWER AND THE ANOINTING

Oodlání believe that the most powerful supernatural force in the universe is God. As charismatic believers, however, for them this assertion is not merely a theological one but a very pragmatic and material one. Oodlání say they experience the power of God all the time, through the mechanism of God's "anointing." The anointing is understood by Oodlání as "the presence of God," or more specifically "the power of God that comes down" (Begay 2008b). The anointing drives the embodied experience of the Holy Spirit that facilitates charismatic behaviors such as speaking in tongues, dancing in the spirit, prophecy, and healing. It is also the name for what anthropologists (following Max Weber) would call the "charismatic authority" of Oodlání preachers, evangelists, and musicians. Those with a large anointing on their ministry will attract followers, change lives, and be able to wield charismatic gifts like healing and driving out demons in the service of others.[42] As such, the anointing underpins the affective power of all of the expressive forms explored in this book.

According to Pastor Wallace, the anointing is difficult to explain, "unless you experience it yourself" (Begay 2008b). But he did describe the feeling of the anointing as taking different forms: sometimes it is experienced as chills down a person's back or as a warmth rising from the feet to the head. "Some people," he said, "feel it in the palm of their hands, like fire" (W. Begay 2008b). He explained that Oodlání view the anointing as "fuel" that helps a person live a Christian life. The relationship with God becomes "a personal relationship." And baptism in the spirit takes a person to "another level" in his or her relationship with God.

To help me understand what the anointing was like, Pastor Wallace recalled in detail his own initial encounter with the Holy Spirit:

> When I got baptized with the Holy Spirit, I was at a Pentecostal meeting and I was standing up there in the bleachers. . . . I never knew about the Holy Spirit. I was . . . Christian Reformed. . . . but I got up and I raised my hand and I asked God to fill me. . . . The anointing fell, people were dancing, they were shouting, and all of a sudden . . . I heard, like a wind, like some kind of force that was coming. And . . . a force, a tremendous power just hit me, threw me back against the wall. I blacked out right there.

> And my cousin Rita and [others] were around me, they . . . they had never seen . . . you know, anything like that. And they said, "Man, it's just like, it's like something just threw you back against the wall. . . . You really hit the wall hard," you know? . . . I'd probably say for like two or three minutes I was . . . lost. And when I came to, I was speaking in tongues and my, my hands were just shaking . . . I was just shaking all over, just, you know. . . . When I tried to say something . . . words were just coming out in tongues. (Begay 2008b)

According to Pastor Wallace, if a church service is going well and people are really worshiping and "the Body of Christ becomes as one," then the anointing comes down onto the service and begins to "fill the hearts of people" (Begay 2008b).

So the anointing, in some senses, is at the root of how God is experienced by Oodláni. It is the present power of God, required fuel for all the more visible charismatic "gifts of the spirit." The power of the anointing, however, is diminished when it is mixed with other forms of power. As a Navajo pastor once told me, "It's like diluting a strong cup of coffee."[43] There are many secular ways in which the anointing of a ministry can be diminished, such as committing adultery, monetary corruption, drinking alcohol, etc. But most typically, the anointing is threatened by a contrasting (and fundamentally evil) supernatural power. As

I explore later, Oodlání see themselves as being embroiled in a cosmic battle between God and the Devil. God is preeminently victorious, but the Devil and his demons are constantly working to tempt humans away from this victory and the divine control it secured. Demon forces do this by introducing misfortune and suffering into daily life, and Oodlání are instructed on how to meet these demon forces and engage them as "spiritual warriors."[44]

Because of the warfare metaphors that undergird Oodlání theology, boundary policing becomes an immediate and material concern (Engelke 2010, 184; Daswani 2013, 468). Often, this boundary protection engages directly with traditional and cultural practices. Outsiders may see a mixture of forms at work in Oodlání rituals, mistaking tent revivals for girls' dances, or may see prayers and offerings as essentially stable because they are still called *tsodizin* and *náá'ii niih*. But believers are actually very conscious sentinels—they are especially careful not to mix or confuse their beliefs or rituals with ones they perceive as traditional. This boundary policing was illustrated particularly well by an exchange between community members and an Anglo evangelist who visited local revivals a few years ago. In an attempt to celebrate "Indian culture" and preach Christianity in (what she perceived to be) a culturally sensitive way, the Anglo evangelist arrived at the camp meeting with "miracle pouches" to give away. They were little rawhide pouches containing small bottles of anointing oil. But, by her own admission, they bore striking resemblance to traditional "medicine pouches." She found that Oodlání categorically refused to take them. For Oodlání, medicine bundles do not represent Navajo cultural heritage. Rather, these miracle pouches and the jish medicine bundles they referenced represented the traditional ceremonial complex, driven by a power other than (and opposed to) the anointing.[45]

The continued destruction of jish is significant because it reflects underlying Oodlání understandings of supernatural power. The way in which jish burning represents both rupture and (a kind of) continuity illustrates what Robbins has named one of the "paradoxes" of Pentecostalism: the way in which it "becomes local without ever taking the local into itself" (Robbins 2003b, 223). The essence of the neo-Pentecostal story of localization, as Casanova has pointed out, is that it is more than a story of rupture. By engaging in spiritual warfare with their "own roots," global Pentecostal movements like the Oodlání "prove how very locally rooted they are" (2001, 437–38). This attitude toward head-on spiritual warfare is reflected in the comments of Pastor Franklin (one of the Navajo pastors who destroyed jish, described earlier). When interviewed by Frisbie, he maintained the rightness of his actions, saying, "I know I did right by breaking way from the Navajo religion," and then adding biblical justification from Corinthians 1:10, reciting: "They are sacrificing to demons, not to God. Do not have fellowship with those who worship demons" (Frisbie 1987, 308). Some Navajo things, argue Oodlání I know, cannot be incorporated into Navajo neo-Pentecostalism; not because traditional ways are not efficacious but because they employ the wrong kind of power for their efficacy. They are not anointed.

Conclusion

I have focused on the rituals of Navajo neo-Pentecostals in order to highlight the ways that this religious movement has found success by capitalizing on a kind of resonant rupture. I have focused not on the way neo-Pentecostal doctrine was learned by some Navajos but rather on the ritual practice of this community, both public and private. This focus on religion as it is practiced shows how neo-Pentecostalism has been made locally relevant by Navajos, who simultaneously hold fast to religious rupture.

Tent revivals are the performative events that hold the key to this resonant rupture, and they are enormously popular evening activities among large portions of the Navajo population. As Frisbie commented in 1987, "Anyone who has spent time on the reservation in the last twenty-five years can vouch for the ever-increasing number of tents . . . erected for 'revival meetings'" (1987, 201). When a large social gathering is sought in the pleasant desert evening of the vast Navajo Nation, there are only a select number of events (within a few hours' drive) that are available as options. We might imagine that tent revivals did provide (and still provide) this kind of communal function, and that social factor may indeed have contributed to their success over the staid, formal, and Sunday-morning nature of denominational mission churches. The mixing of sacred and secular facets present in the tent revival is not unique in Navajo social gatherings but rather the norm.

And yet we should not rush to declare continuity simply because the atmosphere of a tent revival resembles, in some ways, the social nature of the Enemy Way public dances. Robbins cautions that ethnographers may be too quick to assume cultural continuity (2003b, 230). Therefore, I contrast these public rituals of continuity with other, private rituals that indicate deep levels of rupture, even as they continue to endow jish with supernatural power.

The quest for beauty and aesthetic coherence may lead people to adopt practices that resonate (are amplified by) past practice. But continuity in form is not necessarily reflective of continuity in meaning. For Oodláni, the beauty of the tent revival lies not in its social nature but in the powerful movement of the anointing of God. As Pastor Wallace put it:

> [God] moves in a beautiful way when he moves among his people. And miracles take place. Healing takes place. Salvation, deliverance takes place . . . when the anointing comes down. And it is the anointing that breaks the yokes, you know. You can sing a beautiful song, and it will just be a song. But if there's an anointing that flows . . . lives will be changed, people will be touched. And . . . and people will feel the presence of God there. (Begay 2008b)

By focusing on the way in which faith is *practiced* by Oodláni, this chapter has demonstrated the complex ties between Oodláni rituals and the past. In public and private ways, through tent revivals and jish burning, Oodláni practice both feelingful continuity and dramatic rupture.

CHAPTER 3

Háálá Ayóo Diyin
The Resonant Rupture of Language

Dalia danced with reserved steps, like a traditional powwow dancer, and her hands made words. Although Diné (Navajo), Dalia had grown up away from Diné Bikeya, the land between the Four Sacred Mountains. At a revival one windy night in early July, she told the gathered audience of her sadness at never having learned "her language." Wearing a long red broomstick skirt, velveteen blouse, and large silver-work belt (her most Navajo of garb), she told us how her family had moved to Colorado and taught her no Navajo because they felt it would "cripple" her. Growing up, Dalia said, she felt a calling from God to learn another language. But instead of Navajo, as she had expected, God led her to learn sign language. As an adult, she moved to a border town and began attending a church where she was exposed to liturgical dance, which she began to combine with sign language.

In the cool desert evening red dust swirled around her on the revival platform as she spoke. She said that after a few years, the Lord told her she was going to receive a dance to a song sung by a Navajo woman. She was led to the piece Háálá Ayóo Diyin, but not knowing Navajo, she did not understand it. She prayed to God to understand the message of this song. And as she was praying, a Navajo policeman showed up at her door. He translated the song for her. And now she danced its message. "Jesus saved me . . . Jesus healed me . . . Jesus I praise . . . Oh how Holy, and amazingly beautiful. How very, very Holy."[1]

This is just one story from the life of the song *Háálá Ayóo Diyin*. This song is a favorite of Navajo neo-Pentecostals (Oodlání), among whom music plays a central role in worship and the manifestation of spiritual gifts. The song is regularly performed at revivals by both practiced musicians and untrained but inspired believers. It has been recorded by many Navajo gospel bands and is commonly broadcast across local airwaves. And yet despite its popularity, *Háálá Ayóo Diyin* is an anomaly. It stands alone as the only widely known and actively performed Christian song originally composed in the Navajo language and not derived from an English-language piece. The uniqueness of *Háálá Ayóo Diyin* contrasts with the more common linguistic reality among Navajo neo-Pentecostals that largely favors creative Navajo-language expressive culture: prayers, sermons, and testimonies are all extemporized in Navajo. Music is different. The fact that nearly all Oodlání music is composed in (or translated from) English suggests that tangible barriers exist to musical composition in the Navajo language for this faith community. I argue that these barriers lie in the resonant rupture between Navajo "performative" language ideologies and a neo-Pentecostal theologies of "exclusivity."

Choices about when and if to use heritage languages are shaped by what linguistic anthropologists call "language ideologies."[2] Our language choices are shaped by our beliefs and feelings about words. For instance, there may be some words we use around our friends that we might feel are too "vulgar" to use around our grandparents. For Oodlání, choices about appropriate words are also shaped by religious beliefs. And while their theology may have changed to one shaped by Pentecostal Christianity, their language ideologies (beliefs and feelings about the Navajo language) have often not undergone this shift. Religious beliefs and language ideologies thus sometimes conflict. One of the most problematic aspects of Navajo language ideologies for Oodlání is its "performative" dimension. Navajo words are understood to contain the power literally to perform actions in the world, such as healing. This applies particularly to the poetic language of traditional Navajo ceremonial practitioners, speech and song commonly referred to by Oodlání as "medicine man chant."[3] This performative aspect of Navajo poetic language creates tension for Oodlání who are actively trying to practice religious exclusivity by separating themselves from traditional Navajo religion.

These tensions are especially evident in the composition of new Christian music, where Navajo poetic texts must be set to music in a way that does not evoke the aesthetic signifiers of medicine man chant.

In an environment where elderly Navajo grandmothers may greet new musical composition negatively by standing and loudly "shouting the Devil" out of the musicians, how did *Háálá Ayóo Diyin* become so popular?[4] In this chapter I argue that this song has gained success by capitalizing on the productivity of resonant rupture. As with ritual, explored in the previous chapter, resonant rupture accounts for both aesthetic continuity and denotative denial of continuity, present here in the language ideologies of Navajo neo-Pentecostalism. Resonant rupture recognizes the emotional force of continuity in expressive forms while still taking seriously the projects of rupture in which Oodlání understand themselves to be engaged. I discuss how *Háálá Ayóo Diyin* avoids the perils of a performative language ideologies by using poetic devices and aesthetic signifiers that evoke continuity without actually sounding like medicine man chant. *Háálá Ayóo Diyin* may use aesthetically familiar forms, but it actually uses these forms to promote theological rupture.

Navajo Language Ideologies

The Navajo language is an important medium through which Oodlání preach, worship, and testify, at both church services and revivals. Navajo language use is a common and accepted part of Oodlání life. I never heard a single pastor or evangelist preach against its use, and several extolled its virtues. In fact, Oodlání church services and revivals are often one of the most prominent places for the public performance of spoken Navajo.[5] Texts such as the Bible, a hymn book, and several song books are available in Navajo. Pastor Wallace took the time each church service to read the weekly Bible verse in both English and Navajo. And as the vignette about Dalia opening this chapter illustrates, even those who cannot speak Navajo hold strong beliefs and feelings about the language (Silverstein 1979). Although the messages communicated in Navajo by Oodlání are different from those found in more traditional Navajo contexts, there is a great deal of continuity in their language ideologies.[6]

First, Oodlání continue to regard Navajo language use as strongly tied to an "authentic" Navajo identity. Navajo linguists have identified this link to identity as an important aspect of a generalized Navajo language ideologies (House 2002; Webster 2009; Peterson and Webster 2013). The link to identity holds that speaking Navajo is "what Navajos do" (Webster 2009, 85).[7] When Diné Navajo speakers falter, it is not their language ability that is questioned; it is their very identity.[8] As Dalia commented, she had never learned "her" language.[9]

The vast majority of Navajos today speak some English, and many of the younger generation are monolingual English speakers. Since 1975 Navajo children have been transitioning to English monolingualism (Field 2009, 41), and a 1992 study showed that nearly 55 percent of Navajo preschoolers were monolingual English speakers (Platero 1992). Dalia is representative of this trend. Her parents, like many Navajo parents, chose not to encourage more than a passive (receptive) competency in Navajo for their children, primarily because they saw native competence in English as an important way to "get ahead" (Field 2009, 41–42). More and more Navajo children cannot understand or speak with their own grandparents, and yet those elders, "who are the best speakers of the language are, more often than one would think, the least willing to tolerate or cooperate with young Navajo students of the language" (House 2002, 55). In part, the impatience of the elders is rooted in the elision between language skills and identity.

For example, the contention about the eligibility of Christopher Deschene as a candidate in the 2014 runoff election for Navajo Nation president highlighted the ideological connection between Navajo language and Navajo identity. Deschene's eligibility for the office was legally called into question based on doubts about his fluency in the Navajo language.[10] Deschene refused to take a fluency test as ordered by the Navajo Nation Supreme Court, and in a hearing on October 9, 2014, refused to answer questions in Navajo before a tribal hearing officer (Landry 2014). However, in multiple statements to the press and supporters, Deschene has repeatedly insisted (in English and in Navajo), "Diné Nishli," or "I am Navajo."[11]

Like other Navajos, Oodláni also view Navajo language skills as a marker of a kind of "authentic" Navajo identity. One of my first introductions to Pastor Wallace's congregations was as a language learner looking for a public forum in which to observe spoken Navajo. In fact, my role as a language learner remained one of my primary identities in the community throughout my fieldwork. On several occasions Pastor Wallace would explain my presence to visiting evangelists through this framework, occasionally handing me the microphone and asking me say certain basic words or to introduce myself in Navajo.[12] Much more uncomfortable for me than being put on the spot, however, were the instances in which Pastor Wallace used me as a foil through which to chastise the youth of the congregation publicly for their linguistic failings. For instance, the first time I attended a Sunday service at Pastor Wallace's church I arrived early and introduced myself to Pastor Wallace as a student at Diné College, learning the Navajo language, and at his church to observe public use of Navajo. Later in the service he introduced me to the congregation and commented that if white people could learn the Navajo language, then "You can too, especially you young people!" He launched into a fifteen-minute lecture on how young Navajos should be proud to be Diné and not ashamed of their language.[13]

Another major aspect of Navajo language ideologies that remains in circulation among Oodláni is the nostalgic association between the Navajo language and the past. In part, this aspect of Navajo language ideologies is rooted in economic reality. Navajos who held more livestock and grazing land were able to maintain a "traditional" pastoral lifestyle, including traditional religion (Field 2009, 44). Navajos who did not possess these economic resources were forced into interactions with Anglo wage and migrant labor, and these interactions led to higher levels of assimilation (including linguistic assimilation). Over the past few decades these material and social conditions have created an ideological association between the Navajo language, rurality, livestock, and traditional lifeways (Field 2009, 43).

In the Oodlání context, the nostalgia associated with the Navajo language is reflected in the attitudes toward Navajo-language hymns. Unlike in other Native Christian contexts, hymns are not usually a part of Oodlání worship.[14] While hymns have been available in the Navajo language for nearly a century, and became widely accessible in the Navajo hymnbook *Jesus Woodlaaji Sin* in 1979, they are primarily used by and associated with denominational, not Pentecostal, church worship.[15] Hymnbooks are not present in Oodlání worship services, song leaders only rarely lead group songs from the hymnal (in English or in Navajo), and they virtually never identify these songs by hymn number.[16]

Like the traditional pastoral lifestyle, Navajo language hymns are regarded, primarily, as "old-fashioned." In part, this association has come about because hymns were regularly sung at the denominational churches in which many of the older Oodlání were raised (Norton 2012). But the language ideologies that connect the Navajo language with a pastoral, rural past is evident in Pastor Wallace's discourse as well. He explained that if he performed a hymn, he would sing it at an evening service (not a morning one) because they were "restful" and "comforting" and appropriate for "when the sun is setting" (Begay 2012).

As these examples illustrate, several of the important themes of Navajo language ideologies remain intact and operational within Oodlání contexts.[17] Despite their neo-Pentecostal religious affiliation, Oodlání still regard the Navajo language as a marker of authentic identity and as a nostalgic index of the past. These two associations do not cause significant dissonance when paired with neo-Pentecostal theology. The Western tonal harmony of Navajo-language hymns may be regarded as "old-fashioned," but it is unlikely to cause controversy. The same cannot be said for a more metaphysical aspect of Navajo language ideologies: their performativity. Oodlání strive to keep separate the realms of traditional religion and Pentecostal Christianity. When the speaking and signing of Navajo words is regarded as having the power to change the fabric of reality, stable language ideologies begin to come into direct conflict with the Oodlání theology of exclusivity.

Medicine Man Chant and the Theology of Exclusivity

When the Northern Navajo Fair comes to Shiprock, everyone joins the parade. I had arrived just before dawn and, even at that early hour, there were cars lined up along the highway for miles, full of families who had camped out the night before to join the fun. The parade went on for more than three hours. Floats contained school groups, music groups, contest royalty, and government officials. All floats displayed the theme phrase for the year: "Ye'ii Bi Chei—Spiritual Blessing," indicating the association between the Northern Navajo Fair each October and the annual public dance of the Ye'ii (a special group of Diyin Diné'é or "Holy People"). This dance concludes the annual nine-night Night Way ceremony, a major curative ceremony in the traditional ceremonial complex that aims to restore harmony. Many Oodlání churches had floats in the parade, and several of those contained gospel bands. On one float, decorated with palm trees and draped with Hawaiian leis, the Gary Jack Band belted out Háálá Ayóo Diyin. The ladies sitting along the parade route next to me sang along. I noted that instead of "Ye'ii Bi Chei—Spiritual Blessing," the float's banner read "You Bet Cha Spiritual Blessing."[18]

At its core the Oodlání worldview is founded on a theology of exclusivity. While Oodlání are led by Navajo pastors, and believers value their Navajo identity, they are distinct in the Navajo religious landscape in that they adamantly avoid mixing religious practices.[19] Instead, they encourage rupture with the past and are exclusive in their dedication to Christianity—hence the switch from "Ye'ii Bi Chei" to "You Bet Cha." This theology of exclusivity is common in the growing neo-Pentecostal movement globally and is grounded in the fact that traditional religious systems (healing sings, divination, witchcraft) are reinterpreted, rather than dismissed, by converts.[20]

As explored in the previous chapter, Oodlání rarely dismiss the power of traditional healers as "superstitious nonsense." Rather, they reinterpret the very efficacy of that tradition within a neo-Pentecostal framework of divine warfare between Jesus and the Devil (and his host of demons), which is manifest in the trials of the everyday lives of believers. For dedicated Oodlání, this framework necessitates a theology of exclusivity—a rupture with past practice and a dedication solely to neo-Pentecostal solutions. To do otherwise, as I was variously told, would be to "serve two Gods," "dilute a strong cup of coffee," or to "bring the Devil into the church."[21]

This theology of exclusivity has implications for Oodláni musical practice and new composition. One of the primary barriers to new song composition in the Navajo language is the lack of a traditional category for "secular" music. As McAllester found, even when investigating the jovial courting music of the "social" portions of the traditional Navajo Enemy Way ceremony, "It is hard to discuss with a Navaho what music is 'holy' and what music is not. The first reaction of nearly all of my informants was that all of their songs were sacred" (McAllester 1954, 63).[22] Although upon further probing Navajos he spoke with showed some consensus in ordering certain types of music as "more" or "less" sacred, this statement of principle that "all of their songs were sacred" led McAllester to conclude that at the heart of Navajo musical aesthetics lies *nizhóni:* an elision between concepts of "good" and "beautiful" (McAllester 1954, 71).

Song holds an important place in the traditional Navajo ceremonial complex as well. In brief, Navajos have traditionally held ceremonies (also called chants, ways, or sings, depending on the translation of the Navajo enclitic -*jí*) whenever there is a need felt for one, most commonly by an individual and often in response to a concern about health (Gill 1981, 58).[23] Once the proper ceremony (or "Way") has been diagnosed, a *hataałii,* or "singer" (also called a medicine man) is hired to perform the ceremony, or "sing." Sings last between one and nine nights and are communal gatherings that take place in a ceremonial hogan, a traditional Navajo dwelling (Gill 1981, 59). The singer and the patient, more accurately named "the one-sung-over," are the focus of this sing, but everyone who attends the ceremony benefits from the healing and restoration that is done there (Reichard 1963, xxxvii).[24]

Within these contexts, songs constitute a major part of the ritual activities that aim to restore harmony and balance (*hózhǫ́;* Witherspoon 1977, 155), restating and reemphasizing things already stated in prayer. In part, songs have the power to restore *hózhǫ́* during ceremonies because spoken and sung forms of poetic language (or "chant") are seen as closely related within the traditional Navajo worldview, and both can be used in intensified form as prayer. "Music is so much a part of religion," says McAllester, "that it can hardly be conceived of apart from its function," leading Navajos to ask about a song not "How does it sound?" but "What is it for?" (McAllester 1954, 71). The strong connection between song and effect is linguistically evidenced in Navajo as well. According to Reichard, the word for song in the Navajo language has, "a complicated series of corresponding verb-stems, referring, however, not to singing or song but to holiness, reverence, prayer, and, in the passive voice, to sorcery" (1963, 297–98). For Navajo Pentecostals, who equate traditional religion with the Devil, this association between sung Navajo words and traditional forms of poetic ceremonial language is problematic.

The musical compositions of Anglo missionary Ben Stoner provide a compelling contemporary example of the charged nature of the associations between Navajo language, song, and traditional Navajo religion. Stoner has been a missionary at the Brethren of Christ mission in Bloomfield, New Mexico, for more than forty-five years and is widely recognized as one of a handful of Anglos not raised among Navajos who has ever gained fluency in the Navajo language. Disturbed by the lack of "Navajo hymnody," Stoner has been working for years on a project that would "set scripture to music" by cuing off the melodic aspects of the Navajo language (in this case Navajo language biblical passages) when read aloud (Baldridge 2000, 68). Navajo vowels can be short or long, high tone or low tone, and rising or falling. Stoner's project is to "musicalize" these aspects, using a quarter note for a long vowel and an eighth note for a short vowel, raising or lowering the pitch of the "chant" for the high or low tone vowels, and slurring the pitch up or down for rising or falling vowel tones.[25] By Stoner's own admission, the result sounds "much like a traditional chant" (Baldridge 2000, 68).

Despite efforts by Stoner and a handful of Navajo gospel musicians (Daniel Smiley, Andrew Begay, and Julie Redhouse) to popularize this type of music that they claim will help build a "true Navajo church" (Baldridge 2000, 94), the emotional associations of traditional Navajo chant and the theological associations of traditional religion as still containing the efficacious power of demons are simply too strong for the majority of Oodláni to support.[26] As one believer told me, to her this music "sounds like the medicine man singing . . . really Navajo style, swingy-like, like a medicine man . . . and it throws my mind off the real Christianity . . . those that are followers of the Lord already know it's not a good idea to teach our children [this music]."[27] From radio hosts to pastors to lay participants, there seems to be a near universal Oodláni condemnation of this type of musical blending (Baldridge 2000; Marshall 2011a).

The theology of exclusivity thus sets up real challenges to new composition for Oodláni who want to sing in Navajo but avoid sounding like medicine men.[28] However, the problematic associations of poetic Navajo language when set to song go even further. For Oodláni, it is not simply a matter of avoiding the past, of not "going back" (B. Joe 2008). It is also that Navajo language continues to maintain its performative force, particularly when set to song.

Navajo Performative Language

Navajo language, and particularly Navajo language within ritual contexts, has been widely documented to emphasize performativity (Reichard 1966; Witherspoon 1977; Gill 1987; Field and Blackhorse 2002). Even English language ideologies recognize that certain phrases have performative (sometimes called "pragmatic") force. For instance, using one of J. L. Austin's classic examples, saying "I name this ship" in the context of a christening ceremony is the actual act of naming, not a reference to that naming (Austin 1970, 235). In the Navajo ceremonial context the performative force of language is the central mechanism by which the rituals are understood to have efficacy. But this very performative force inherent in the language creates problems when imported into new contexts, such as Oodláni revivals.

Navajo language ideologies are distinctive from Euro-American language ideologies (but similar to other Native American language ideologies) in that they privilege the performative nature of language. Euro-American language ideologies regard language as primarily "reflectionist"-assuming that the primary function of language is in providing names for things (Field and Kroskrity 2009, 10). Many Native Americans, on the other hand, possess language ideologies that "view language and speech more 'performatively'—as a more powerful and creative force that 'makes' the natural and social worlds they inhabit" (Field and Kroskrity 2009, 10).[29]

The performative nature of Navajo ritual language is linked to Navajo mythology, philosophy, and cosmology. In the creation myths the world was created out of the thoughts of the Holy People but did not come into being until these thoughts were spoken and sung (Witherspoon 1977, 47). In this view of creation, transformative acts proceed from knowledge, "organized in thought, patterned in language, and realized in speech" (Witherspoon 1977, 34). As Navajo educator Wilson Aronilth Jr. explains:

> Everything has been created as a result of thought and feeling. . . . Diné philosophy's teaching [holds] that everything in existence is the result of thoughts, all form maintains itself as long as the thought is held positively. But as the thoughts change, so does the form. . . . Through the power of the Holy People [and] the process of development . . . you will see desire being projected in to the universal mind and returning in physical reality." (Aronilth 1994, 62)

Because of this contingent relationship between thought, language, and effects in the world, Witherspoon makes the claim that for Navajos, "language is not a mirror of reality; reality is a mirror of language" (1977, 34). A theology that places the burden for creation in the directed and enacted thought of the Holy People is not just focused on actions from the Navajo past, however. Navajo ceremonies ("sings") consistently revisit this act of creation through the reenacting of the positive thoughts, words, chants, and songs of the mythic past as a fundamental part of the curing ceremonies. The prayers and songs are spoken again, restoring the world to the state of balance and harmony with which it first came into being (Witherspoon 1977, 25).

Prayer, in particular, is recognized as a performative act: signaling a special frame of experience that opens up a mode of communication between humans and nonhumans (Reichard 1966; Gill 1987). As explored in the previous chapter, in the Navajo ceremonial healing context, prayers—and, in emphatic form, sung prayers—address deities by kin terms (which obligates them to act in kin-appropriate ways); prayers also point out the offerings made, declare the binding relationship of reciprocity that obliges the deities to act in certain ways, and recite the removal of the illness and the return to health (Gill 1987, 122). These words are not seen as describing a situation but as performative action: actually creating the effect that they name with illocutionary force (Austin 1970). In all these ways Navajo ceremonial language relies upon the performative power of the Navajo language.

The referential (naming) and performative (acting) aspects of language thus contend in the context of Oodlání new musical composition. While Stoner and Baldridge argue that Navajo words become meaningless when set to Western tonal harmony that does not preserve linguistically necessary high and low tones (Baldridge 2000, 67), Oodlání themselves are much more concerned with the performative connotations of the "newly composed Christian chant."[30] Given language ideologies that hear performative power in Navajo chant, paired with theologies that equate that power with the forces of evil, bringing anything that sounds like "medicine man chant" into the church is not just irrelevant—it is potentially very dangerous.

Háálá Ayóo Diyin

A special guest was addressing the annual camp meeting of Pastor Wallace's church. A Navajo politician had come to greet his constituents and to pass on spiritual encouragement. His sister, co-pastor Alice Norton, stood by his side. The speaker exhorted the assembled to love one another and not put some people above others, reading from several passages in the Bible that described the interdependent parts of the "Body of Christ." He said, "There's nothing more that we can do than praise the Lord tonight." He talked about how he'd been all over the country, even Washington DC, and wherever he went, he noticed that people were always searching for answers, not knowing that "there's an answer in the Lord Jesus Christ, Amen." Then he took up his guitar, and as he adjusted the guitar strap, his siblings and maternal cousins gathered around him, the first time they had shared a stage in nearly twenty years. "I'd like to sing you a song," he announced, "A song that the Lord has blessed me with." As he began to strum his guitar the audience recognized the familiar tune and broke out in cheers, clapping and shouting. He then asked the understated question with the obvious answer, "And, um, how many of you know Háálá Ayóo Diyin?[31]

The unique success of *Háálá Ayóo Diyin* as the only widely accepted Oodlání song with original Navajo lyrics suggests a way that Navajo words can be set to song without evoking medicine man chant. Its popularity lies in its ability to capitalize on what I call resonant rupture.

Háálá Ayóo Diyin is a song composed by the family group, the Kinlichini Singers.[32] This group was formed in the 1980s as a traveling group sponsored by the Southern Baptist denominational mission. This group was composed of the children of two sisters, cousins who would be classified in Navajo kinship reckoning as brothers and sisters. Ranging in age from teenagers to young adults at the time, the Kinlichini Singers traveled around the Navajo Nation in a large bus (provided by the Southern Baptist denomination). The bus was covered in psychedelic paintings and the words "American Indian Gospel Movement." They traveled to remote areas to conduct revivals: setting up a generator and getting out their guitars. Now an active Navajo politician, Raymond Yazzie was one of the leading members of the Kinlichini Singers.[33] According to him, the revivals led by the Kinlichini Singers were different from the great miracle healing revivals also happening at the time. Coming out of the Baptist church, they emphasized bonding with the community through shared food and games of basketball rather than charismatic gifts of the spirit (Raymond Yazzie 2008). They did hold "church services," however, and at those church services their music was key. Live performances of electric instruments themselves (guitar, bass, drums) were still novel, especially in the remote areas of the reservation, where even today electricity is available only through generators.

Háálá Ayóo Diyin arose out of the creative energy of this group: traveling, rehearsing, and playing together. Although there is some contention about who composed which parts of the song, it would not exist at all without the combined energies of Raymond Yazzie, his brother Russell Yazzie, his sister Alice Norton and his "cousin-sister" Julia Redhouse.

Structurally, *Háálá Ayóo Diyin* includes extensive use of repetition and what Raymond Yazzie describes as "short phrase beats" (1–2, 1–2) characteristic of Navajo "social song and dance" (Yazzie 2008). Although it is composed linearly, its highly repetitive structure allows for a certain degree of flexibility in performance. During my research I heard this song performed in a number of ways, from a simple chorus-bridge-chorus form to a more complex mix of chorus, bridge, and nonlinear verse choices. New verses have been created to fit into the poetic framework of the song. The ability of this song to be used in free, nonlinear repetition allows it to be performed as a praise song, with an emergent form based upon the interaction between the resources of the performer and the interest of the audience (Bauman 1975).

The song is lyrically noncomplex, emphasizing a few main ideas. Although Navajo lyrics and English translation are provided in table 1, this is not a bilingual song: this is a song composed and exclusively performed in Navajo. The English version is a translation provided for English readers but is an artificial creation, not an ethnographic reality.

Resonant Rupture: Sounding the Paradox

The key to understanding the success of *Háálá Ayóo Diyin* lies in our ability to see how it *resonates* with inherent aesthetic forms of Navajo poetic language. As discussed in the introduction, resonance is an acoustical principle that explains how certain vibrations amplify other vibrations but without assuming identical frequencies. Musicians use this principle all the time. Because

Table 1. *Háálá Ayóo Diyin*

CHORUS

Háálá Ayóo Diyin	Oh how Holy
doo lá dó' nizhóní da	And amazingly beautiful
Háálá . . . Háálá Ayóo Diyin	How very, very Holy
Jesus Ayóo Diyin	Jesus, very Holy
doo lá dó' nizhóní da	And amazingly beautiful
Háálá . . . háálá Ayóo Diyin	How very, very Holy

VERSE 1

Jesus yisdá shííłtxį	Jesus saved me
doo lá dó' nizhóní da	How very beautiful
Háálá . . . háálá Ayóo Diyin	How very, very Holy
Jesus ná shííłdzíí'	Jesus healed me
doo lá dó' nizhóní da	How very beautiful
Háálá . . . háálá Ayóo Diyin	How very, very Holy
Chorus	

VERSE 2

Jesus ayóo shik'is	Jesus is my best friend
t'áá íyisí shik'is	Without a doubt, my friend
Háálá . . . háálá Ayóo Diyin	How very, very Holy
Jesus baa hashniih	Jesus I praise
t'áábí baa hashniih	He, himself, I praise
Háálá . . . háálá Ayóo Diyin	How very, very Holy
Chorus	

BRIDGE

hiiná, hiiná dooleeł	I will live, I will live
hiiná, hiiná dooleeł	I will live, I will live
. . . Lá	. . . because of it

VERSE 3

Jesus Nánádááh	Jesus will return
doo lá dó' nizhóní da	How very beautiful
Háálá . . . háálá Ayóo Diyin	How very, very Holy
[Repeat]	
Chorus	

VERSE 4

Jesus ayóo shó'ní	Jesus loves me so much
doo lá dó' nizhóní da	How very beautiful
Háálá . . . háálá Ayóo Diyin	How very, very Holy
[Repeat]	
Chorus	

of the way "resonance" explains the amplifying but not equivalent aspects of two things, it is a particularly useful concept for exploring the complex type of rupture enacted in neo-Pentecostal localization. Ethnographers who have worked closely with neo-Pentecostal communities globally are struck by how focused believers are on enacting rupture in their lives or, as Birgit Meyer has put it, on making "a complete break with the past" (1998).[34] Some scholars have argued that this religious change actually represents a kind of cultural stability, since "spiritual warfare" is framed within preserved traditional terms (converts still seek protection from witchcraft and healing from curses, for example). But scholars who specialize in neo-Pentecostalism have continued to insist that these apparent continuities represent more of a "paradox" (Robbins 2003b) than evidence for stability, since the ontologies are really only preserved insofar as believers can make war against them.[35]

As established earlier in the present chapter, Diné Oodlání are dedicated to preserving a theology of exclusivity that frames their cosmological world as completely set apart from traditional Navajo cosmology. And yet beliefs and feelings about the beauty, value, and identity-defining features of the Navajo language remain, even if the more performative aspects of this ideology cause difficulties in certain circumstances. As Webster has stated, Navajos regard themselves as "natural" poets because of the natural descriptive beauty of the Navajo language (Webster 2009, 85).[36] Because of their inherent ambiguity, aesthetic forms like poetic language are ideal places for making productive use of resonant amplification, even in acts of rupture.

The aesthetic practices of expressive culture are a realm in which the sense of something being "similar but different" gains a powerful expression, as mentioned in the introduction. In situations of culture change as dramatic as Pentecostal conversion, the "feeling for form" that Michael Owen Jones (1987) identifies as one of the hallmarks of aesthetics can remain the same while the meanings can vary greatly. The "feelingful" nature of signs is often tied to the connotations gained through local historicity (Samuels 2004). Similarities in aesthetic form, then, can amplify affective attachment between two things (such as song forms), without also assuming their equivalence. *Háálá Ayóo Diyin* maintains the aesthetic form of Navajo poetic language in two primary ways: incremental repetition and the invocation of a generalized Native American identity.

Resonance and *Háálá Ayóo Diyin*

Háálá Ayóo Diyin resonates with traditional Navajo expressive culture in two important ways. First is its use of incremental repetition, or what Field and Blackhorse call *metonymy* or "parallelism in meaning rather than sound" (2002, 218). A well-known hallmark of complex oral literature like traditional Navajo ceremonials, incremental repetition aids with the memorization of long texts by altering the verses only slightly at each iteration. Navajo repetition, in particular, makes use of what Field and Blackhorse call "inventories," so that "members of a set (such as anatomical relations) are the basis of the verbal patterning" (Field and Blackhorse 2002, 218). This incremental repetition is a quality that Raymond Yazzie himself calls the "soaking quality" of *Háálá Ayóo Diyin,* like the gentle soaking rain Navajos call "female rain" (Yazzie 2008). The "soaking quality" of incremental repetition in Navajo poetic language can be seen in a well-known daily Navajo prayer:

With beauty before me, I walk.
With beauty behind me, I walk.
With beauty above me, I walk.
With beauty below me, I walk.
From the East beauty has been restored.
From the South beauty has been restored.
From the West beauty has been restored.
From the North beauty has been restored.
From the zenith of the sky beauty has been restored.
From the nadir of the earth beauty has been restored.
All around me beauty has been restored.

—(WITHERSPOON 1977, 153-54)

In this text, the repetition of "With beauty ____, I walk" is altered in each repetition with the incremental change of the modifying phrases "before me, behind me, above me, below me." This pattern of incremental repetition is used extensively in the text of Navajo ceremonials, as has been widely documented.[37] In *Háálá Ayóo Diyin* the incremental repetition is the slight alteration of the "A" line of the verse, with the "B" and "C" lines remaining nearly identical. The slight alteration of the A line is a repetition of the many things that Jesus "does" for the faithful: Jesus is very Holy, saved me, healed me (*Jesus Ayóo Diyin, yisdá shííłtx̨į, ná shííłdzíí'*); and Jesus is my best friend, will return, loves me so much (*ayóo shik'is, Nánádááh, ayóo shó'ni*).

Like a traditional prayer, the incremental repetition of *Háálá Ayóo Diyin* has a "soaking" quality (Yazzie 2008). However, for Oodlání who are fully dedicated to the neo-Pentecostal theology of exclusivity, the suggestion that this Christian song sounds like a traditional prayer would be horrifying, an ethnographic fact we cannot readily ignore. Their focus is on the significantly different meanings communicated by this song.

In fact, when I asked Pastor Alice Norton (an original member of the Kinlichini Singers) why *Háálá Ayóo Diyin* had remained so popular over the years, she commented that it was the *meanings* emphasized by the repetitions that gave the song so much power, because they emphasize salvation, healing, happiness and restoration. The bridge, *hiiná dooleeł Lá* (I will live because of it), drives home the point for her that "since all these things are comin' out, now we are livin'" (Norton 2012). This insight cannot be overemphasized: the meanings communicated by the incremental repetition in *Háálá Ayóo Diyin* claim that through *salvation* (not through beauty, *hózhǫ́*) we are healed, happy, restored. For Oodlání, it is through the choice to follow Jesus, not through the performative power of the language of the Holy People, that "we live." No matter how affectively resonant is the form of incremental repetition, the denotative meaning of the song suggests profound disjuncture: it emphasized concepts at the very core of neo-Pentecostal Christianity.

The other primary way that *Háálá Ayóo Diyin* represents a

point of resonance is through its "Native feel." Raymond Yazzie claims that the "melody" for this song was taken from a Cree chant he heard from Jimmy Anderson (Cree) while at college in California. Furthermore, the melody for the bridge (*hiiná*) is taken from a song by Red Bone, a Native American popular music group from the 1970s (Yazzie 2008). These musical influences give *Háálá Ayóo Diyin* a non-Western feeling that resonates with Navajo converts and feels somewhat more familiar than the songs derived from Western vertical harmony. The appeal of *Háálá Ayóo Diyin*'s "Native feel," however, is in that it feels "Native" without being actually *Navajo*. Thus the danger of new composition in Navajo sounding like medicine man chant is mitigated by using the musical traditions of other tribes and Native pop culture. In incorporating pan-Indian musical influences, *Háálá Ayóo Diyin* succeeds where other new composition fails in Oodláni contexts. The Native influences are similar enough to resonate but different enough to allow for the attachment of new meanings. These two "points of resonance" provide the familiarity that *Háálá Ayóo Diyin* needed to become popular, while maintaining a safe distance from Navajo traditional religion, ingredients necessary for the success of this Navajo Christian musical composition in Oodláni contexts.

Conclusion

Háálá Ayóo Diyin is a beautiful song. But the importance of this song stretches beyond its aesthetic appeal. As the only widely known Navajo Christian song composed in the Navajo language, *Háálá Ayóo Diyin* has achieved a level of acceptance that suggests it has been able to overcome the dual barriers of a neo-Pentecostal theologies of exclusivity and stable "performative" language ideologies. It has been able to do so through the productivity of resonant rupture.

Without doubt, *Háálá Ayóo Diyin*'s success has been aided by its soaking quality. This soaking quality represents one point of resonance for the song, in that its emotional force is amplified by related musical practices. And yet it is also clear that *Háálá Ayóo Diyin* does not forge continuity with traditional medicine man chant. The denotative meaning communicated through the words of the song suggest a complete remaking of cosmological worlds.

In this sense, resonant rupture is a way of understanding the aspects of continuity that are nearly always a facet of culture change. Resonant rupture, however, speaks about change as much as continuity. Regardless of how strong is the bridge formed by expressive culture, the destination is a different realm. The paradoxical nature of *Háálá Ayóo Diyin* lies in the fact that rather than reflecting cultural continuity, the song sings transformation and rupture through the medium of the Navajo language.

CHAPTER 4

"God Never Listened to Country"

The Resonant Rupture of Music

In July 2012 the original members of the band the Chinle Galileans staged a reunion concert on the fairgrounds in Shiprock, New Mexico. Although they were nicely dressed in blue jeans and button-up country dress shirts, with several band members wearing sharp cowboy hats and boots, they were no longer the young men who graced the cover of their self-titled recordings in the 1970s. As they stood on the large stage surrounded by towering speakers and amps and illuminated by dozens of can spotlights, it also became obvious that they had not played together in decades. Vocalist Roland Vixon was notably flat, and Emerson Luther's drum set struggled to keep the guitar and bass players (Pastor Jerry Tom, Able Arthur, and Lee Begay) from dragging down the tempo. But when Vixon launched into the opening phrase of the band's signature tune, "Clingin' to a Savin' Hand," it was clear that the audience didn't care. As one fan commented: "These guys are the Beatles of the Navajo Nation." With plenty of country twang, Vixon sang:

Sing me a song of praise and glory
Help this wanderin' child to understand
So when I close my eyes in sleep eternal
I'll be clingin' to a savin' hand

If live music is being performed at a Navajo neo-Pentecostal (Oodlání) revival, there is a good chance that music is country gospel. Despite the existence of a Navajo-language hymn book and its continued use in denominational Protestant churches on the Navajo Nation, Oodlání hardly ever sing hymns. By my second week of fieldwork I had stopped bringing my hymn book to church. It was clear that if I wanted to learn something about

Oodlání music culture, I needed to pay less attention to Charles Wesley and more attention to Johnny Cash.

The prominence of country-style gospel fits quite naturally with the larger musical culture of the Navajo Nation. As you drive across its wide-open landscape, your car radio is more likely to play country music than anything else (and may actually pick up nothing else). Country music features prominently on the local Navajo-operated stations like KTNN and KNDN as well. Country has been "king" on the Navajo Nation for decades, leading ethnomusicologist David McAllester to note in 1979 that although the traditional music he studied was still important to Navajos, it was not the music that "fills the airwaves in the Navajo Nation" (McAllester 1979, 182). That music was country.

And yet, despite the sonic similarity of secular country and country gospel, secular country music is widely denounced by Oodlání as dangerous and immoral. Country music, say many Oodlání, will "lead you straight to the Devil." Pastor Wallace regularly cautioned his congregation to stay away from the frequent country western dances on the reservation lest they be pulled into immoral behavior. This anti–country music sentiment was summarized concisely by one Oodlání woman, who declared, "God never listened to country music!" (both comments relayed in L. Joe 2014).

In this chapter I explore country music as another point of resonant rupture for Oodlání. While country gospel music is sonically identical to (and rising from the same history as) the secular country music that is fundamental to Navajo "cowboy culture," the meaning ascribed to country gospel is new. I suggest that the continuity of the sonic form reflects the importance of country music to Navajo identity, but that the ascription of new meanings stems from Oodlání emphasis on rupture with the past. This discourse of rupture has particular meaning for musicians, who are cautioned against mixing secular and religious music because their musical ability is framed as both enabled by and a transmitting medium of the active presence of God: the anointing.

One of the better known poems of influential Navajo poet Luci Tapahonso is called "Raisin Eyes," in reference to Navajo cowboys with "raisin eyes" and "pointed boots" who are as alluring as they are troublesome (Tapahonso 1993, 42). Cowboy culture is deeply meaningful for many Navajo, based in the common importance of a rural, Western, land-based and livestock-based way of life. The strength of cowboy identity for Navajos has a powerful impact on contemporary Navajo expressive culture—especially music making. There are more than forty country bands in operation on the Navajo Nation today, and these bands perform regularly in a very active secular country music scene, which has been documented extensively by Kristina Jacobsen Bia (Jacobsen 2009; 2012; forthcoming).[1]

Because of its ubiquity in everyday life on the Navajo Nation, secular country music is understood by Navajos as more than assimilation to Anglo identity. Rather, country music has become deeply associated with a traditional Navajo way of life and thus authentically Navajo. Even Navajos who do not like country music are expected to know who the first "rez bands" were, knowledge that is likened to "to knowing one's own Navajo history and culture" (Jacobsen 2009, 460). It is this very association with traditional life that makes country music such a powerful point of resonance for Navajo Oodlání: both deeply meaningful and deeply problematic.

The sounds of country music enter the Oodlání revival through the genre of country gospel. Country gospel is a subgenre of music blending the influences of black gospel, Anglo-American hymns, and secular country music. In some senses country gospel (or "Christian country music") is a natural outgrowth of the evangelical faith of many well-known country artists and a reflection of the often implicitly Christian cultural milieu of country music more broadly. Many well-known country music variety shows incorporated country gospel tunes into their programming.[2] And nearly all the best-known secular country music artists from the 1950s, '60s, and '70s have released religious ("gospel") albums.[3]

In this section I discuss the continuities of country gospel with the broader Navajo country music scene. I demonstrate that through a shared history, shared songs and symbols, and shared class identity, the power of country gospel at Oodláni revivals is amplified by Navajo cowboy culture. Oodláni country gospel draws appeal from the irresistible romanticism of the cowboy that Tapahonso captures in her poem: "he just smiles that way, you know, / and then I end up paying entry fees / . . . It's not hard" (Tapahonso 1993, 41).

SHARED HISTORY

Country music gained popularity among Navajos beginning in the 1950s, as broadcast radio became commonplace across all parts of desert Southwest. Even remote Navajo sheep camps started to acquire battery-operated radios. The impact of broadcast radio on Native expressive culture in the Southwest has been traced both by Kristina Jacobsen and, in the San Carlos Apache case, by David Samuels. The musicians with whom Jacobsen worked often shared with her stories from the 1960s and '70s of listening to one prominent station, KOMA (AM 1520) out of Oklahoma City (Jacobsen 2012, 308).[4] KOMA played a mix of country, rock'n'roll, the Beatles and other popular hits and represented for these young listeners the cosmopolitan world beyond the reservation (Jacobsen 2012, 313).

The connections between country music and Navajo identity were not cemented through passive listening as a kind of aural colonization, however. Samuels has argued that by enacting the cognate Apache/Navajo concept of "to run after them"—*bikéé' anáshdááh*, (I follow in his/her footsteps), which Louise Lamphere (1977) has described as the Navajo model for cooperation—reservation listeners got their own guitars and learned to play them in a kind of dialogue with the radio. According to Samuels, this dialogue was packed with all the associated meanings of *bikéé' anáshdááh*, including concepts of cooperation, desire, and longing (Samuels 2004, 109).[5] The participatory style of listening practiced by young Navajo and Apache musicians often led to the formation of their own bands. The popularity of these local bands fed what Samuels calls the "band era" among San Carlos Apaches (Samuels 2004, 109). A similar band era existed on the Navajo Nation with the formation of "chapter house bands." Some of the best known chapter house bands of this era included the Fenders, Aces Wild, the Wingate Valley Boys, and the Sundowners (see Jacobsen 2009).

The roots of Navajo country gospel music lie within this band era as well. Just as young Navajos encountering secular country music over the airwaves were not content simply to listen, neither were young Navajos being swept up in the spreading Oodláni religious movement (Marshall 2015a). One of the best-known Navajo country gospel bands to form in this era was the Chinle Galileans. This band was the first Navajo group to record a country gospel sound, on three different self-titled volumes for Canyon Records between 1975 and 1979, and they paved the way for dozens of Navajo Christian bands to follow.

Like well-known Navajo secular country groups of this era, the country gospel recordings of the Chinle Galileans are only lightly marked as Navajo: with Navajo-accented English and a flat, mono-channel A M radio sound.[6] And yet, as with these other groups, the popularity of the Chinle Galileans with the Navajo Christian audience was unmatched. Through the generations of Christian bands they inspired, the twangy English-language country gospel of the Chinle Galileans also set the precedent for Navajo Christian musical aesthetics.

Because of their roots in the Navajo band era, both sacred and secular Navajo country music blossomed through similar performance venues: live rural music contexts and radio airplay. Secular country music reached far into the interior of Navajo country through the structural mechanism of chapter houses. Starting in the 1920s, the Navajo Nation was divided into more than a hundred local "chapters," which allowed local concerns to be communicated to the central tribal government in Window Rock. Most of these chapters have community buildings ("chapter houses") that serve as community meeting and recreation centers. It was in these chapter houses that early secular country western bands performed, leading them to be called chapter house bands.

Starting in the 1960s, Navajo chapter house bands like the Ramah Ramblers, Murphy Brothers, Fenders, and Wingate Valley Boys began covering nationally known tunes at local chapter house dances (Jacobsen 2009). Although the country songs performed by these chapter house bands were in English with standard country band instrumentation, Jacobsen argues that there are certain sonic markers that characterize the "chapter house sound." These markers include a mono-channel flatness derived both from the mono-channel A M radio sound and the lower-quality instruments and public address and recording systems with which early chapter house bands often made do (Jacobsen 2012, 335). This sound is also often marked by heavily accented English, and a strong duple beat, and is occasionally emplaced by the substitution of local place names (Jacobsen 2009, 472; 2012, 335).[7] This sound is identified by contemporary Navajo bands as "mono," "rez," or "Jáán" (discussed later).

Chapter house country western dances continue to be incredibly popular on the reservation, helping to perpetuate the influence of Navajo cowboy culture. During my fieldwork large home-made signs would be posted every weekend at the main intersections in Shiprock, advertising the live music of Navajo country bands at various chapter houses and other reservation venues in the area. Contemporary Navajo country bands maintain continuity with the "authentic" sounds of the chapter house bands and occasionally make direct reference to their influence, such as by calling themselves names like Fenders II.[8]

Live performances in the deep, rural heart of Navajo country played a role in the development of Navajo country gospel as well. Early Navajo Christian groups like the Chinle Galileans did not play at chapter houses, however. Instead, they performed at the increasingly popular open-air tent revivals of the early Oodláni movement. Throughout the 1970s and early 1980s, the Chinle Galileans were an actively touring band, playing numerous revival gigs in summer. Navajo Christian guitarist Larry Emerson began touring and playing with the Chinle Galileans during the summers when school was out, and he recalled that they performed at revivals nearly every night during the summertime.[9] According to Emerson, they would perform in Chinle, Arizona (near the heart of the Navajo Reservation), at evangelist Luke Yazzie's church for Sunday morning and evening services. Then on Monday, "We pitched a tent, and then Monday night we're at it, and then it's every night from there" (Emerson 2008). Their performances at revivals ranged across the entire reservation "deep into Arizona . . . the whole reservation practically," from Newcomb and Shiprock in the east to Tuba City and Cameron in the west to Page and Kayenta in the north (Emerson 2008).

Live music performances in rural locales were important to the development of both secular Navajo country and Navajo country gospel music. But the dominance of these secular and sacred genres was cemented through the increasingly popular prominence of broadcast radio. McAllester noted decades ago that Navajo requests to local radio channels (such as KTNN and KNDN) tend to favor the Navajo covers of popular hits. Through this mechanism, the music of the chapter house bands achieved a wide reach. So often were their covers of national hits broadcast that, according to Jacobsen, being able to associate famous chapter house bands with their signature songs has become part of Navajo "cultural patrimony" (Jacobsen 2009, 458).[10]

Through this same mechanism of Navajo-centered radio broadcast, the Chinle Galileans' version of "Clinging to a Saving Hand" became the first mega-hit of the Navajo Christian community. It also gained some celebrity nationally (at least among ethnomusicologists) when it was incorporated by David McAllester into his contribution to Jeff Todd Titon's widely used ethnomusicology textbook *Worlds of Music*.[11] More important, the radio play of songs by the Chinle Galileans inspired generations of Navajo Christian musicians who came after them. Before Larry Emerson began playing with the Chinle Galileans, he first heard them on the radio. He recounted for me a story about that exciting moment in his life when the broadcast influence of the Chinle Galileans met their performance practice, and he got to see them live for the first time:

LE: they had already put their first album out, so they were, like I said they were on the Native station and I would listen to them. And, uh, then I would pick off of what they sang and I would play along with them [their record] . . . so by the time they came to our church—

KM: You already knew all their songs.

LE: Yeah! The [Anglo] pastor . . . knew that I was pretty excited about this particular group . . . and so one morning . . . Sister Davis, she goes, "Larry, guess who's, who we have coming for our revival?" And, I said, "I don't know," and she said "The Chinle Galileans are coming here." . . . Boy! The excitement. You know, "Wow . . ." These guys because, like I said they were the first Navajo [Christian] group to record professionally, in a professional recording studio. . . . I believe they kind of blazed the trail on the Navajo Reservation . . . and that's how exciting it was for me.

—(EMERSON 2008)

The combination of influence, from radio play to live music contexts in revivals across the reservation, fueled (literally "amplified") by a resonant connection to the secular country music gaining popularity in Navajo popular culture, helps to explain how the Chinle Galileans set the tone for Navajo Christian music aesthetics up to the present moment.

SHARED SONGS, SHARED SYMBOLS

Another important aspect of the aesthetic continuity between country gospel and the broader Navajo country music scene lies in shared songs and symbols. As mentioned, there is deep historical precedent for semi-professional Navajo bands to perform covers of nationally popular songs. Among Oodlání bands, the sources for these songs were never strictly Christian artists or lyricists but were typically from nationally known country musicians who became famous for their secular country music. For example, one of the most widely performed and recorded Navajo Christian covers is the tune "Scarlet Purple Robe," first popularized by the Stanley Brothers. Other common Navajo versions of country tunes include "I Shall Not Be Moved," "Where Could I Go (but to the Lord)," "The Unclouded Day," and "House of Gold."[12] These sources cement the sacred music practice of Navajo Christian bands squarely within the national secular country western music scene.

The close ties between Navajo country gospel and the national development of country western music is best revealed in the signature tune of the Chinle Galileans. Their version of "Clinging to a Saving Hand" is a cover of a song written by Bill Mack, a famous radio DJ out of Fort Worth, Texas. Because of his through-the-night broadcasts on WBAP, Mack was nicknamed "the midnight cowboy" (Mack 2004, 247), and he collaborated with many famous country music artists over the years. His song "Blue" (recorded by LeAnn Rimes) won the Grammy Award for the Best Country Song in 1997, and his song "Drinkin' Champagne" was recorded by Cal Smith in 1968 and George Strait in 1990. The deep influence of country music aesthetics is present in his song "Clinging to a Saving Hand," which was first recorded by Connie Smith on her album *Where Is My Castle* in 1971.

Navajo country gospel does not just draw upon secular country western music for songs, however. Many Navajo Christian artists utilize the broader symbolic vocabulary of country western as well. This includes the prominence of cowboy hats and boots, blue jeans, big shiny belt buckles, and button-up country dress shirts on the covers of many Navajo Christian albums. Even those covers without explicit reference to "cowboy dress" often showcase the rural backdrop of the Navajo Reservation. For example, on the cover of Thomas Arviso's 2006 album *How Great Thou Art*, Arviso appears in the foreground of the shot wearing a button-up plaid shirt and holding an electric guitar. Behind him runs a barbed-wire fence attached to a rustic post, and the red dirt and scrub juniper-covered hills of the Navajo Nation spread into the distance.[13]

The symbolic prominence of rurality is an important point of commonality between Navajo secular country music and Navajo country gospel. Secular chapter house bands found rural symbolism a powerful mode of connection to their audiences, who were often first exposed to country music sounds while listening to radio stations like KOMA from the dirt floor of a rural hogan or cabin, without running water or electricity. This "traditional" way of Navajo life (increasingly infrequent on the contemporary Navajo Nation) amplifies the sentimental power of country music's common use of rural nostalgia (Jacobsen 2012, 308–10). It has the same kind of symbolic power for Oodlání who (as explored later) often find themselves alienated from this type of rural traditionality.

SHARED CLASS

Beyond a simple affinity for country sound, songs, or symbols, Navajo country gospel exhibits continuity with a broader Navajo cowboy culture through a certain type of class identity. Country music globally romanticizes a rural and farming way of life but often expresses the deeply embedded grammars and poetics of working-class people living marginally in urban and peri-urban contexts (Fox 2004; Dent 2009; Murphy 2014).[14] Although the popularity of country music among Navajos has been attributed by some to the shared traditions of living off the land and raising livestock, I argue that it is also the way country music expresses marginalization and class inequality that makes it so appealing, especially to Navajo neo-Pentecostals.

Although Navajos are typically viewed by outside observers as a monolithic culture group, there are certainly socioeconomic distinctions within Navajo communities. Class distinctions among Navajos have existed since at least the mid-nineteenth century, as families with good grazing land (and therefore large herds of livestock) became wealthier than other Navajos (Field 2009, 43). However, as Leighton Peterson has pointed out, discussions of Navajo class dynamics have to take into account not just economic capital but, following Bourdieu, social capital as well. Certainly there are Navajo "lawyers, doctors, and engineers" who have great material wealth (Peterson 2006, 101). But there are also individuals with high on-reservation prestige (medicine men, matriarchs) who may be rich in sheep herds or medicine bundles (*jish*) and ceremonial knowledge but who have very little access to disposable wealth (Peterson 2006, 101). Whether they have wealth or not, individuals with high social capital on the reservation do often have practical control of access to important community economic and political resources, "such as school boards and/or chapter houses" (Field 2009, 44). Living in a remote (rural) area, herding sheep, weaving, and speaking in "proper" Navajo are all practices that gain one access to high social capital in Navajo society.

Navajos who convert to neo-Pentecostal Christianity are usually the Navajos who are most disenfranchised: both from the social capital of Navajo traditionalism and from the monetary capital of a lucrative career in the Western wage economy.[15] This class alienation is experienced in two ways: through patterns of migrant work off-reservation and through changing on-reservation residence patterns. Migrant work off-reservation is written into the life histories of many of the Oodlání I know. The story of Amanda Yazzie's family is telling. Although Navajo, she was raised in an off-reservation mining camp in Colorado in the 1960s, where her father found work. Her family was introduced to Christianity there, and her mother "fell in love" with the faith, eventually converting the entire family. When they moved back to the reservation, their family land (on the edge of Shiprock) was parched and barren and could not support any significant number of sheep. Yazzie's father started a church there instead. The church her father founded made the couple central to new Christian networks that included both Navajos and Anglos, enhanced their local reputation, and allowed them a means to provide for their family financially. Christianity gave Yazzie and her family a way to manage a deficit in both symbolic and material capital (A. Yazzie 2008). When I interviewed Yazzie in 2008, her connection to the prestige system of rural traditionalism was so fragmented that despite having lived on the reservation since the 1970s, she could not even name her clans.

Another reason that Navajo Pentecostals seek alternative forms of social capital is because of changing on-reservation residence patterns. As Peterson explains:

> With the advent of publicly funded schools, families transitioned to housing near major roads during the school year, so that their

children could attend day schools rather than the dreaded boarding school. . . . For a variety of reasons some Navajo families would rather live in town or in a housing development, where electricity, plumbing, and telecommunications are becoming the norm. (Peterson 2006, 107)

These Navajos view their choice as having exchanged the symbolic prestige of traditionalism for modern conveniences, even if it means that they "are regarded by many Navajos and others to be much less traditional" (Peterson 2006, 118). These choices were and are particularly salient for members of Pastor Wallace's congregation, since his church is located on the outskirts of Shiprock, one of the largest "border communities" on the reservation.[16] Most of his congregation lived in federally funded Navajo Housing Authority complexes in or around Shiprock. Some of these complexes are new, but most of them are decades old and their graffiti-tagged, vandalized, and run-down appearance resembles ghettos more than "developments." But access to centralized services (the Laundromat, telecommunications, electricity, plumbing) makes this housing, for many Navajos, the preferable choice to the symbolic prestige of sheep herding "up on the mountain" or "at grandma's" (Peterson 2006, 116).

The case of Lynda Kelly shows this deliberate change in on-reservation residence.[17] She was raised on rural family land in the 1970s. After the death of her parents and her flight from an abusive marriage, Lynda struggled to find a safe place to raise her children. She tried to return to her family's land, but without her mother and father around, she felt the land was too remote, unbearably "lonely," and she began engaging in self-destructive behavior. After encountering the Pentecostal influence of Pastor Wallace and his mother, Lynda applied for public housing in Shiprock and moved her family to Shiprock so that she could attend church regularly, make friends, and secure steady employment with the tribe, eventually teaching for the Navajo Headstart Program (Kelly 2008).

For both Amanda Yazzie and Lynda Kelly, aligning with neo-

Pentecostalism allowed them to gain social capital in a system that had excluded them as too poor to access rural forms of prestige and too "rez" to prosper in the Western wage economy. This class position has a particular characterization among Navajos, the stereotypical figure of the *Jáán*, and Navajo country music (particularly the mono chapter house sound) is strongly associated with a Jáán identity. Like the term *redneck*, Jáán is both a derogatory designation of the "backward hick" and a prideful label of authenticity—an alternative form of social capital.[18]

The roots of the term *Jáán* lie in the very migrant work that introduced many Navajos to Christianity. According to Robert Young (a linguist who worked extensively with the Navajo language), the word was incorporated into slang Navajo in the 1940s, when non-English-speaking Navajo men sought work with non-Navajo-speaking Anglos. "Consequently," said Young, "a Navajo is often dubbed 'John,' or is referred to as 'John' when a white man addresses him (as we commonly refer to strangers as Bub, Mac, and the like)" (Young 1948, 87). This off-reservation usage was then adopted "half in jest, perhaps" as "Johns" or Jáán (Young 1948, 88).

In some senses Jáán resembles the stereotype of the "failed modern," and (like other "failed modern" stereotypes such as the "greenhorn" or "wannabe") indicates someone unsuccessful at being either "traditional" or "assimilated" (Jacobsen 2012, 328; Peterson 2006, 104). Someone with high symbolic capital like a traditional singer (*hataałii*), for example, would not be considered Jáán, even if he had access to very little disposable wealth (Jacobsen 2012, 328). A Jáán identity thus represents an alternative form of social capital for Navajos disenfranchised by the very rural traditionalism they romanticize in song.[19]

Navajo country music has long been the medium for just such marginalization. The music produced by the Jáán is the lo-fidelity, tinny, mono-channel and heavily accented English of the chapter house band (Jacobsen 2009). It is a sound associated with "authentic" Navajo country music. And it expresses sentiments continuous to the class experience of many who have addressed their class alienation through the alterative social capital afforded by the Oodlání movement.

It is early afternoon in the small kitchen off the main church room. Hours before, that room was filled with church members, praising loudly and worshiping together. I had spent most of the morning helping Ma Beverly cook and serve these believers a meal. Now the dishes are done, the kitchen is clean, and the church is deserted. She and I alone remain, sitting in metal folding chairs at a table covered in a green plastic tablecloth. I ask her about the improvised speech Pastor Wallace had given earlier in the morning's service. I had not been able to follow all of the Navajo he rapidly and passionately preached, but I had picked up the main idea: mixing country music with Christian music was bad. Given that I had been listening to what I thought was country music at Oodláni revivals for more than a year, I ask her to clarify.

She begins by telling me about country dances. She says, "It's a place where you can just, you know, open up for sin. And the married woman, the married husband, they can . . . dance with the opposite sex . . . that's not right. You know?"

She pauses to reflect on the moral force undergirding the distinction. "[Us] elderlies . . ." she says, "we are supposed to be, you know, be an example for our young ones . . . for our family. That wisdom should be in there. But there's no wisdom in country and western."

"Have you even gone to one of these dances?" I ask.

"No," she says, "I never went to a country and western dance. I just heard about it." It doesn't matter, she says, because "I know . . . for sure there's always people fighting and drinking and . . . doing adultery within that dance. . . . And then, Christians, you know, we're being taught not to do those things." (B. Joe 2008)

Despite the strong continuity of country sounds, symbols, and class identity between secular Navajo country music and Oodláni country gospel, there is significant pressure on Oodláni not to mix these genres. Oodláni are cautioned (both from the pulpit and from peers) not to attend chapter house dances, or live country music concerts, or to even listen to country music on the radio. Thus despite its sonic similarity, country gospel is regarded as a completely separate genre from secular country western, and policing the boundaries between the two genres is a community project of cultural rupture.

DISCOURSES OF BEHAVIOR

Boundaries between sacred and secular country are constructed along two main lines of argument: discourses of behavior and discourses of exclusion. Discourses of behavior are those engaged by Ma Beverly in our kitchen conversation, saying that believers should not attend chapter house dances because it will lead them to immoral behavior, such as adultery.[20] And while these meanings certainly attach to live music venues, they also seem to attach to the music itself, causing Oodláni who do enjoy country music to distance themselves from the social worlds represented by this form of music. For example, Layne Joe was one dedicated Oodláni who actively participated in Pastor Wallace's church. She was always at church and traveled with Pastor Wallace to revivals, and she often helped Ma Beverly out in the kitchen as well. From informal conversations with her, I knew her to be a big fan of country music and cowboy culture, with a healthy crush on both musician George Strait and bull rider Adriano Moraes. When I asked her how she reconciles the peer criticism she receives, she commented:

> Sometimes people tell me, "God said you're not supposed to listen to country music. It even says that in the Bible."
> And I tell them, "There's nowhere in the Bible that is says 'Don't listen to country music.'"
> . . . For me, how I think of country music, it's just a song but, you know, you don't live by it. It's just something that you listen to. (L. Joe 2014)[21]

For Joe, the primary rupture with Navajo cowboy culture is behavioral: how one lives. As long as one does not engage in the "hell raising" enshrined by some secular country music, there is no harm in listening to it.

However, there was one behavioral boundary that even country music fan Joe would not cross as an Oodláni: attending chapter house dances. In part this was because of the concentration of immoral behavior she believed existed at these dances: drinking, flirting with married men or women, and brawling.[22] But her vow to avoid country dances had a spiritual root as well. She commented, "They say when you go to country dances it makes you have an evil spirit on you" (L. Joe 2014).[23] Thus chapter house dances provide another venue where Oodláni believe the behavioral choices of individuals meet the cosmic spiritual battle between God and the Devil. An individual's choice to attend a chapter house dance is not automatically damning but does open that individual up to attack by demon spirits. A wiser choice, according to Oodláni, is to avoid the places (like chapter house dances) where evil spirits congregate.

DISCOURSES OF EXCLUSION

The other primary way that Oodláni create boundaries between sacred and secular country music is through discourses of exclusion: encouraging believers not to mix these genres. Musicians, for instance, are cautioned not to adopt the performance pattern of many African American gospel and soul artists, playing secular venues on Saturday nights and sacred venues on Sunday mornings (Burnim 2006, 416). Instead, Oodláni musicians tended to segment their participation in each venue to particular points in their lives. They typically grow up playing music only at church, later (as young adults) playing only secular music at bars and dances, and then going through a period of becoming "saved," whereupon they decide to "use their talent for the Lord" and play only gospel music at church, revivals, and "singspiration" gospel concerts. They may later go through a period of "backsliding," again playing only in secular contexts, but the alternation between the two is typically episodic in the lifespan of an Oodláni musician.[24]

The example of Navajo country musician Travis Friday demonstrates the power of these discourses of exclusion. Friday gained prominence as the lead musician for the chapter house band Stateline. Although well known in the secular country music scene, the band went on hiatus in 2007 while Friday "renewed his religious faith" (Patterson 2009), composing and performing country gospel. In 2008 Stateline began performing secular venues again. And even though Friday's reasoning for performing in secular venues is explicitly evangelistic ("I just felt that I couldn't go to heaven by myself"), and concerts always include country gospel tunes, Friday has come under criticism from Navajo Christians for mixing the two (Patterson 2009). The discourses of exclusivity wrap the performance of country music into larger tropes of things "anointed" and "not anointed"; things "of the Lord" and things "not of the Lord."

Discourses of exclusivity tie debates about musical practice to larger anti-pluralistic sentiment within Oodlání communities. The event that precipitated my kitchen conversation with Ma Beverly was the emotional public testimony of one of the leading members of Pastor Wallace's church. That hot July morning in 2008, she got up to pray about a troubling event that had recently happened in Shiprock. There had been a large singspiration (gospel) concert, but it included both gospel music and secular country music. From reports that I heard afterward, Oodlání were troubled by critical comments from some of the country musicians, who mocked the ecstatic states of worship central to Oodlání ritual (i.e., "dancing in the spirit"). Church members were also concerned about the atmosphere of the concert, which (reportedly) eventually included one woman taking off her clothes. Pastor Wallace reassured the hurt feelings of his church (no one likes to have their most personal and sacred things mocked) by engaging in a heated mini-sermon on the topic of mixing Christian music. While this is in some ways a simple reiteration of the concerns about the "immoral" behavior celebrated by country music (drinking and carousing), a broader anti-pluralistic discourse is enshrined in the connections Pastor Wallace makes between secular country music, powwow music, and traditional medicine man chant (all very different genres). This connection is suggestive of a concern with mixing conceived much more broadly than simply a sacred/secular country music split. The original text (mixed English and Navajo) appears on the left, with a fully English translation appearing on the right.

Table 2. Pastor Wallace's country music sermon, July 6, 2008

(1)

If you're going to live for the Lord you're gonna have to have a good attitude, Amen? And you're gonna have to have a good spirit, Amen. Oh, I tell you, Amen, praise God. Sister Tandy mentioned the singspiration. . . . and it was a gathering where *t'áá ał'ąą ádaat'áo*.

(2)

Yeah, *ásaa' da deił haałgo*.

I hear about this all the time, different music being mixed, and over here they're playing "Alligator Man," I hear this one was singing over here. And I was sort of questioning that, because I heard there was gospel music going to be over here, and then there was going to be other music.

(3)

And I said, "Is that from God? Is that from the Lord?"

Jó ákonee'?

Oh I tell you, Amen.

Your gifts and your talents and your abilities—

are to be used—

for the kingdom—

and only the kingdom of God.—

We don't mix the good—

with the evil—

because when you mix the good—

with the evil—

when you mix the anointing—

and demonic spirits together—

you create confusion, *eii lá yáada?*

Confusion, *aaníí?*

Diné naaki bił nidahaleeh áhwíjít̜įgo!

(4)

Amen.

Have you ever seen *eii t'áá le'é da nijiiłniihgo?*

If you buy something it says "to be used only for the surfaces." *Ah'eh* Pine Sol [mimes drinking it]

yił didoodzih.

<Audience laughter>

(5)

Oh, but I tell you, Amen.

And praise God, Amen.

Mixing the powwow with the church, Amen.

It gets people confused, *aaníí lá?*

But *ła' yoołkááł jó akonee' níléí church baa*

nida'aldeehgo

[mimics mock-powwow singing]

(1)

If you're going to live for the Lord you're gonna have to have a good
attitude, Amen? And you're gonna have to have a good spirit, Amen. Oh, I
tell you, Amen, praise God. Sister Tandy mentioned the singspiration. . . .
and it was a gathering where {everything is mixed}.

(2)

Yeah, {they were banging on the drum}.
I hear about this all the time, different music being mixed, and over here
they're playing "Alligator Man," I hear this one was singing over here. And
I was sort of questioning that, because I heard there was gospel music going
to be over here, and then there was going to be other music.

(3)

And I said, "Is that from God? Is that from the Lord?"
{See?}
Oh I tell you, Amen.
Your gifts and your talents and your abilities—
are to be used—
for the kingdom—
and only the kingdom of God.—
We don't mix the good—
with the evil—
because when you mix the good—
with the evil—
when you mix the anointing—
and demonic spirits together—
you create confusion, {don't you realize?}
Confusion, {true?}
{You confuse people if you do that!}

(4)

Amen.
Have you ever seen {to be used only for}?
If you buy something it says "to be used only for the surfaces." *Ah'eh* Pine
Sol [mimes drinking it]
{You'll choke on it}.
<Audience laughter>

(5)

Oh, but I tell you, Amen.
And praise God, Amen.
Mixing the powwow with the church, Amen.
It gets people confused, {true?}
But {when the day comes around and church is happening, and as people
came in and gather they hear powwow}
[mimics mock-powwow singing]

yits'a'go jó akonee'?
Áádóó níléí ásaa' da deiłhaał dóó at'a' da deełmazgo.
(6)
And it's supposed to be a Christian powwow,
but *níléídą́ą́' yii' nidaaskai dóó yah adaheeskaiígí*
azee' deiyá dóó traditionalism *yiyi'dę́ę́'*
hadaheeskaiyę́ę́ bitsiits'iin deich'id
nít'ę́ę́' ádaanií lá
'eii t'áál'ii át'éé lá.
The powwow, NAC, traditionalism
'eii t'áál'ii át'éé lá.
t'áá aanií lá t'áál'ii át'éé la'.
T'áála'ii bich'į' tsodadiilzin.
(7)
Doo bił da haadaat'eií da
(8)
Oh, the powwow people,
ts'os da yee naanída'įįlzhíísh ásaa' da deiłhaał.
At'a' da kwídeeł naanída 'įį dó' Diyin God da yaa dahaniih.
Níłch'i Diyinii da yee da'alzhishgo.
"Oh it's no different!"
Áála'ii át'éé lá daaní!

(9)
T'óó 'ahayói
Diné bił naaki dahazlį́į' Diné be'oodla'yę́ę́!
(10)
They went back into traditionalism, they went back into powwow, they
went back into peyote, *jó ákonee'?*
A spirit—
of confusion—
came in—
and entered, *jó ákonee'?*
Ałtsxo eii lá yáada?
And some of them—
are not serving the Lord anymore.
<Shouts of approval>
(11)
You can't mix the Country, amen.
Country music and gospel, *jó ákonee'?*
It brings confusion and compromise, *jó ákonee'?*

{This is how it sounds, see?
They're drumming, and twirling feathers}.
(6)
And it's supposed to be a Christian powwow,
but {they went into powwow, the ones who entered
those who had left NAC and traditionalism
those ones are scratching their heads, confused
and so they say:
"It's all one."
"The powwow, NAC, traditionalism
it's all one.
They really they mean the same thing.
We all pray to the same One."}
(7)
{They don't even see the differences.}
(8)
Oh, the powwow people,
{Here they are swinging around with their feathers and they're banging on
the drum.
They're doing this with feathers at the same time they praise God.
And that the Holy Spirit empowers them to dance.}
"Oh it's no different!"
{They say "It is all one!"}
(9)
{Many
people are confused in their beliefs!}
(10)
They went back into traditionalism, they went back into powwow, they
went back into peyote, {see?}
A spirit—
of confusion—
came in—
and entered, {see?}
{Don't you realize (emphasized)?}
And some of them—
are not serving the Lord anymore.
<Shouts of approval>
(11)
You can't mix the Country, amen.
Country music and gospel, {see?}
It brings confusion and compromise, {see?}

So despite the sonic similarity between secular country music and country gospel, these two are regarded by Oodláni as more than separate genres. They are genres that must literally be *separated*, or kept separate, as a community project of cultural rupture with the broader Navajo cowboy culture. To do less would be to cause "confusion" and "compromise" that would weaken the healing and transformative power of the Oodláni faith.

Discourses of behavior and discourses of exclusion frame secular country music as appropriately avoided in the same way as music of the powwow, the Native American Church, or the traditional ceremony ("sing"). As discussed in chapter 2, these things are viewed by Oodláni as important to avoid entirely because of the danger of their enlivened presence: the manner in which they can "open the door" to demonic attack. And, as we shall see in the final section of this chapter, this theology of exclusivity has particular implications for musicians.

Oodláni Musicians and the Anointing

The first time that Rose Yazzie got the Holy Spirit, she was performing as a backup singer for Pastor Wallace at a revival service in Mescalero, New Mexico. She felt a cool chill running from her head to her toes, and then she lost consciousness. Later, she asked Ma Beverly what had happened. "You got the Holy Spirit in you," explained Ma Beverly, but she also added a warning: "Don't sell yourself to no one. . . . Once you're into it like that, you know, it's dangerous. Don't go back. Don't do anything. Don't sell yourself." (Rose Yazzie 2008)

Hearing these comments, I was initially quite puzzled. How could one "sell" the ability to be filled by the Holy Spirit, and who exactly would be in the market? What exactly makes this spiritual gift "dangerous," and how is that danger related to the context in which the infilling took place: the making of Christian music?

The tensions between sacred and secular country music often converge in the bodies of individual Navajo musicians. Their ability to play instruments (guitars, bass, drum set) or sing in a country style with a band prove valuable skills in the live-music contexts of Oodláni church services and revivals. And

FIG. 14. Layne Joe. Photo courtesy of Layne Joe.

yet, I argue that while musicians can capitalize on the transfer of skills between secular country and country gospel, discourses of exclusion put particular pressure on them not to mix. This special pressure is exerted on musicians because of the unique nature of their skills and the special place they hold within the church. Their musical ability is framed as both enabled by and a transmitting medium of the active presence of God: the anointing. As such, Oodlání musicians actually embody musical resonant rupture. It is the simultaneous continuity of form and active rejection of a prior (false) meaning that makes Navajo country gospel such a powerful aesthetic medium.

MUSICAL GIFTS, TALENTS, AND PRIDE

One of the reasons that Oodlání musicians come under particular pressure to avoid secular musical contexts is the prevailing view that their skills are a gift from God, a "talent" as in the Parable of the Talents (Matthew 25:14–30), that should be used only to increase God's kingdom.[25] This was the primary meaning behind Ma Beverly's warning to Rose Yazzie. When I asked Yazzie to clarify Ma Beverly's statements, she said, "You know, like a [country] western dance. If they ask you, you know . . . 'Wow, your voice is nice. You sing like one of those professional [musicians]. Can you sing for us?' . . . Just say 'I'm not for sale'" (Yazzie 2008). Since her talent for singing with power came from God, Yazzie believed that she should only use it in certain contexts.

Pastor Wallace preached many sermons about using one's "talents" and "gifts" correctly for the Lord. In his sermon from July 20, 2008 he provides an important conceptual framework for understanding the "proper" use of talent by contrasting it with "pride":

> Your giftings are for service.
> Your talents are for service.
> Your abilities are for service.
> It is all for serving the Lord.

Later he adds:

> Your giftings are not for your own personal glory.
> People have a lot of problems with pride these days.
> Preachers, singers, teachers, musicians, and on down the road . . .
> You're gonna run into trouble because of pride.
>
> —(BEGAY 2008C)

This dichotomy of humility and pride is an important one for Oodlání (especially musicians) because it is set up with the paired dichotomy of using your gifts to "serve the Lord" versus "serve yourself" (by making a profit through your musical skills).

The idea that there may be more or less appropriate uses for one's musical talent was brought home for me in an interview with the Navajo gospel band Mighty Wind, which I often saw perform at Shiprock area revivals. The lead guitar player for Mighty Wind had spent time playing revivals in the 1980s and 1990s, and now he and his children had formed a touring band. His daughter, Mariah Wagner, was in her early twenties when I interviewed her in 2008 and had quite a good singing voice. I asked her if she had any aspirations of becoming a professional musician. She paused thoughtfully and then answered, "I'm not sure. . . . I'm not doing it for the fame." Given that she and her family were performing at more than thirty revivals each summer and traveling long distances to do so, I asked why she *was* doing it. "I'm just doing it because it pleases the Lord." She answered, "So that other people get encouraged, you know?" (Wagner 2008). This attitude of humility and gratitude, and caution about the perils of pride, characterizes the broader Oodlání attitude toward musical ability.

Consequently, musicians were under near constant threat of leveling gossip directed them for having excessive pride.[26] After Pastor Wallace's 2008 camp meeting, for example, I asked a focus group to identify who they thought the "best" guitar player of the revival was. While many agreed that one musician had the best technical skill, there was also some consensus that his music lacked power because his excessive skill had led to excessive pride.[27] Interestingly, one of the focus group members, Pastor Fred (Navajo), commented that the excessive pride of this musician decreased through his very participation in the camp meeting. In Pastor Fred's estimation, as the guitarist's pride decreased, his efficacy as a musician increased. Said Pastor Fred, "It's amazing when a guy that knows how to play and sing . . . responds to what's happening in his life, and changing his life. And you can see that difference . . . in the camp meeting" (F. Begay 2008).

Conversely, musicians who are perceived as humble servants are praised. The comments of Richard Kuntz (the Navajo owner of the only Christian bookstore in Gallup, New Mexico) illustrate this point. In discussing the Navajo Christian musical group that sells the best, he commented, "they are real humble and they do really rely on God for what they're doing. . . . Their walk with Christ is solid and they, they do believe that what they're doing is of God. It's not for their glory. So I think that comes through" (Kuntz 2008). By way of evidence for the power of their humility, Kuntz described how their music brings people to tears, even when their music is merely playing on the store's stereo system.

MUSICIANS AS A VESSEL

Beyond simply using their talents in correct ways, however, musicians are under particular pressure to practice exclusivity because their talent is seen as more than a gift from God. It is literally the means by which the gifts of God are transmitted to others. According to Pentecostal theology, the power of God is called the "anointing," and this anointing is what literally *empowers* believers both with spiritual gifts and in their daily lives. Musicians are regarded, then, as "vessels"—containers that receive this power (anointing) of God in order to pour it out onto others.

Navajo pastor and musician Naomi Joe, for instance, mentioned to me that she did not perform at singspiration (gospel) concerts anymore. She explained that she played only at revivals and church services because too many performances "drained" her of the anointing. She said that when making sacred music for people, she feels that "a lot of anointing is going, overflowing them. And when you get back home it's just like they drain you out real good" (N. Joe 2008). This anointing must flow out from the musicians, according to Joe, because that is how people "get recovered" and "get healed." But once God's anointing has been poured out of a musician, that power must be recovered through Bible meditation and prayer. Joe comments that after a performance, "I had to be refilled again, to get my song, to get my Bible together and start praying. Get prayed up, get ready again" (N. Joe 2008). Pastor Naomi sees her primary role as being a musician to serve as this transmitting medium of God's anointing power.

Oodláni musicians strive to create music that has this anointing in it. Navajo pastor and musician Elizabeth Bryant described her recording process, which includes prayer over every song she and her band record. They pray, "Lord, just send this music to people out there. Touch their hearts with it. Just lift up their spirit" (Bryant 2008). And given the feedback she has received, she feels that God's power is actually transmitted through the music. One woman told Bryant that she was dying of cancer but that one of their songs touched her heart. "And the Lord healed her, she said. And that was about—how many? Five years ago that she was supposed to die . . ." (Bryant 2008). So when used correctly, the music of Oodláni bands can act as a conduit for the power of God, a miraculous power with the ability to overcome any barrier, including cancer.

Musicians who act as conduits for the anointing of God are regarded as having the proper relationship to their "God-given" musical skills. This image of the properly humble Oodláni musicians is in stark contrast to the much-maligned "prideful" musician. Deriving personal profit from these skills (as in the case of secular country musicians) is seen by Oodláni as taking the credit for the work of God. And sullying one's God-given gifts in the questionable moral contexts of bars and country dances limits one's ability to act as a conduit for the anointing of God. The two are seen as interconnected: the less mixing done by musicians, the more powerful will be their ability to transmit the anointing. Keeping the "vessel" pure, then, is seen as a community project of boundary policing. So while their skills may be transferable between the secular country and country gospel contexts, discourses of exclusion and community pressure work to encourage musicians not to mix the genres.

Conclusion

Country gospel is the soundtrack of Navajo Pentecostalism. The strumming guitars and twang-filled praise songs of Oodláni musicians are appealing because they create a bridge of continuity to the broader Navajo cowboy culture. Navajo Christian bands like the Chinle Galileans developed in the same historical period as the secular country chapter house bands, when Navajos began playing their own guitars in dialogue with broadcast radio before forming their own touring bands. Arising from a similar position of class marginalization (marked by migrant off-reservation labor and changing on-reservation residence patterns), the sounds of both chapter house bands and country gospel bands express the shared romantic image of a rural way of life. In these ways country gospel was, and continues to be, a way of amplifying the appeal of the Oodláni message through reference to a broader Navajo country music scene.

However, despite the sonic similarity between secular country and country gospel, there is significant pressure on Oodláni not to listen to secular country, either in live music contexts (such as chapter house dances) or on the radio. Country music is regarded by many Oodláni not only as a dangerous influence on behavior but also as a way of making oneself vulnerable to attack by evil spirits. In this way, a parallel is drawn between musical anti-pluralism and religious anti-pluralism. And as with other contexts of Oodláni anti-pluralism, rupture with practices "not of God" is encouraged. This applies particularly for Oodláni musicians who are regarded as prone to the temptation of pride but also a powerful conduit for the anointing power of God.

CHAPTER 5

Dancing in the Spirit
The Resonant Rupture of Nonhuman Actors

I make my way across the dusty ground to the entrance of a massive white tent. Inside, accompanied by a deafening din of repetitive music, projected through eight-foot-tall speaker towers, are hundreds of Navajos with their hands raised in the air. At the front of the tent, beside the platform for the musicians and preachers, are a dozen or so believers, set apart from the others. Their arms are not raised but are held bent, close to their bodies, pumping back and forth. Their hands shake and tears fall down faces contorted in expressions of agony or bliss. They step forward and backward slowly, erratically, completely out of time with the music. To a newcomer, these bodies seem to be seizing uncontrollably. In fact, Navajos outside of the tent describe these believers as tsí haayá: *going crazy. But for Navajos inside the tent, this movement is a dance, brought about through intense contact with the Holy Spirit. And it is full of beauty. They call it* ajilzhish: *rejoicing "with joy unspeakable."*

Dancing in the spirit is one of the distinctive "charismatic" practices that set the various neo-Pentecostal Oodlání churches apart from all the other Christian denominations that have attempted to establish a mission presence on the Navajo Nation. In previous chapters I have argued that the neo-Pentecostal Oodlání movement found success among Navajos where other Christian denominations did not because the forms of neo-Pentecostal Christianity provide a type of deeply felt aesthetic continuity, despite the inversion of meanings communicated by those forms. Charismatic dancing in the spirit, however, does not seem to fit this pattern. Unlike many African and African-derived religious traditions, and unlike shamanic practices common to other

Native American traditions, "spirit possession" was never a central part of traditional Navajo ceremonialism. There is no deep resonance in this type of spirit-filled dancing for Oodlání. Why, then, has it localized so easily?

In this chapter, I explore how spirit-filled dancing is an aesthetic practice that actually reflects a different kind of resonant amplification—that of the relationship between human and non-human actors such as spirits, demons, deities, ghosts, and witches. In contrast to rational Protestantism, neo-Pentecostalism takes seriously the traditional Navajo concerns about the threat of witchcraft and curses as well as the spiritual root of illness.[1] Neo-Pentecostalism provides ontological continuity by acknowledging the very real influence of nonhuman actors in the daily lives of believers. As with other aspects of neo-Pentecostalism, many scholars have interpreted this kind of ontological continuity as evidence for flexible religious pluralism among Navajos. Christianity is often portrayed as providing Navajos with new sources of supernatural power, with which they can protect themselves from traditionally understood threats like witchcraft, curses, or ghost sickness (Aberle 1982, 219). This perspective portrays Navajo culture as essentially continuous through time, accommodating only those aspects of Christianity that can be synthesized with traditional Navajo philosophy (Blanchard 1977, 192). While this approach emphasizes the empowerment of Native actors making strategic choices, it also concludes that such empowering choices by Navajo Christian "converts" results in a Christianity relatively devoid of theological depth (Blanchard 1977, 198).

In contrast to these portrayals, I emphasize that practices such as dancing in the spirit reflect not just empowered choices toward cultural continuity but also empowered choices toward cultural rupture. While cultivating relationships with powerful nonhuman actors is a practice amplified by aspects of Navajo traditionalism, among Oodlání there is also significant difference in who these actors are understood to be and what proper conduct toward them entails. Through a close examination of the aesthetics of spirit-filled dancing, I argue that we can see how Pentecostalism resonates with traditional Navajo religion, while still representing a fundamental rupture for believers. I structure this chapter around four points. First, I explain the practice of dancing in the spirit among Navajos, focusing on the aesthetic boundaries that define the form of this dance. Second, I introduce the idea of ethno-aesthetics and reexamine the dance through this lens, demonstrating the centrality of the Holy Spirit. Third, I compare this ethno-aesthetic principle with the embodied experience of nonhuman actors in traditional Navajo philosophy. Finally, I argue that the aesthetics of dancing in the spirit operate as resonant rupture by emphasizing the continued importance of nonhuman actors but in importantly novel ways.

Oodlání Dancing in the Spirit

It was almost dusk at the revival by the river. The mosquitoes had dissipated, as had the wind that was blowing up dust. The musicians had been playing for a while, but the tent was still relatively empty. The Holy Spirit had yet to descend. Pastor Wallace took up the mic and began to sing. Usually his powerful voice would create the atmosphere ("accord") needed to invite the outpouring of God's anointing. And after a few songs, one woman fell out of her seat, rolling on the ground, covering herself with dirt and knocking over chairs. She got up and started dancing wildly around: swinging her arms and covering large amounts of ground. In my fieldnotes I scribbled, "She's endangering people!" Church members tried to move her up to the front where she could dance freely. But her movements did not seem right—even to me, a relative newcomer to charismatic gatherings. Her movements were violent. When she got to the front of the tent, right before the altar, she sat on the ground, spasming wildly. Then she got up again, danced wildly some more, then sat down again. No other dancers joined her. After a few songs and while she was still up front, Pastor Wallace signaled the musicians to stop playing and started reading loudly from the Bible in preparation for his sermon, deliberately ignoring her. Discussion after this event made it clear that community members knew that she didn't have "a true spirit." She was simply "seeking attention" they said. How did they know?[2]

Dancing in the spirit is often described by outsiders as "out of control" movement. In some sense, this is true: Oodlání filled with the Holy Spirit are not performing a choreographed dance. They are not following step patterns, have never been taught proper arm or leg positions, and although their movement is repetitive, it is markedly out of time with the beat of the music. And yet, as the preceding vignette suggests, it is movement bound by certain informal rules, most obvious when those rules of proper form are broken. Furthermore, it is movement described by Oodlání as "dancing" and thus presents itself as subject to evaluation not just in terms of correct and incorrect behavior but also along an aesthetic spectrum of beauty.[3]

AESTHETICS AND DANCE

Aesthetics are systems of evaluations based on the concept of "beauty" broadly conceived. As dance scholar Judith Hamera has pointed out, systems of aesthetics operate as a kind of "communicative currency" that is both "developed by and circulating between" different actors in the social worlds of dance: artists, audiences, and critics (Hamera 2007, 3). In some ways these aesthetic principles provide a sort of restrictive binding on creative free expression, because even the creative bending of long-held aesthetic principles (if well received) simply institutes a new set of rules (Royce 1977, 178). But in some ways aesthetic systems also help us to appreciate the beauty around us. As folklorist Henry Glassie has argued, the best way to understand the principle of aesthetics is to think of its etymological opposite: the anesthetic. Anesthetics help us feel nothing, or feel deadened. Aesthetics, on the other hand, help us to understand the world in ways that energize and enliven us. Glassie says, "When the nerves are excited, when the senses are seeking their own pleasure, leaving no room for boredom, preventing any feeling of alienation, an act is aesthetic and it has met the first requirement of art" (1986, 270).

In either case, whether a blinding or a blessing, aesthetic systems of beauty are ultimately socially determined. Creations that reflect the social values of their interpretive communities tend to be judged as beautiful, while ugliness is a category that can include antisocial behavior.[4] The entangled relationship between aesthetics systems of valuation and social systems of valuation is particularly evident when studying expressive forms cross-culturally. Cross-cultural dance scholarship (sometimes called "dance ethnology" or the "anthropology of dance") has proven a particularly valuable pathway into studying the social values inscribed in aesthetic systems, since dance is a way of physically manifesting these social values in embodied form.[5] As Hamera puts it, "dance techniques put aesthetics in motion" (Hamera 2007, 4).[6]

Dance scholarship has not always been interested in the relationship between culture, body, and movement (Reed 1998 505). Prior to 1970, dance scholars were primarily interested in recording the history and choreography of the world's dances, while anthropologists were less interested in the technical form of the dances than in the social functions they served.[7] In the 1960s, scholars such as Gertrude Kurath began to try to pull these threads together into a coherent field of dance ethnology. Her 1960 article, commissioned by Sol Tax and included in the inaugural issue of *Current Anthropology*, both "defined and laid out the shape" of anthropological dance research in America (Royce 2008, 224).[8]

Early dance ethnologists attempted to highlight the way that cultural meaning shapes movement by investigating the very boundaries of dance itself. In many societies, dance is inextricably imbedded in ritual, musical, and social events (Shay 2008, 106). Anya Peterson Royce provided an extensive cross-cultural survey of the parameters of dance, and devised an early universal definition, pointing out that dance is a unique kind of motion that involves the human body "making patterns in time and space" (1977, 3).[9] She further clarifies that these patterns are repetitive and non-utilitarian. Weeding a garden, for instance, requires repetitive and patterned movement but would not be considered a dance by most.[10] Universally, then, the boundaries of dance are not defined by choreography or virtuosic artistry but as motion with aesthetic value.[11]

Aesthetics shape dance through constraining the form of individual movement. Recognizing that aesthetic judgments are socially defined, aesthetic evaluation forces dancers to align their movements to a common (socially determined) vocabulary of form. Because these vocabularies of "beautiful movement" differ from culture to culture, one of the tasks of dance ethnographers, in fact, is to map diligently the form of dances. Describing the structural analysis of dance done by Kaeppler (of Tongan dance) and Martin and Pésovar (of Hungarian dance), Royce argues, "Until one has a 'grammar' of the dance, one does not know what the rules are and hence has no way of knowing how those rules are being bent or broken to incorporate change" (Royce 1977, 71).[12] In later works, Royce continues to push us to think about the grammar of dance (now called *technique*), and the way this technique interacts with individual artistry (Royce 2004, 24). Just as with classical ballet, the social pressure of aesthetic criteria encourages Oodlání spirit-filled dance to conform to a certain technique.[13]

THE TECHNIQUE OF DANCING IN THE SPIRIT

Technique is one way that dance ethnographers describe the rules of the dance genre. Discussions of technique assume that dance can combine an "almost limitless number of possibilities" for movement, and that technique informs not only what movements are combined but also the rules for combining them (Royce 2004, 7). Techniques are specific to different genres, and the technique for Oodlání dancing in the spirit dictates specific interactions between bodily movement and music.

Dancing in the spirit is nearly always initiated through music—specifically music that has started slowly (at under 100 beats per minute) and gradually increased in tempo to over 125 bpm. Preferably, this will be music that has tightened in repetitions as the tempo has increased. The tightening of repetitions is made possible by the interaction in the call-and-response pattern between the caller (the music leader, usually a pastor or evangelist) and the response (usually provided by audience members). The typical performance by Pastor Wallace of the praise song "My God Is a Good God" provides a good example of the way repetitions can tighten over time, through a comparison of the same thirty-two-beat phrase.

CALL:	My God is a good God
RESPONSE:	Yes He is
CALL:	My God is a good God
RESPONSE:	Yes He is
CALL:	My God is a good God
RESPONSE:	Yes He is
TOGETHER:	Yes he is, Yes he is,
	Yes he is.

This form of the call-and-response pattern is repeated an indeterminate number of times but usually goes on for several minutes. As the performance continues, however, the caller can tighten the repetitions of the full iteration of the song, and it begins to condense:

CALL:	Yes He is
RESPONSE:	Yes He is
CALL:	Yes He is
RESPONSE:	Yes He is
[repeat 3 more times]	

Finally, when really stoking the energy of the crowd, the caller can tighten the repetitions so much that the call and response become a sing-word back-and-forth pattern:

CALL:	Yes
RESPONSE:	Yes
CALL:	Yes
RESPONSE:	Yes
[repeat 7 more times]	

The idea behind the tightening of repetitions is that the energy of the song is increased not just by the increasing of tempo; the tightening of repetitions within phrases is also necessary for bringing about the dance.

Another important element of Oodlání dance technique is the way in which it is initiated. Dancers begin dancing at their seats and gradually move to the front and center of the gathering—often they have to be guided there, unaware, by others. Dancing usually begins with handfuls of people at around the same time, not individually, as if the dancing of a few people sets off a chain reaction in others. The woman in the preceding vignette chose to come out and dance in front of everyone, thus breaching both Oodlání and more general Navajo social norms that discourage calling attention to oneself (Kluckhohn and Leighton 1946, 302).

As mentioned, aesthetically guided technique also constrains the body position of the dancers. Again, these rules are not formally taught. As in a folk dance, newcomers learn by watching. Instead of the expansive violent motions evidenced in the vignette, dancers with a "true spirit" typically lean forward, with their heads down. As noted, their arms are typically bent, and pump forward and back, and their hands may be noticeably trembling.[14] Although this dance begins with music, once it begins the dancer falls completely out of time with the beat, moving repetitively but at a tempo all her own. Given these aesthetic boundaries, the motions of the out-of-control dancer described were clearly apparent to participants who understand the unspoken aesthetic rules about what proper dancing in the spirit looks like.[15]

What was significant about the motions of this dancer for community members, however, was not just that they looked wrong, it was that they conveyed the wrong meaning. Since the 1970s, dance ethnologists have emphasized that bodies in motion can tell us so much more about cultures than the form of their dances. This is because dance (constrained by aesthetic boundaries) brings cultural values to life. Deeply held cultural meanings are literally *embodied* through the motions of dancers (Ness 1992, 233). Furthermore, the cultural meanings embodied in dance are not identical to those conveyed in language, because movement communicates on a different and less referential level (Royce 1977, 155; Bull 1997, 270).[16] Through dance, then, we can reveal and unpack "the webs of meaning created through the dance event" (Bull 1997, 269). One way of accessing these broader webs of meaning in the dance event is through the lens of ethno-aesthetics.

Ethno-aesthetics are aesthetic spectrums of beauty (broadly conceived), as applied by cultural actors themselves. Often, ethno-aesthetic spectrums can and do make room for valuation judgments about beauty that are not normally encompassed by our narrow Western art-critic definition of color, balance, and proportion.[17] For instance, Kenneth Goldstein's study of folk singers revealed that their aesthetic evaluation centered on a quality they called "bigness" that incorporated not only the forceful and expressive nature of a singer's voice but also the number of songs a singer knew and how lengthy and complete those songs were (Goldstein 1991). David Coplan's study of poetic song from Lesotho demonstrated that the ethno-aesthetic value of hearing over seeing helped explain the continued use of this sung poetry in socially constituting communal sentiment, even in migrant and Western hegemonic contexts (Coplan 1988). And Cynthia Bull (1997) argued that in Ghana, aesthetic beauty in dance is determined by the way in which dance promotes social relationships.[18] She says, "The structural parameters of Ghanaian dance encourage a balance of control and variation and a sense of participation by all" (Bull 1997, 284). Ethno-aesthetics thus challenge the sensory privilege of sight, often ascribed to the West (Porcello et al. 2010), and account for other sensory ways of determining beauty. Ethno-aesthetics can account for definitions of beauty that include the completeness of repertoire, the harmonic sounds of a community acting together, or even the technique of Trobriand yam gardening (F. Myers 1997, 166).[19]

Similarly, when I asked Navajo consultants about what made dancing in the spirit beautiful, my questions about body posture, musical triggers, and embodied sensations were consistently redirected into discussions about the Holy Spirit. At first I assumed that my Oodlání interlocutors were more interested in theology than aesthetics. But after hearing repeated evaluative comments about this type of dancing framed around whether or not someone had "a true spirit," I began to think about the incorporative nature of ethno-aesthetics. In considering this "divine choreography" (Browning 1995), Oodlání evaluation of aesthetic beauty certainly incorporated more than simple ideas about technical skill or artistry. According to the ethno-aesthetic system of Oodlání, theology and aesthetics are not entirely separate categories.[20]

Pastor Wallace and I are sitting at a little table in the Farmington loca-
tion of Furr's Cafeteria. Over sliced ham, mashed potatoes, biscuits, and
Jello, with plenty of refills on coffee, I ask him about his music ministry. He
answers me with a story. "I had never sung, or anything" he says. "And I
was at a revival one night and the Holy Spirit just spoke to my heart and
told me to sing a song. . . . And I got up there and I started singing, and the
anointing fell. People were dancing, shouting, and um . . . I got scared!"
he laughs heartily. "I just put my microphone back on the pulpit and I got
up . . ." He pauses and laughs again. "You know, like 'What happened?'
and 'I'm sorry, I didn't mean to do this!'" (Begay 2008b)

Theologically, Oodlání are Pentecostal or charismatic.[21] The root
of charismatic belief is that the gifts of the Holy Spirit that were
evident during apostolic times (such as speaking in tongues) are
available to modern Christians as well. There are many "gifts"
attributed to the Holy Spirit, some of the major ones being speaking in tongues, healing, and spirit-filled dancing. In English, charismatics talk about being "filled" with the Holy Spirit, where the
Holy Spirit is understood as the power (or "anointing") of God
interacting with humans. Following the translation of these concepts in the Navajo Bible, specifically in the book of Acts, Oodlání also talk about "being filled," or say in Navajo, "*Nílch'i diyini*
nii hádee biid" (The Holy Spirit filled them). They may also say,
"*Biih ííyá*" (Something entered him or her). Once the Holy Spirit
has "entered" or "filled" someone, Oodlání say "*Naa biił ná*" (It
moved him/her). Thus we can see that movement, motion, and
what we might call dancing must proceed from the actions of an
outside, nonhuman actor (the Holy Spirit) in order to be judged
aesthetically pleasing or done well.

Interviews with Oodlání community members revealed this
aesthetic focus as well. One elderly Navajo pastor told me, "What
makes the change [to dance] is that, when you yield to the Spirit. . . .
And then the Holy Spirit will start working. That's how it does it.
That's what makes it change. If you put pride in there. . . it won't
work" (F. Begay 2008). Dancers must yield their will and pride
(by which he means their desire to be the center of attention)

FIG. 15. Oodlání praying to be filled by the Holy Spirit (*Nítch'i Diyini*). Photo courtesy of Eugene B. Joe.

over to the control of the Holy Spirit.[22] Sometimes this surrender to the Holy Spirit is described in forceful or even nearly violent terms. Rose Yazzie commented that "when the Holy Spirit is moving, you can feel that power coming towards you. . . . You can hang onto your chair like this, but it still can throw you out" (Yazzie 2008). Another community member commented that the spirit will "jump you up" (literally make you jump up), and "the Holy Spirit gonna grab you" (Mann 2008). The words *throw, jump,* and *grab* all suggest a type of interaction with a powerful actor.

Often Oodlání describe their interactions with the Holy Spirit in terms of surprise and lack of control. Pastor Wallace's comments in Furr's Cafeteria suggest both these emotions as well as something near embarrassment. Rose Yazzie mentioned surprise and lack of control as well, saying that when you feel the power of the Holy Spirit coming on, "You try to stop yourself but it won't stop" (Yazzie 2008).

Who is this nonhuman but very real actor in the lives of Oodlání? Most Oodlání are Trinitarian, so the Holy Spirit is understood to be one aspect of a triune Godhead composed of Father, Son, and Holy Spirit. The Father, who is referred to by the English word "God" (sometimes with the addition of the Navajo descriptor *Diyin*, "Holy," as in the phrase *Diyin God*) is considered both the creator and all-powerful ruler of the universe but also a personified force interacting with Oodlání in personal ways and in daily life.[23] Tanya Luhrman has written extensively about the kind of intimate involvement in everyday matters that God can have for Christians like Oodlání (Luhrman 2012). The second member of the trinity, the Son, who is referred to by the proper name Jesus Christ is taught to have made the atoning sacrifice on the cross that saved humanity from eternal torment in hell, and Oodlání join fundamentalist Christian theology in preaching that only those who repent of their sins and believe in Jesus will be reunited with God in heaven after death; the rest will spend the afterlife paying for their sins with eternal corporal punishment in hell (Warrington 2008, 37). Both the protecting power of God and the atoning sacrifice of Jesus are understood to have real material consequences in the lives of believers in *this* world. It is the role of the Holy Spirit to work as the transmitting conduit of this power, or "anointing."

As charismatics, Oodlání are deeply invested in the manifestation of spiritual gifts, facilitated by God's anointing through the Holy Spirit. Unlike the proper names untranslated for God or Jesus, Oodlání do regularly employ a Navajo word for the Holy Spirit: *Nítch'i Diyinii* (*nítch'i*, "wind"; *diyinii*, "the one that is holy"). Alternately, they may refer to the Holy Spirit as *Nítch'i Yá'át'ééhii* (wind that is good) or *Nítch'i Nizhóní* (wind that is beautiful). For Oodlání this Holy Wind is active in the world today, not only in transmitting spiritual gifts but also in aiding the worship (and thus warfare) of Oodlání against the devil.

When comments about the quality of a spirit-filled dancer center on whether that person has "a true spirit," it is the presence or absence of *Nítch'i Diyinii* that is being evaluated. This aesthetic judgment can operate along a spectrum. As Pastor Fred pointed out, how well the spirit operates largely depends on how much the dancer yields control and surrenders "pride." In some sense, then, the ethno-aesthetic evaluation of Oodláni spirit-filled dancing is the inverse of typical Western aesthetic judgments. Instead of valuing practiced skill and virtuosity, this dance is judged most beautiful when dancers let go of control and let a nonhuman actor (the Holy Spirit) take control.[24]

The opposite situation exists as well. If a good dance is judged beautiful because of the absorbing presence of the Holy Spirit, the really awful, worst kind of dance is that which is driven by the wrong kind of spirit. Pastor Alice Norton (Navajo) told me a story once about a woman who was afraid to pray (Norton 2012). Sitting next to Pastor Alice, this woman confided that every time she began to pray in the spirit, it was painful: the spirit threw her around, bruised her hands on chairs and poles, and made her whole chest fill with pain. Pastor Alice told her, "I know what this is. I recognize this spirit. You don't have the right spirit, because the Holy Spirit does not work like that. . . . I'm gonna come against the defiling spirit that is inside of you." Pastor Alice prayed with the woman and told her to pray too. "And now pretty soon that thing [was] jumping. . . . So we come against it, we rebuke it, we asked it to leave out of her in the name of Jesus. And then it just . . . it just left her." The woman deflated like a balloon. She told Pastor Alice, "I felt it leavin' me. . . . Now I'm gonna seek the right spirit." But, driving home the lesson of *yielding* versus *seeking*, Pastor Alice told her, "You don't have to seek it. The Lord's gonna give it to you at your own time."

Because the actions of the Holy Spirit are somewhat unpredictable, spirit-filled dancing can walk a line very close to demon possession.[25] Thus the presence of not just a nonhuman actor but the *right kind* of nonhuman actor becomes central to the ethno-aesthetic evaluation of spirit-filled dancing.

Traditional Nonhuman Actors

The agency of nonhuman actors is a concept that has deep roots in traditional Navajo religious practice, philosophy, and cosmology. As mentioned in previous chapters, traditional Navajo religion is more accurately understood not as a belief system but as an all-encompassing lifeway or "matrix" that is experiential at its core. *Diné Binahagha'*—the traditional Navajo ceremonial complex most accurately translated as "walking about ceremonially,"—has as an underlying philosophical core the restoration of *hózhǫ́* (beauty or balance). In a broad perspective, then, Navajo ceremonies are about healing. They restore the patient to the "corn pollen path" (L. Lee 2014, 5) of *Sa'ah Naagháí Bik'eh Hózhǫ́ǫ́n*, translated loosely as "one's journey of striving to live a long and harmonious life" (Cajete 2014, ix). The efficacy of these healing ceremonials in restoring a state of *hózhǫ́* is achieved by recruiting the aid of nonhuman actors, the *Diyin Diné'é* or "Holy People." The traditional matrix of SNBH presumes that the active involvement (or threat) of nonhuman actors has very real consequences for the living.[26]

Navajo healing ceremonials take place whenever there is a need felt for one but often in response to a concern about ill-health.[27] According to traditional practitioners, the world was created in a state of balance (harmony, or in Navajo *hózhǫ́*). Furthermore, the imbalance caused by the in-fighting of early proto-humans was negated by the actions of the hero-twins (Monster Slayer and Born-for-Water) and their benevolent mother Changing Woman (Yazzie 1984). The actions and teachings of these mythic figures provided a template through which *hózhǫ́* could be preserved and ceremonially restored.[28] This "sunwise" or "corn pollen path" is regarded as the "natural law" of the universe, which can be seen "to work all the time and every minute of our life, . . . in every breath we take, and in the working process we call Sa'ah Naagháí Bik'eh Hózhóón" (Aronilth 1994, 10). The sunwise or corn pollen road of life is seen as walking in the "sacred foot prints of white corn and yellow corn" laid out by the *Diyin Diné'é* (Holy People; Aronilth 1994, 92).[29]

Unlike the Judeo-Christian concept of a supreme, all-knowing, and wholly good God, the *Diyin Diné'é* (Holy People) are a class of beings set in contrast to the *Nihookáá Dine'é* (Earth Surface People). Just like Earth Surface People, the *Diyin Diné'é* are multitudinous, have personalities, and contain the capacity to work for good or evil (Reichard 1963, 381–505). In fact, according to anthropologist Gladys Reichard, some "are almost wholly evil"

(Reichard 1963, 49). They are distinguished from Earth Surface People not because they are more perfect or morally upright but by the strength of their power to influence the natural world and human thought and behavior (Frisbie 1987, 2). Through the ceremonial and ritual framework, the Holy People may be persuaded to restore a state of health, long life, and happiness: a state of *Sa'ah Naaghái Bik'eh Hózhǫ́ǫn*.[30]

In addition to the *Diyin Diné'é*, two other important nonhuman actors animate the traditional Navajo world: *ch'įįdii* and the *Nilch'i Diyini*. *Ch'įįdii* are understood by traditional Navajos to be the malevolent ghosts of the departed, and in the past Navajos have practiced strict avoidance of the dead for fear of contamination by the malevolent *ch'įįdii* (ghost) that remains near the body of even the most kindly deceased Navajo mother.[31] Frisbie argues that although standard translations gloss this word as "ghost," the English-language concept of ghost is inadequate for understanding the full meaning of this term, which can encompass things imbued with evil power as well.[32] In embodied form, *ch'įįdii* are conceived of as shadowy and ethereal beings, sometimes said to live in a ghostland called *ch'įįdiitah* located to the north (Frisbie 1978, 304). According to the traditional view of most Navajos, *ch'įįdii* can influence events around the living, returning at night to "avenge wrongdoings" (Frisbie 1978, 304), and can cause illness, misfortune, and premature or unnatural death. Consequently, according to Frisbie, "*Ch'įįdii* are dangerous and greatly feared by the Navajos: much attention is directed toward avoiding them" (Frisbie 1978, 304).[33]

The *Nilch'i Diyini*, on the other hand, is primarily benevolent and is considered by most traditional Navajos to be one of the *Diyin Diné'é* (Holy People). *Nilch'i Diyini* means "Holy Wind" and, as a Holy Person, is much more than a simple breeze. In some ways this Holy Wind is understood to be the experiential force of the Holy People "who stand in the four directions" and are themselves the "symbolic representation of the power of Sa'ah Naaghái Bik'eh Hózhǫ́ǫn" (Aronilth 1994, 96). According to scholar James McNeley, the term *Nilch'i* indicates "the air or atmosphere in its entirety, including such air when in motion, conceived as having a holy quality and powers that are not acknowledged in Western culture" (McNeley 1981, xviii).

In traditional Navajo philosophy, Wind is an animating force in all living things, giving both life and breath, but also thought, motion and communication (McNeley 1981, 1). In the mythic creation of Diné, *Níłch'i Diyini* "entered between the covers of the sacred deer skin and gave us the precious breath of life. It also entered at the top of our heads and [exited] our fingers and toes, this is why we can still see the Wind's trail at the tips" (Aronilth 1994, 33). As the internal personification of SNBH, the "indwelling" wind inside one is also a moral force, providing moral guidance when in combination with proper instruction, thoughtful reflection, and correct actions (McNeley 1981, 36–49). It facilitates growth, speech, and even thought. As McNeley beautifully summarizes: "Winds exist all around and within the individual, entering and departing through respiratory organs and whorls on the body's surface. That which is within and that which surrounds one is all the same and it is holy" (1981, 35). In this sense, wind is a nonhuman actor, a Holy Person experienced by traditional Navajos in every breath, through markings on the body, and through the very thoughts and speech of each individual. As Aronilth sums up, through the *Níłch'i Diyini*, "We are SNBH" (1994, 96).

In good ways and in bad, then, nonhuman actors like the *Diyin Diné'é*, the *ch'įįdii*, and the *Níłch'i Diyini* exert concrete influence on the daily lives of traditionally oriented Navajos. This is the spiritual-cultural matrix that has grounded Navajos for centuries, and contemporary Navajos continue to use these principles to "achieve happiness, prosperity, and well-being" in the present moment (Lee 2014a, 3).

Spirit-Filled Dance as Continuity

There are many ways in which the continued relevance of active nonhuman agents represents a type of deeply felt continuity for Oodláni. Both linguistic and aesthetic practices suggest that strong ties exist between Oodláni spirit-filled dancing and traditional Navajo ceremonialism. I argue, however, that a close examination of the types of nonhuman actors understood to be interacting with believers in these two contexts reveals as many rifts as continuities. This amplifying (but not equivalent) relationship, then, exhibits the quality of resonant rupture.

Clearly part of the success of Navajo Pentecostalism is rooted in the fact that this form of Christianity continues to recognize and incorporate the real and materially manifest presence of nonhuman actors. Being Diyin (Holy) and involved in the lives of humans implies an inherently useful power in matters of healing, whether from the *Diyin Diné'é* (Holy People) in the traditional context or Diyin God in the Oodlání context. The next chapter explores the resonance of Oodlání healing in more depth and the deeply felt similarity between the protective power of God in place of the protective power of the *Diyin Diné'é*.

Another type of deeply felt continuity exists between evil forces as well. Both the malevolent ghosts of traditional Navajo cosmology and the malevolent demons of Pentecostal Christianity exert negative effects in the lives of Navajos. Further emphasizing their connection, Oodlání refer to the Devil and his troupe of torturing demons in Navajo as *ch'įįdii*—the same word used to describe traditional malevolent ghosts. Just as with traditional ghost *ch'įįdii*, Oodlání demon *ch'įįdii* can cause illness and misfortune. For example, when one pastor visiting a revival could not sing because of laryngitis, one of her congregants explained to the assembled, "The devil is taking my pastor's voice away."[34] *Ch'įįdii* were also seen to be constantly trying to stop the worship of God among the Oodlání, which is viewed as "doing spiritual warfare with your praise."[35] They try to interrupt worship in many ways, including controlling the weather. One evening during camp meeting, the sky was gray and windy, threatening to bring down the tent and ruin the service. Pastor Wallace kept walking through the kitchen to check on the weather through the window, repeatedly declaring, "We rebuke you, devil!"[36] In one of the more dramatic moments of my fieldwork, a bad storm hit during one of the nights of Pastor Wallace's camp meeting. I had sheltered with some of the church ladies in the temporary lean-to kitchen that had been built beside the church, and the wind came through so strongly that all of us had to hold the walls up to keep the kitchen from collapsing. As terrifying as the event was, the calm voice of Ma Beverly kept declaring throughout "I rebuke you, devil, I rebuke you!"[37] When bad things happen to faithful Oodlání (whether bodily or financial), the malevolent influence of ch'įįdii is suspected, just as it has been among Navajos for generations.

Finally, the traditional matrix and Oodlání Christianity appear to have a strong degree of continuity in the nonhuman actor called the Nílch'i Diyini. As mentioned, this figure is understood by traditionally oriented Navajos to be a sort of animating wind, suffusing all of nature, and giving "life, thought, speech, and the power of motion to all living things" (McNeley 1981, 1). The term Nílch'i Diyini is used by Oodlání as well to describe the Holy Spirit who animates expressive practices like spirit-filled dancing. Given this philosophy, the traditional Navajo and Oodlání concepts of Holy Wind share some characteristics. Both are able to dwell within a person. And just like the Holy Wind of traditional Navajo philosophy, the Oodlání Nílch'i Diyini causes material effects in this world.

For instance, one very hot afternoon in June 2008, the church community had donned work clothes and people were laboring together to raise the large tent under which the annual camp meeting would be held the following week. Raising a massive tent that can hold hundreds of people is a difficult task, taking dozens of people many hours of physical effort: pounding stakes, lacing canvas, and tying lines. As the mercury topped one hundred degrees in the late afternoon, the preparations reached a critical stage: the raising of hundreds of feet of heavy canvas on the three main weight-bearing poles. Women and children took hold of the edges of the tent and lifted a bit while handfuls of men, bent halfway over, walked the poles into the center of the large sheet of the tent. Once the tops of the center poles were tied in place, they began to count down to coordinate the extraordinary physical strength it would take for the team to raise the roof of the tent off the ground.

At precisely this moment, the hot and still air was broken by a strong whirlwind that blew through, lifting the tent and allow-

FIG. 16. Raising the tent. Photo by author.

ing the poles to be raised effortlessly under it. This wind was joyfully interpreted as the Holy Spirit, assisting in the holy battle, and the video footage I had been absent-mindedly recording throughout the afternoon became an instant hit in the community, with several people asking for a copy and Pastor Wallace asking me to post it to the church website as a testimony to the active support of *Niłch'i Diyinii*.

The Resonant Rupture of Spirit-Filled Dance

Although the active involvement of nonhuman actors in both traditional Navajo religion and Oodlání Christianity seems to indicate a great deal of continuity, believers themselves do not understand what they are doing as continuity. In fact, as established in previous chapters, they set themselves as diametrically opposed to traditional Navajo religion. The power of the medicine man is equated by Oodlání with the power of the Devil, and the tools of the medicine man are a gateway through which demons can enter an Oodlání home. Pentecostal Christianity is grounded in born-again theology, and for Navajo neo-Pentecostals, becoming a believer is fundamentally about making a break with the past. Although still valuing their identity as Navajos, Oodlání emphasize not continuity but rupture.

Which brings us, finally, back to the ethno-aesthetics of dancing in the spirit. As established, the ethno-aesthetics of Navajo neo-Pentecostal dancing in the spirit holds that the most valued, most beautiful performers of this dance are dancers who surrender to the will of the spirit and let the actions of the Holy Spirit move through them. There is great agency, here, with a nonhuman actor: the Holy Spirit. In form, this is similar to the great agency of the traditional Navajo nonhuman actors: the *Diyin Diné'é*, the *ch'įįdii*, and the Holy Wind. The agency of nonhuman actors resonates.

And yet resonant tones are not identical tones. Resonance also implies difference, and a careful comparison of traditional Navajo and Oodlání human actors reveals that believers interact with Oodlání nonhuman actors in importantly novel ways. For instance, dancing in the spirit (and, frankly, any kind of "spirit possession" behavior) is absent from traditional Navajo healing ceremonies. Traditional Navajo forms of healing are achieved not through a shamanic and other-worldly intermediary but through rational compliance to the guidelines for good living set out by the Holy People.[38] In particular, Changing Woman taught Navajos how to maintain the balance of harmony, *hózhǫ́* through ritual observances, songs, prayers, and avoidances (Frisbie 1987, 2). The restoration of *hózhǫ́* is the primary way of curing illness, since in restoring the balance that has been disrupted, a singer is also negating the underlying cause of the illness. This restoration, within the ceremonial context, often involves recruiting the aid of nonhuman actors but primarily by seeking to remind the *Diyin Diné'é* of the mutually obligating rules of reciprocity. As discussed in chapter 2, the primacy of the reciprocity principle organizes interactions between humans and nonhuman actors, encouraging powerful supernaturals to "remember" their less-powerful human kin and behave toward them in a socially appropriate way.[39]

Oodlání may identify themselves as *Diyin God bee awéé*: literally the "baby" of God, and thus signal a type of childlike dependence. But a major difference in this new kinship arrangement is that the Judeo-Christian God is not beholden to preestablished rules or social norms of reciprocity. His will is "divine and unknowable." He may be worshiped and His aid may be beseeched, but in important contrast to traditional Navajo nonhuman actors, His cooperation can never be *compelled*, by social graces or otherwise. Oodlání are assured in general terms that God loves them and wants them to be happy. But the response of God to any particular petition or event is never totally secure. Between Oodlání and the Judeo-Christian *Diyin*, the rules of reciprocity are *not* mutually obligating.

Oodlání *ch'įįdii* are also a bit different than the traditional *ch'įįdii*.[40] Their form is different: while still invisible and mysterious, they are not understood by Oodlání to be the ghosts of the deceased. Among Oodlání, the term *ch'įįdii* refers more specifically to an unspecified class of demons, devils, and bad spirits. The devil (when distinguished) is referred to as *Ch'įįdii binant'a'íí* or the "boss" of the *ch'įįdii* (*binant'a'íí* is "boss" or "leader"). And in contrast to the generalized sense of *ch'įįdii* as any of a class of things associated with the dead, for Oodlání *ch'įįdii* are strictly conceptualized as personified actors.[41] *Ch'įįdiitah* continues to be the dwelling place of these demons, since it is the Navajo term used to identify the Christian hell. But for Oodlání the cosmography of *ch'įįdiitah* is different. Instead of a shadowy location to the north, the *ch'įįdiitah* of the Oodlání is very Christian in location: existing in an underworld directly below this world.

The easy continuity of the *Nílch'i Diyini* (Holy Wind/Holy Spirit) becomes less clear upon closer examination as well. According to McNeley, the Holy Wind in Navajo philosophy is said to control normal bodily processes like life, breath, thought, communication, and personality. As Aronilth points out, "By the Holy Wind, our behavior is controlled through different teachings" (Aronilth 1994, 33). The *Nílch'i Diyini* of the Oodlání, on the other hand, is a separate entity—one that visits the believer on occasion but does not dwell within the believer at all times. Being "filled" by the Holy Spirit is a special event, a liminal frame, with a beginning and ending point. Spirit-filled dancing highlights this difference. When the Holy Spirit causes people to dance, believers experience bodily sensations set apart from everyday reality: chills down the back, a warmth rising from the feet to the head, or a warmth on the palms of their hands, "like fire" (Begay 2008b). As mentioned, believers begin to dance when they "let go" and let the spirit take control and drive their actions. Some dancers remember what was happening around them while they danced, observed as if from the outside. Often dancers black out: they are unaware of what their bodies are doing and do not recall these events afterward. The dance usually ends with the dancer being "slain" by the spirit and collapsing to the ground.[42] After a while the slain dancer will "come to," returning to regular consciousness. Brushing off the wood chips or dust from the ground, sometimes tearful and with bowed head, the dancer will return to his or her seat. The visit by the Holy Spirit, then, is just that: a visit. It is a markedly liminal activity: a time out of normal time. In dramatic contrast to the *Nítch'i Diyini* of traditional Navajo philosophy, the visit of the nonhuman actor most responsible for spirit-filled dancing is not a normal part of daily life.

Last but certainly not least, Oodlání themselves understand the practice of spirit-filled dancing as diametrically opposed to the patterned motions of Navajo ceremonialism. From an Oodlání perspective, one is the province of the anointing of God, and the other is the province of the devil. And their opinion about what it is they are doing does, in fact, matter.

Conclusion

Oodlání value their Navajo identity. They preach and sing in the Navajo language, share meals of mutton stew and frybread, and dress up with vivid velveteen skirts and large turquoise squash blossom necklaces. And yet the religious orientation of Oodlání is not incorporative. Converts will tell you that what they are doing is different, new, and a deliberate effort to change.

However, there is great emotional significance invested in a world that is enlivened with the presence of unseen but influential beings. Dancing in the spirit is an expressive practice that reflects the continuity of this nonhuman investment in the world of humans. Expressive practices are particularly "potent" points of resonance because, as symbolic forms of communication, they are notoriously ambiguous. This ambiguity allows them to incorporate multiple meanings, providing a kind of enacted bridge across which cultural meanings can be punned, contested, and ultimately rewritten.

When Rose Yazzie dances in the spirit, she feels a cool chill moving from the top of her head all the way down to her toes (Yazzie 2008). When she dances, she experiences the presence of a nonhuman actor deeply invested in her personal health and well-being. The embodied effects of a spiritual being resonate with a deep groove of Navajo spirituality, experienced by her grandmothers before her. For centuries, the Navajo cultural matrix has presumed that the active involvement (or threat) of nonhuman actors has very real consequences for the living. Rose certainly understands and interacts with these nonhuman actors differently than did her grandmothers: yielding instead of compelling, rebuking instead of avoiding. But by tapping into this affective echo of Navajo spirituality, Rose's dance is amplified with power and significance. Resonant rupture helps to make her dance beautiful.

CHAPTER 6

Embodying Healing
The Resonant Rupture of Faith Healing

The camp meeting has been going on for several hours, and after nearly an hour of preaching, the shouting of the Navajo evangelist has been joined by the occasional riffs of a few background musicians. He shouts "The Devil has been defeated!" and the guitar player responds with a struck cord, and the drummer with a hit. He shouts "You are an overcomer!" and the musicians again respond. Gradually, seamlessly, through nonmelodic vamping of increasing length, the musicians and the evangelist work together to build the energy of the assembled. By the time the preacher is ready to turn from the "lesson" to the application of that lesson (through healing), the musicians are cooking and people are already on their feet.

The evangelist signals to the musicians, and they play more softly as he addresses the crowd. "And if anyone in here wants some healing prayer," he shouts, "come on up here and let the Lord heal you." The musicians crank up the volume again as most of the Navajos in the tent (literally hundreds of people) line up along the side of the tent and proceed single-file across the platform at the front where the healing evangelist is standing. One by one, the healing evangelist consults with the "patients," and then lays a hand on them and prays loudly, beseeching God to intervene or commanding demons to be gone. Usually the patients respond emotionally; some at this point are filled with the Holy Spirit and are escorted off the stage to the ground below, where they can dance in the spirit freely. Most proceed past the evangelist fairly quickly, without much more than a touch on their forehead, and return to their seats with a "prayer handkerchief," soaked in anointing oil and handed out by the evangelist's helpers. But occasionally the evangelist pauses the line to point out to everyone the healing of a particular supplicant: to demonstrate a blind man being given sight or a woman in a wheelchair able to walk in response to his prayer.

As all of this activity is happening on the platform, the repetitive and rhythmic vamping of the musicians behind the evangelist has transformed the soundscape of the tent revival into an energetic sonic atmosphere. Their playing is projected at deafening levels through eight-foot-tall speaker towers. As supplicants wait for their turn with the evangelist, they file directly past these massive speakers, so the bass can be felt vibrating within their bodies. When they actually have their turn with the healing evangelist, the pair stands less than two feet from the front of the drum set, so the thumping of the bass drum pounds within the patient's chest. The soundscape in which Oodlání healing takes place is an aural assault that envelops the patient completely.

Healing is central to Navajo culture. So crucial are concerns about curing bodily ills that healing has been called an "underlying cultural archetype" specific to Navajos (Schwarz 2008, 76). For centuries Navajos have understood bodily health as the physical manifestation of an inner spiritual state, and healing as a religious process. The two, as Thomas Csordas has put it, are "intimately entwined" (Csordas 2000, 463).[1] As new religious and ceremonial systems were introduced among Navajos, they localized and became relevant to converts in large part by emphasizing their ability to heal (Csordas 2000; Pavlik 1997). The centrality of healing helps to explain the popularity of two of the most influential new religions to be adopted by Navajos in the past century: the Native American Church (NAC) and the neo-Pentecostal (Oodlání) movement.

Healing is an embodied and multi-sensorial experience, incorporating aspects of sight, hearing, and touch. And yet too often analysis of ritual healing focuses on the discursive (or spoken) aspects of healing rituals at the expense of the phenomenological (lived) experience itself (Csordas 2002, 3). One way that ethnographers have attempted to break through this verbal barrier to embodied experience is to focus attention on the way that the world is encountered by the various senses; to conduct multisensorial ethnography (Stoller 1997). Examining the expressive forms of Oodlání revivals helps to tap into how these healing rituals sound, feel, and smell, in both their material form and as they are constituted poetically.

For example, the soundscape described is unique in the Navajo ritual healing landscape. It is a markedly different sonic environment than that of the traditional healing ceremonial, where the *hataałii* (medicine man) soulfully chants unaccompanied prayers.[2] It is also fundamentally different from the soundscape of the NAC healing ritual, where the rapid shaking of a gourd rattle and high-pitched water drum accompany devotional songs. For participants, inhabiting the sonic space of an Oodlání revival communicates in nonverbal ways a special type of acoustic epistemology: a sonic way of knowing the world.[3] Navajo healing soundscapes are notably distinct from one another and thus communicate a principle of *separation*: respecting the distinctive nature of each type of healing.

Despite what the sonic landscape suggests about the uniqueness of these three types of ritual healing, there are some crucial continuities that recent scholars have highlighted as common to traditional Navajo ceremonialism, NAC ritual healing, and Navajo Christian faith healing. These continuities have allegedly allowed the latter two forms of ritual healing to be adopted rather effortlessly by Navajos.[4] These continuities include: (1) the emphasis of all Navajo ritual healing systems on the restoration of kin relations (Lewton and Bydone 2000), (2) the way each healing system allows access to new forms of supernatural power (Garrity 2000), and (3) the common thread of each system in accessing healing by talking to a patient "so they understand" the causes of their illness (Csordas 1999, 11).

As with other aspects of Oodlání religious practice, however, my research suggests that the bridge of continuity between different ritual healing systems may be overemphasized by scholars. Rather, I argue that the primary embodied orientation of Oodlání ritual healing, communicated through expressive form, is one of resonant rupture.[5] While capitalizing on the kind of affective amplification it gains from connection to the broader Navajo healing "archetype," Oodlání faith healing simultaneously embodies a great deal of rupture with the other ritual healing systems. It is not only distinct from traditional and NAC healing but actually oriented in opposition to these systems. In this chapter, I examine continuity and rupture as they manifest in the kin building and harmony restoration of motion, the supernatural power of material items, and the performative language of testimony. Each of these expressive forms helps to reveal a fuller of picture of the ways in which resonant rupture is performatively embodied and enacted.

The Kin Restoration of Motion

The healing revival is in full swing. It is late and the desert night is dark. But the atmosphere inside the lighted tent is vibrant: Oodlání would say that the anointing of the Holy Spirit is flowing. Dozens of Navajos file past the healing evangelist at the front of the tent. She is standing on the platform, elevated above the wood chips on the ground by about two feet. She leans over to lay her hand on the heads of those who stand in front of her. "I felt her energy flowing," Michelle later told me. "I went through the prayer line . . . she's positive, and she's agreeing with me." For all the people who come past, the evangelist presses her hand on their forehead and prays over them. Most people take the handkerchief soaked in anointing oil that she gives out and return to their seats. But some people experience her touch like an electric shock. They are thrown backward, unconscious. Others react to her touch by seizing uncontrollably, "dancing" in the spirit without awareness of objects or people around them. I've heard stories about the first big tent revivals brought by healing evangelists to Shiprock. They say people were so caught up in the spirit they ran into tent poles. Tonight, though, those who are filled with the spirit have watchful guardians to protect them from harm or embarrassment. A handful of church men, the ushers, carefully watch how each person reacts to the evangelist. They help guide the unaware dancers into safe spaces. They catch any who fall back, lay them gently on the ground, and cover them with a red cloth. Regardless of whether those in the prayer line are Oodlání or not, they can see that if the Holy Spirit fills their bodies, tonight these men will protect them.

Part of the success of the Oodlání movement relies on the way that Ooldání churches function as surrogate families. Often both pastors and participants in this movement come out of troubled family lives shaped by extreme poverty and marked by both substance abuse and domestic violence.[6] The support of a new "church family" is defined not just in the kin terms (brother/sister) that church members call one another; it is experienced in bodily ways, as in the preceding vignette, through the supportive hands of an usher laying your body gently to the ground.

In some ways, the kin-making aspects of Oodlání interactions are amplified by the fundamental Diné cultural matrix that grounds traditional Navajo healing: *Sa'ąh Naagháí Bik'eh Hózhǫ́ǫ́n*.[7] Although this matrix of Diné life has been studied for decades, recent scholars have emphasized the concrete ways in which this matrix is made manifest: in Navajo forms of healing through the restoration of harmonious relationships between family, land, and tradition (Lewton and Bydone 2000; Lee 2014a). And yet, while the making of a church family is important in the Oodlání context, this kinship restoration does not etiologically heal. By focusing on the way healing is embodied in the motion of Oodlání, I argue that kin restoration is better understood as a resonant aspect of a healing system that is based on rupture.

SA'ĄH NAAGHÁÍ BIK'EH HÓZHǪ́Ǫ́N

According to Lewton and Bydone (2000), Christian healing has found success among Navajos because it relies for healing on the same fundamental principle central to traditional Navajo healing: *Sa'ąh Naagháí Bik'eh Hózhǫ́ǫ́n*.[8] This philosophical stance (abbreviated SNBH), has been mentioned in previous chapters.[9] It is notoriously difficult to translate, and although a strict translation might approximate it as "long life/happiness," it would be more accurately rendered "one's journey of striving to live a long and harmonious life" (Cajete 2014, ix). The SNBH matrix is based upon the idea of journeying in *hózhǫ́* (sometimes rendered as "walking in balance/beauty"), and is experienced in the Diné way of life through "language, land, cultural knowledge, protocols, trades, and living [in] a distinct sustainable way" (Lee 2014a, 7).

In particular, the SNBH matrix has important implications for

Diné health and healing. According to Lewton and Bydone, SNBH applies to healing by teaching that a proper state of health (beauty/harmony/long life/happiness) requires the "establishment and maintenance of proper relationships" based upon "respect, reverence, kindness, and cooperation" (Lewton and Bydone 2000, 492). SNBH holds that once people have oriented themselves in proper relation and connection to their kin, the land, tradition, and the Holy People, heath will be restored. Proper relations are, under this principle, a "precondition" for health and well-being (Lewton and Bydone 2000, 479). The fundamental underlying function of traditional Navajo healing ceremonies is the restoration of these relationships.

Traditional healing rituals restore SNBH through several "grounded phenomena" (Lewton and Bydone 2000, 492). Patients feel supported by the family members who contributed to the great cost of the ceremony. Patients also restore their connections to their traditions and their environment by hearing the great mythological stories of their ancestors, emplaced in the landscape. Finally, relations are restored between the patient and the *Diyin Diné'é*, who are referred to by familial terms, and upon whose reciprocal care the healing depends. Through these processes, the restorative principle of SNBH is understood to effect healing.

Lewton and Bydone argue that the SNBH principle has continued salience in NAC and Christian healing in the Navajo context. For NAC members, healing is grounded in teaching patients their connections to both Navajo lands and mythology and the broader "intertribal Native American community" (Lewton and Bydone 2000, 485). Furthermore, part of NAC therapeutic process relies on counseling the patient in NAC origins, history, and teachings, including the important theme of good family relations (Lewton and Bydone 2000, 486–87). Lewton and Bydone argue that this SNBH principle continues to ground Navajo Christian healing as well. They maintain that Christian healing depends not only on being "right with God" but also in being "right with one's fellow Christians" (Lewton and Bydone 2000, 489).

While the creation of a church family is certainly one reason that neo-Pentecostalism appeals to some Navajos, I argue that a close look at Oodlání healing etiology (theory of causation) and the way healing is embodied during Oodlání tent revivals also shows rupture with the SNBH principle.[10] While the motions of the church family are supportive, they are not etiologically effective. For Oodlání, it is only the motion inspired by a direct connection to the Holy Spirit in this context that actually heals.

EMBODYING A CHURCH FAMILY

The healing testimony of Ma Beverly helps to illustrate the ways that church families are embodied. In many ways her narrative fits a common healing testimony formula. She feels chronically ill, her problem is divined by a healing evangelist, he prays over her, and she is healed, to the astonishment of medical doctors. But her healing testimony also contains several descriptions suggestive of how community members were involved in her healing in bodily ways. She says:

I had problem with my feet and my knees. . . . They would just swell without doing anything . . . . I don't know the reason why, it just got swollen from my knee on down to my ankle. When I go to bed my knees would be, you know, kind of just like this [she gestures toward her knee]. But when I get up in the morning my knees and my feet would be just all puffy. . . . And then when I try to put my feet down, it would hurt. . . . And then my shoes would pop . . . they would just pop open, that's how bad my legs were.

Then one time we were passing by a revival . . . there was an evangelist there that was having that revival . . . we sat down for a moment. And he started preaching . . . the preaching was real good, you know? I understood it and my spirit, you know, agreed with everything. I wanted to be there.

And I never knew that he was gonna call me out. And then he said, "Sister, you in the"—I had a pink suit . . . pantsuit on. And he said, "the lady in the pink, I want you to come up." And I was looking around and there was no one. [She laughs]. I thought he meant somebody else. . . . But one of the ushers . . . he pointed out to me . . . "That lady! That lady!" he said. And then the usher came running

"It's you sister, come up!" And then he took me out and I went to the altar.

. . . And I was up there, and then he [the evangelist] said, "The Lord told me that He's gonna heal you." And that's what he said: "You're having problems with your legs, from your knees down to your ankles." He described everything that was wrong with me.

. . . He laid his hand on my head, he prayed for me.

. . . There was a lady usher. He sent one of them to come over and touch my knees . . . she probably already had [anointing oil] on her hands, so, went and touched my ankles up to my knees, just keep massaging it. Then that's it. He said, "Sister, you're gonna be healed. You're never gonna have that kind of problem from this day forward."

And then, to this day, I never have it. . . . And I went to the doctor to see what was wrong with it, they never found out anything . . . what was wrong with me. They took tests, my blood, and . . . they did all sort of things just to find out but they said everything just comes out negative, there's nothing wrong with you. (B. Joe 2008)

In this healing encounter, Ma Beverly had several interactions with community members other than the healing evangelist. Both male and female ushers had a role in supporting her healing, and they communicated their support in embodied ways. The male usher pointed her out, "came running" to her, and walked with her up to the altar. The female usher massaged her ankles, legs, and knees with anointing oil.[11] Neither of these ushers is mentioned by name, and it is likely they are people who did not know Ma Beverly and whom she never saw again. This is also the case with the ushers who support those who dance in the spirit at Oodlání revivals. With their bodies, ushers protect, guide, and hold supplicants for healing, and the lack of actual blood-kin relations is regarded as unimportant. As Rose Yazzie put it, "Over there at revivals . . . people are really nice over there and they call you "shichei" [my granddaughter] in Navajo and they even give you a hug and kiss you on the cheek" (Yazzie 2008). Through the rather intimate sensation of touch (in massages and hugs) the supportive nature of the Oodlání community is established. The embodied actions of protective ushers and elderly Oodlání grandmothers help to constitute a church family.

This type of familial intimacy is wrapped into the neo-Pentecostal healing encounter and, as pointed out by Lewton and Bydone, taps into a deep groove of Navajo ideas about healing. However, while the embodiment of kin relationships is important in facilitating the healing ritual, its relationship is one more of resonant amplification than continuity. When looking closely at the relationship between motion and healing, it is clear that the importance of kin is being rewritten by Oodlání healing, and that the bodily experience of the Holy Spirit is the only really important relationship embodied in the Oodlání healing ritual.

EMBODYING HEALING

When I first observed ushers covering people with red cloths, I was puzzled about what they were doing and why, so I asked Pastor Wallace for clarification. He explained there was nothing spiritually significant about the cloths, they just helped to preserve the modesty of people whose clothing may become displaced as they fall to the ground. "It's a courtesy" he said, "we do that just to take care of people . . . *because there's people that will shake in the presence of God*" (Begay 2008b, my emphasis). Certainly the care of a congregation is experienced in bodily ways at revivals, as in ushers covering strangers with cloths to protect their modesty. But there is only one kind of relationship that is understood by Oodlání to facilitate healing: the embodied presence of God.

God's presence is experienced through the anointing, transmitted by the Holy Spirit. Although this anointing is assumed to be invisible, its presence is made visible through the embodied motion of believers: being slain (falling to the ground unconscious) and dancing "in the spirit." As I established in the previous chapter, spirit-filled dancing is understood as a direct form of communication with a nonhuman other (the Holy Spirit). It is movement that happens when control of one's body is surrendered completely to the spirit.

The anointing, embodied in spirit-filled dancing, is the etiological key to Oodlání healing. As Pastor Wallace explained,

"He moves in a beautiful way when He moves among His people. And miracles take place. Healing takes place.... It is the anointing that breaks the yokes, you know" (Begay 2008b). If healing evangelists have any power to heal, it is because they are acting as conduits for the anointing power of God. The same is true for the laying on of hands by community members.[12]

Etiologically, this suggests that the only relationship that needs to be restored in order for Oodlání healing to be effective is the unilinear relationship with God. Oodlání will identify themselves descriptively as *Diyin God bee awéé* ("child of God," or literally, "baby of God"). And by someone placing complete faith in God, like a child, health can be restored. In contrast to the SNBH healing principle, which is about achieving all-enveloping harmony and restoring relations with all kinds of kin, for Oodlání faith in and correct alignment with God are the sole road to healing.

In Oodlání healing rituals, the creation of a church family is more of an effect than a precondition. It is helpful to have the oil-covered hand of an usher massaging aching legs, or the strong arms of an usher to catch falling bodies, or even the open palm of a healing evangelist pressed on foreheads. But according to the Oodlání healing etiology, none of these alone is performative. In contrast to the relationship-based healing etiology of Navajo traditional ceremonialism, none of these actions of church-based family making will facilitate healing without the anointing power that comes only from God.

The Power of Material Culture

> *And so it says that on the day of Pentecost, that while they were in the upper room they were praying and, you know, they were fasting and they were all in one accord and then all of a sudden . . . there came a sound like a mighty rushing wind. And it filled the whole upper room, and it says they had, you know, cloven tongues [of fire] that . . . rested on them. In other words, the anointing fell, the power of God came down. And they were submerged with power. Before they were powerless . . . they had just scattered. But something happened . . . when the anointing fell on them. (Begay 2008b)*

Pastor Wallace recounted this story for me one day after I had asked him to clarify the Oodlání concept of the anointing. This is the biblical story of Pentecost, from Acts 2:1–4, recounted in his own words. It is an important orienting passage for Oodlání, who as neo-Pentecostals feel that their modern charismatic practice has biblical precedent in this encounter in the upper room. But Pastor Wallace's paraphrase of this story also emphasizes some themes important to understanding the Oodlání perspective on healing. In this vignette, the phrases "the power of God came down," "they were submerged with power," and "before they were powerless," all suggest that the concept of power is central to understanding anointing and, by extension, healing.

Access to new forms of supernatural power has fueled the growth of the Oodlání movement. According to Garrity (2000), the "ethos of power" is as central to understanding different forms of contemporary Navajo ritual healing as is the "ethos of harmony."[13] He also claims that Navajo Christian healing has been adopted because of this etiological continuity of power. Just as in the traditional ceremonial system and the NAC, supernatural power is accessed by Oodlání through a material point of contact. In the Oodlání context this material point of contact is anointing oil. And yet, while material culture seems to provide a point of continuity, the meaning attached to these powerful material objects has changed dramatically in the Oodlání context. By carefully examining the healing power that lies behind anointing oil, I argue that Oodlání material substances like anointing oil are better understood as resonant rupture even when similar Navajo words are used to describe their manipulation.

MATERIALITY AND THE ETHOS OF POWER

According to John Garrity, accessing supernatural power is as important to Navajo healing as the restoration of harmonious relations (Garrity 2000, 537).[14] In all forms of Navajo ritual healing, material substances play an important role in accessing this supernatural power, and the manipulation of these material substances has a role in influencing divine intervention. In traditional healing rituals, one centrally powerful material substance is corn pollen (*tádídíín*). *Tádídíín* is used to demarcate ritual healing space and to consecrate and sanctify "patient, hogan, paraphernalia, drypaintings, [and] spectators" (Wyman 1983, 541). *Tádídíín* is used in "maintaining the proper relationships to the Holy People" (Kluckhohn and Leighton 1946, 203) and thus has a part in the daily maintenance of a blessed state, being rubbed on limbs and in daily dawn prayers that begin by the sprinkling of *tádídíín* (Kluckhohn and Leighton 1946, 203). According to Diné scholar Lloyd Lee, "Corn pollen represents the essence of life and will always be the security of a person and the community" (Lee 2014a, 5). The maintenance of this blessed state between the patient and the Holy People is important precisely because of the greater access Holy People have to power. Therefore, offerings of corn pollen to nonhuman "relations" become a way of accessing healing power.

According to Garrity, the power of material substances has continued salience in the NAC and Christian healing contexts. NAC rituals use the peyote plant (called an "herb" or "medicine") to access healing, as a supernaturally imbued substance that facilitates introspection and self-understanding. As Garrity states, "Patients are cured by partaking of peyote and absorbing its 'pure healing power'" (Garrity 2000, 529). When used correctly, this power can lead to outcomes of health. It is particularly effective, argues Garrity, by being able to address directly patients' problems with alcohol and substance abuse (Garrity 2000, 530).

Garrity suggests that Oodlání healing appeals to Navajos because it also provides believers another way to "seek power" for use in healing (Garrity 2000, 537). My research with Oodlání suggests that this quest for supernatural power has a material dimension as well, through the substance of anointing oil. In fact, the same Navajo word (*yisįį'*) is used to describe the way that both corn pollen (in traditional healing rituals) and anointing oil (in Oodlání healing rituals) are applied.[15] However, by examining the meaning ascribed to the material objects, I argue that Oodlání anointing oil actually represents resonant echoes over deeper rupture. While appearing to be a similar material object to *tádídíín*, or to peyote, anointing oil is understood by believers to gain its healing efficacy from an entirely new source: God's anointing.

OIL WITH WHICH YOU PRAY

Anointing oil is a regular part of any Oodlání service or revival. Usually contained in bottles at the front of the church (before the altar), it is provided for believers to use freely, at almost any point during the service. The oil can be scented (Pastor Wallace likes to scent it with frankincense and myrrh, scents available through a Christian bookstore in Farmington), and the oil is usually prayed over by church leaders before being put to use. Oodlání rub anointing oil on their hands before praying, literally spreading a holy scent on their own skin. The first act of many devout believers upon entering a church or revival space is to proceed directly to the altar, rub anointing oil on their hands, and kneel down in front of the altar to begin fervent (and often emotional) personal prayer. Anointing oil can also be carried with one in small plastic bottles and may be shared with those standing around one in a church or revival service. The slippery feel of the anointing oil, in some ways, lubricates the praise of believers, and the sweet scent of the oil wafts around the sacred space.

Anointing oil is also a substance used to bless things and people. For example, I observed new musical equipment being anointed with oil and prayed over before being put to use.[16] In an interview, Rose Yazzie described putting anointing oil on the shoes and backpacks and things carried to school by her children in order to try to protect them. She said, "Even though they're not there, I know their bag, I put anointing oil on their shoes, the things they carry I anoint them all" (Yazzie 2008). And anointing oil plays a large role in healing. As in the healing testimony Ma Beverly gave, both the healing evangelist and the ushers "anoint their hands with oil" (rub the anointing oil on their hands) before praying over someone during the healing ritual. Specifically, it is rubbed over any particular area of the body causing distress.

In Navajo, Oodlání call anointing oil *Ak'ah bee tsodizinígii* (*Ak'ah,* "oil"; *bee tsodizin,* "with which you pray"; *-ígii,* "the one that is") or, literally, prayer oil.[17] But more than simply being an aid in prayer, anointing oil is understood by Oodláni as a way of accessing the power of God in the sense of getting the attention of the benevolent powers in Heaven. As Pastor Wallace put it, "It's just like the shofar. They say that when they blow the shofar that Heaven hears it. . . . Amongst all the other trumpets, it says there's significance with the shofar . . . the heavens stop, stand still when they hear the shofar" (Begay 2008b). In a similar way, angels attend to the anointing oil. "It's a point of contact," said Pastor Wallace. "The angels . . . they recognize it" (Begay 2008b). Once a point of contact to divine power has been established through the material substance of the oil, the anointing of God can flow out and effect healing.

MEANING OVER MATERIALITY

There is some degree of continuity in the Oodláni use of a material substance to access supernatural power. The connection between traditional *tádídíín* and Oodláni anointing oil, in particular, is emphasized by the continued use of the term *yisį́į'* (to anoint) to describe how that material substance is used. However, when examining the significance of material culture, we need to take into account the meanings associated with these substances, and especially the source from whence their power to heal derives. In both traditional and Christian contexts, there is an overriding narrative that the power of the substance does not lie in the substance itself. Pastor Wallace cautioned me not to read too much into the power of the oil. "It's just symbolic," he said, "God hears your prayer whether you have oil or not" (Begay 2008b). In a similar way, the *tádídíín* is "not a medicine but a [holy] food" (Wyman 1970, 30).[18] The importance of meaning in understanding the different uses of material forms cannot be overemphasized. For example, Matthew Engelke found that Apostolic "Masowe" churches in Zimbabwe used objects like honey for healing in both traditional and Christian contexts. But he also found that "a major concern in the Masowe churches is the relationship between the circulation of therapeutic materials . . . and the meanings people associate with that material"

(Engelke 2007, 225). Even though they participated in practices that may be perceived by outsiders as expressing continuity, the meanings assigned to the practices by converts expressed disjuncture. They maintained that what mattered was not the materiality of the honey but rather "the blessing conferred on it by the Holy Spirit" (Engelke 2007, 226).

In similar fashion, Oodlání regard anointing oil as having the power to heal not because of its materiality but because it transmits the anointing of God.[19] Anointing oil, according to Oodlání, is used to set aside things as special and "of God." As Pastor Wallace noted, it is a practice that harkens back to the priests of the Old Testament who would use special oil to mark, set aside, and consecrate certain objects for the temple or a king as belonging to God, "almost like a seal of the Holy Spirit" (Begay 2008b). This is significant because from an Oodlání perspective, anointing oil gives them access not just to a different form of supernatural power than does *tádídíín*—it gives them access to a *superior* form of power. As one Pentecostal Navajo woman told Lewton and Bydone, "A long time ago men use to pray like that—'I will walk in beauty and live in beauty with my children.' Now everybody just relies on God. We pray, 'Take care of us, God.' That's more powerful that way" (Lewton and Bydone 2000, 488). Even though Oodlání preserve the form of the material anointing substance, the meaning behind that substance has changed substantially, making anointing oil and corn pollen no longer parallel substances. Tellingly, Oodlání are strongly opposed to using corn pollen in church contexts.[20] The resonant power of anointing oil lies not in its materiality but in the anointing of God it accesses. Rather than reflecting cultural continuity, anointing oil makes material the concept of resonant rupture.

The Poetic Language of Testimony

Praise Jesus. Billie Yazzie, that's my name. . . . God is real, he's a miracle-working God. God raised me off my deathbed. Two years ago. He's real. He's not dead. We're serving a real, true God. I was afflicted. I don't know what was wrong with me. Two years ago, I almost died in Phoenix, Arizona. I became . . . one day I got sick. Doctors . . . nobody

knew what was wrong with me. So I had to go . . . I was even in a wheel-
chair. This is what God did for me. I'm a miracle walking person—
aaníí? If you believe in him, if you have faith, if you're obedient . . . he
will raise you off your deathbed. I asked God, I said, "The same power
that raised you off . . . out of your death . . . I need that." . . . I was in
a wheelchair. . . . .

I have a very strong testimony. . . . You see Jesus . . . I go through tri-
als and tribulations, but I'm not giving up. My back might be against
the wall, but there is hope if you believe in him. Even, you know what,
your relatives . . . friends can forsake you. But God will never forsake
you. He's the king of kings . . . and he's the same yesterday, today and
forever.[21]

These comments about faith healing are not scripted theological teachings but rather the improvised, public testimony of an
elderly Oodlání woman. Public testimonies like hers are a regular part of Oodlání revival services. These meetings often extend
long into the early morning hours precisely because they do not
end until everyone in the tent who would like to share a testimony has been given the chance to do so. In Navajo, testifying
is called *Diyin baa hashniih* (Praising the Lord), indicating the
breadth of possible topics. But in practice Oodlání testimonies
almost always deal with illness, health, and healing.[22]

In testifying about their health, however, the words that Oodlání use are not strictly their own. Testifying is a poetic form of
oratory that makes use of a high degree of what we might call
"stock poetic phrases": common and repeated statements used
by testifiers in order to frame their own narratives. Thus improvised testimonies can be authentic to the person's experience
while simultaneously fitting into a larger etiology of disease and
healing.[23] They help to frame the individual therapeutic experience in such a way that listeners can understand their own illness experiences.

Testifying helps individual believers to understand both the
cause of their illness and their subsequent path toward healing and, as such, taps into a long-held Navajo belief that healing is affected by explaining the root causes of an illness to the

patient. This is a principle that Csordas calls "talking to them so they understand" (1999, 11). Without doubt, the testimonies of co-believers have a role to play in helping patients to understand the cause of their illness. But in this section I argue that the poetic language of Oodlání testimonies reveals that, in contrast to traditional and NAC ritual healing, "understanding" alone is not sufficient for healing. As with kin restoration and manipulation of supernatural power, the property of "talking to them so they understand" does not represent continuity so much as resonant rupture.

"TALKING TO THEM SO THEY UNDERSTAND"

In testifying to an audience so that they "understand" their ill-health or misfortune differently, Oodlání testifiers are tapping into a deep groove of Navajo health and healing. According to Csordas, all forms of Navajo ritual healing rely upon the healer talking to the patient "so that they understand" (1999, 11). This is in contrast to, say, Western biomedical healing, where healing is not contingent upon whether a patient understands how cancer spreads or what hormones cause infertility. Csordas argues that making the understanding of the patient a central concern of healing is based in the Navajo philosophical connection between thought, speech, and effect (such as healing). Therefore, regardless of the ritual healing context (traditional, NAC, or Christian), this focus on "understanding" in healing contexts is distinctively Navajo.

According to Csordas, the patient is being made to understand different things about his or her illness in each religious context (traditional, NAC, Christian). Traditional Navajo healing etiology is rooted in a "philosophy of obstacles" whereby ill-health is caused by some sort of event or action that has "blocked up" or unbalanced the state of *hózhǫ́* (balance/beauty) established for humanity by Changing Woman. Healing, therefore, rests upon the diagnostician being able to identify what is causing the obstacle. Once the obstacle has been identified, one of the primary roles of the healer is "didactic": helping the patient to understand why that event or action was an obstacle and how the healing removed it (Csordas 1999, 11). Healing only really occurs if the patient understands how the obstacle and healing are rooted in the entire Navajo lifeway matrix, so that "thought and speech" can be used to return the patient to a state of health (Witherspoon 1977).

In contrast, Csordas claims that Native American Church healing rests on a "philosophy of self-esteem" that is intimately tied to the ingestion of peyote. Ingesting peyote allows one to get in touch with the sacred, including the sacredness inside the self. Ill-health is caused by "immoral" actions (drinking, fighting, adultery, being a bad family member) that go against the teachings of the NAC. Healing, then, is predicated upon confession of these immoral actions (Csordas 1999, 11). By discussing problems, with the guidance of the "medicine" and the support of the church family, NAC members are able to discover the underlying causes of their ill-health and misfortune. Being led to understanding, by finding an answer to the overriding question "what have I done?" empowers NAC members to take control of their own healing.

Csordas argues that a similar process of "understanding" underlies Navajo Christian healing as well. He claims that the overriding ethos of Christian healing is fundamentally tied to ideas about identity, so that the primary therapeutic principle is "conversional" (Csordas 1999, 11). Rather than being led to answer the question "what is blocking my healing?" or "what have I done to bring on this bad health?" Navajo Christians are encouraged to ask the question "who am I?" (Csordas 1999, 11). Healing, they believe, is couched in the proper identity as a Christian, often in contrast to a traditionalist or a peyotist (Csordas 1999, 11). In many ways, then, the "understanding" that Navajo Christian healers are trying to impart is one not of "therapy" in a strict sense but one of converted religious identity.

Oodláni testifying practice shows that talking to potential patients so they "understand" themselves as Christians (and can thus access healing) is not simply the purview of the Oodláni "healer" but rather the business of all believers through testimony. Without doubt, testimonies encourage the conversion of listening non-converts by promising a more effective method for achieving healing than could be accessed in either traditional or NAC healing contexts. And yet an analysis of the stock phrases commonly used in Oodláni testimony reveals both continuity with and rupture from the idea of "talking to them so they understand." Testimonies allow listeners to understand their own distress within a Christian framework, particularly when orienting listeners to ideas about the Prosperity Gospel (see next section). But in contrast to traditional or NAC consultations between patients and healers, the poetic language of testimony also emphasizes the ultimate futility of trying to understand either the causes of illness or reasons for healing. Fundamentally, testimonies are about miracles—events that defy understanding.

THE FRAMING LANGUAGE OF TESTIMONY

The poetic language of Oodláni testimony forges continuity with traditional and NAC healing consultations by helping patients to "understand" the root of their illness. In the Navajo Christian context, according to Csordas, this understanding is "conversional" so that healing is effected when patients understand themselves as Christians (Csordas 1999, 11). But Oodláni testimonies emplace healing distress not just in identity but in a broader cosmological context of supernatural war. Through the use of stock phrases, individual testifiers can frame their anecdotal experiences with illness and healing within larger theological frames, frames that they themselves may not be able to articulate otherwise. The primary theology through which disease and healing are understood by Oodláni is sometimes called the "Gospel of Prosperity" or the "Word of Faith."[24]

The main idea driving the Gospel of Prosperity theology is that God "wants" people to be healthy, wealthy, and living "an abundant life." This theology holds that the major battle between God or Jesus and the Devil has already been fought and (as they often say) "the Devil has been defeated." The victory of God has set up a cosmic order in which God's divine plan has already been established, but the Devil (as if in death throes) is trying to take as many people down to Hell with him as possible. Sickness and misfortune, therefore, can only be caused in humans who fall prey to deceit, temptations, or fear inspired by the Devil.

The stock phrases used in the poetic language of testimony reflect this theology. Those used in the testimony of Billie Yazzie about being raised from her death bed are representative.[25] First, in talking about supernatural actors, such as God and the Devil, she focuses on them both as concretely manifest in the world. For God, she states:

> God is real
> He's a miracle-working God
> We're serving a real, true God

And for the Devil, she uses the phrases:

> [The Devil] is here to destroy, steal, and kill us
> I rebuked the Devil

She also makes reference to the divine supernatural battle between God and the Devil. She emphasizes that God's divine plan (including health and prosperity for humans) has already been established, but the Devil makes people doubt this supreme victory. Healing can be accessed through ignoring the Devil (who is a "liar") and "claiming" the prosperity that the superior power of God has instituted. This theology is evidenced in the following stock poetic phrases used by Yazzie:

> God will never forsake you
> [He's the] king of kings
> Every eye will see him, every knee will bow, every town will believe
> Oh, greater is He
> I claim [healing]
> I stand on [scripture]
> He [the Devil] is under our feet
> The Devil has already been defeated
> [The Doctor said I was sick] but I didn't believe it because the Devil is a liar

Part of the role of these poetic stock phrases used by Oodlání testifiers is to help people understand their distress within a

Prosperity Gospel framework. Stock phrases are "echoes": they are drawn from biblical passages as well as "biblical-sounding" language not used in common parlance (such as "forsake" and "rebuke"). The overall structure of the testimony story (trial resolved by God) also echoes many biblical tales, thus showing the contemporary relevance of biblical stories (Harding 2000, 54). These poetic phrases are echoed through the speech of community members, in testimony and in everyday life, so that if nonbelievers spend enough time around Oodlání revivals (or even Oodlání relatives), they begin to hear these phrases framing their own experiences as well.[26]

According to Susan Harding, who studied the language of witnessing among Christian fundamentalists, framing distress is precisely the point of testimonies. Linguistically, testimonies use minimal details to establish time, place, character, and relationships, use dialogue over narration, and repeat moments of key dialogue, all of which helps to engage the listener in the story (Harding 2000, 54). Fitting this structure, Yazzie's testimony also contains minimal detail, and for the majority of the testimony contains hints of a story, without much linear narration.[27] The stock phrases, therefore, are much more important to the testimony than are the actual details of the illness and healing. This is because the deliberately vague and generic statements about healing wrapped into Oodlání testimony show that the most important aspect of Oodlání healing testimony is not about having "witnessed" (or experienced) a miracle healing. It is that you, too, could experience this kind of healing. Although testimony appears to be a story about one person's healing, Harding argues, these stories "are on a deep level about the listener; you, too, are a character in the stories; these stories are about you" (Harding 2000, 44). Much more than lengthy sermons or theological discussions, Oodlání understanding of healing is framed by these short poetic phrases passed around in testimonies. It is these phrases that help make the connection between the testifier and the listener, helping listeners to understand that through faith, they too could be (as Oodlání say) "walking in divine health and healing."

As already established, the poetic language of testimony does help listeners to "understand" their illness within a Christian framework, providing some continuity with the overriding Navajo healing principle of "talking to them so they understand" (Csordas 1999). However, there is rupture with this principle contained within the language of testimony as well. The language of testimony emphasizes the "miracle" nature of healing, an interaction with divine forces that surpass understanding.

In both traditional and NAC contexts (and in part because of the close Navajo association between thought, speech, and effect), being able to answer the question "what is blocking my healing?" is primary. In the traditional context, healing can be blocked by contact with a multitude of things that Navajos have been directed by the Holy People to avoid (snakes, bears, lightning, tornadoes, the dead). In the NAC context, healing is blocked by a variety of immoral actions (drinking, committing adultery, etc.). In both contexts, understanding the root of the illness and addressing it (through ceremony or confession) provides a clear path to healing. In contrast, the etiological root of illness for Oodlání has been described as "parsimonious" (Milne and Howard 2000, 566) or "stingy." According to Derek Milne and Wilson Howard, all misfortune and sickness are thought by Oodlání to be caused by demons or the Devil.[28] To reiterate: this "stingy" theory of causation (everything bad comes from the Devil) is in stark contrast to the plethora of causes for illness in traditional Navajo or NAC healing contexts. But understanding the cause of illness, or removing demonic obstacles, or even having faith that God has power to heal illness is not always enough to effect healing. Testimonies repeatedly emphasize healing that was unexpected or impossible, because most testimonies are about miracle healing.

Several of the stock phrases used by Yazzie emphasize the miracle nature of her healing, where even doctors could not believe how well she had recovered. She sets up her illness by using phrases that emphasize how dire the situation was:

trials and tribulations
back against the wall
I was afflicted
I was laid in bed

And when discussing her healing, she emphasizes the real power of God to overcome even the most impossible odds. In faming her healing this way, she uses the following stock phrases:

God raised me off my deathbed
Nothing's impossible with God[29]

In general, the themes of these etiological frames indicate that sickness is caused by the unpredictable mischief of the devil and that the healing power of God is founded in miracles. Therefore, testimonies are not so much about talking to patients "so they understand" the roots of their illness as about describing experiences that surpass understanding.

This distinction is highlighted in common tropes across Oodláni testimonies. Many common Oodláni testimonies speak about healing that happens in ways that precede a "converted identity" (what Csordas calls "understanding oneself as a Christian"; Csordas 1999, 11). Lynda Kelly felt that it was this kind of divine encounter that saved her life.[30] In the early 1990s Lynda was the mother of four young children and the unhappy wife of an abusive husband. The death of her mother, and then her father, drove her into massive depression. She said, "At the time I lost my dad . . . I took it so hard." After particularly violent abuse in which her husband broke her wrist and beat her to unconsciousness she fled with her children to her sister's house. Her sister helped her file charges and file for divorce, but she could not stay at her sister's place permanently.

After a few months, Lynda took her children out to her parents' house, now empty. It was very remote, and the isolation drove her deeper into depression. After a while, she said, "It was so lonely and I couldn't take it. My mom and dad weren't home. . . . There's nobody to turn to." One night she started questioning the purpose of living, saying "What am I good for? I'll just go ahead and do something . . . see how it tastes." So she loaded up the kids into the car, dropped them at a friend's house, and drove into town and "did some drinkin' for three days." This pattern of binge drinking repeated several times, even though her kids cried every time she picked them up, asking, "Where'd you go mom?" and telling her, "Now you smell ugly." She told them, "I miss your dad. I miss everybody. I miss my dad. I miss my mom."

One night the loneliness got so bad that she put the kids to bed and then took off for town. It was after midnight and she was driving into town alone, longing for the oblivion of drunkenness. But on an isolated reservation road she passed a remote gas station. She hesitated in inner turmoil, wondering, "What am I doing? Maybe I'll just turn around right here." As she pulled into the convenience store parking lot, full of indecision, she noticed a house on the hill above the gas station with its lights on. She did not know who lived there, but thought, "Well, I'll go up there." At two o'clock in the morning, she randomly knocked on the door of Ma Beverly. She did not know who Ma Beverly was, but told her, "I need help. I don't know what I'm doing."

In reflecting on that encounter, Lynda said, "I didn't even know they were Christian. I just went up to her house and talked to her about it." Ma Beverly listened to her problems, her loneliness and lack of family, and her sense of helplessness. Ma Beverly told her, "You can do it, Lynda," and said, "If you do it, God will help." Then Ma Beverly and Pastor Wallace (who lives next door) came over and started praying for her. Ma Beverly told her, "Go home. Sleep." Lynda answered her, "I can't sleep . . . I haven't slept in so many days . . ." But after they prayed for her, Lynda listened to Ma Beverly and went home and "somehow I went to sleep real good . . . the bed was so comfy! And after that I thought, 'I can do it!'" Thirteen years later Lynda is still a cheerful and faithful member of Pastor Wallace's church, traveling with them to revivals and remaining sober. Her kids all successfully graduated from high school. She feels that God intervened by leading her to Ma Beverly and Pastor Wallace and that night saved her life.

Lynda's testimony of God's miracle intervention demonstrates how Oodláni healing represents resonant rupture more than continuity. When God "led" Lynda to Ma Beverly and Pastor Wallace, she was not a Christian. She had little understanding of Christianity, neither how God could heal nor how becoming a Christian might allow her to access this healing. Certainly her understanding of both of these things deepened as her familiarity with the Oodlání community grew. But at this pivotal moment in her life, when she most needed intervention, God "led" her to a house on a hill, without waiting for her conversion or understanding.

From an Oodlání perspective, this distinction is rather important. Unlike traditional and NAC ritual healing, Oodlání healing etiology is not *necessarily* contingent upon the patient understanding the causes of either disease or healing. Understanding themselves as Christian certainly aids people in being able to access this healing source consciously. But from an Oodlání perspective it is not the understanding of the patient that causes healing in the way that it is for traditional or NAC ritual healing. The *only* thing that Oodlání healing is based upon, fundamentally, is the supreme and ultimately uncontrollable power of God.

Conclusion

Resonant rupture is a concept that encompasses how people navigate their changing cultural surroundings in feelingfully continuous ways. When cultural forms resonate, they are amplified by the presence of deep cultural grooves with affective power. Both NAC and Navajo Christian ritual healing practices are amplified by the fundamental importance of healing as a central aspect of the Navajo cultural matrix. However, Oodlání healing also entails a fundamental rupture in the meaning ascribed to continuous forms and rewrites the meaning of these forms.

The significance of rupture in understanding the way Oodlání healing is embodied was emphasized in a story about soundscapes that Pastor Wallace told one Sunday morning. A few days before, he had been visiting a revival in Arizona as a guest preacher. At the end of the service he was approached by a husband and wife for healing. Pastor Wallace did not know this couple but listened to their problems. Their children were sick, the husband had been laid off from his job, and their car was not working.

They were looking for healing. Pastor Wallace started to pray for them, but when he laid his hands on them, he immediately heard the sound of the NAC gourd rattle. He stopped praying and took his hands off them. He looked around but there was no visible source for such a sound. This happened several times before he stepped away from them and asked them if they had any peyote paraphernalia in their house. Beaded feather fans? Ritual staffs? They answered that yes, they occasionally went to NAC meetings, so they had some of those things in their home. Pastor Wallace said to us, "See? That stuff was blocking up their healing. And the Holy Spirit knew it and that's why I kept hearing that rattle. I told them to throw those things in the trash, and that would bring healing back into their lives."[31]

Expressive forms (soundscapes, bodily motion, material objects, and poetic language) certainly reveal aspects of continuity with traditional and NAC ritual healing. But it is just as important to recognize their underlying rupture. When compared to traditional and NAC healing soundscapes, Oodlání healing rituals do not just recognize separation; they recognize that mixing soundscapes will block up healing. Just as in traditional and NAC ritual healing, the restoration of kin relations is experienced in bodily ways at Oodlání revivals. But in contrast to the other two ritual healing contexts, the only relationship that needs to be restored is with God, embodied through the infilling of the Holy Spirit. Material substances like anointing oil provide powerful points of resonance, and even the action of "anointing" is described using the same Navajo word as refers to the traditional anointing of corn pollen. But the continuity of the material behavior is not as important to believers as the fundamental rift in meaning: that the oil gets its efficacy from a fundamentally more powerful source. Finally, the poetic language of testimony provides an important point of resonance to the "understanding" fundamental to Navajo curing traditions, allowing listeners to understand their own distress within a Christian framework. But just as with the other expressive forms, rupture is wrapped into Oodlání testimony as well, attesting to the fact that sometimes the healing of God surpasses understanding.

As scholars, we can try to make sense of Navajo culture change by relying on the assumption that new technologies are incorporated into a fundamental cultural core in logical ways. But contemporary discussions in anthropology make it quite clear that culture is constituted in ideological positioning and assertions by powerful actors as much as it is an external reality. Culture cores are in actuality quite fractured, and people might be seeking (and asserting) change, not continuity. Choices that favor resonant rupture mean that sometimes change and continuity can coexist in a complex and dynamic tension where people can shape their cultures in ways that sometimes surpasses our understanding as well.

Conclusion
Resonant Rupture, Sovereignty, and Global Pentecostalism

There is a picture that Pastor Wallace asked me to take, late one night after a long and lively camp meeting service. In this photo he is wearing a red vest and Navajo turquoise necklace. His left arm is around a visiting evangelist from New Jersey who is Jewish by heritage but neo-Pentecostal by faith. On the other side Pastor Wallace links arms with three other visiting evangelists: a woman from Jamaica and two men, one from Uganda and one from Juarez, Mexico. All had traveled from their homes to this small town in a remote corner of the desert Southwest to take turns as guest preachers at Pastor Wallace's tent revival. The Ugandan evangelist, in particular, had stirred a praising spirit in the assembled Navajos.

"I am so happy to be here!" he had said in accented but very clear English. "I am from Kampala, Uganda, East Africa, and God sent me to America to be a missionary here. For so many years, Africa lived in darkness. And when missionaries came, they said "there is no hope here." And they named Africa the "dark continent." But God had a plan. . . . Africa is not a dark continent. Africa has seen the light. And Jesus is alive in Africa. . . . Listen. In Africa miracles, sign, and wonders are happening. Somebody say Hallelujah?"

While Navajos in the tent shouted "Amen!" in encouragement, the Ugandan evangelist continued with a biting criticism of American Christianity: "God has blessed America . . . and now people do not want to go to church! . . . But God sent me to tell you, the Navajo Nation, this is a new season. It is a new day. This is your time. This is your moment. God is about to do something big. Something supernatural. Something incredible. Revival is coming to the nations. Get ready. It is a new wave. It is coming. God is gonna do something new. Because the days of the Devil are over. Somebody shout hallelujah! It is a time of miracle new life! It is a time of heal-

ing!" The remainder of his words were drowned out by raucous applause and shouts of "Hallelujah!" and "Praise Jesus!"[1]

I n this book I have shown that resonant rupture is central to understanding how neo-Pentecostalism among Navajos is both locally relevant and decisively nonlocal, both culturally continuous and culturally disruptive. Aside from a generalized aesthetic attachment to familiar form, I have speculated very little about *why* Oodlání employ techniques of resonant rupture. To whit: if ambiguous aesthetic forms can be mistaken so easily for continuity, and Oodlání spend so much time asserting that they are not actually continuous, why not simply stop using these forms altogether? Why not simply give away *jish* bundles, compose music in referential Navajo, perform music for any paying gig, and understand healing as a matter of faith (not blockage)? To return to the conundrum I introduced at the beginning of the book, if Oodlání are committed to reinterpreting the sunwise path teachings to focus only on an upward trajectory, why do they continue to express this message in terms of cardinal directions?

The answer I propose in this conclusion is the somewhat radical notion that, in framing their faith through distinctively Navajo forms, Oodlání are asserting a type of indigenous sovereignty on the global stage. As Pastor Wallace's array of global visiting evangelists attests, Navajo neo-Pentecostals are not an isolated religious community but are (and have always been) socially connected to a broad range of actors: Native, non-Native, American, and international. Furthermore, they are socially connected as among equals: they receive visiting evangelists as guests to the camp meetings they host, but they also travel as visiting evangelists across Indian country, America, and abroad. Oodlání see themselves as a missionizing (not missionized) people. If sovereignty is understood as a type of interdependent interaction between semi-autonomous actors, then continuing to frame themselves as distinctively Navajo in the global Pentecostal community becomes a political act. Culture continues to matter because, as the Ugandan evangelist put it, as Navajos, "This is your time.

FIG. 17. Global Pentecostal evangelists. Photo by author.

This is your moment." Rather than seeing themselves as victims of the structural violence of settler-colonialism, Oodláni see themselves as distinct but equal partners in a global project. From an Oodláni perspective, the Navajo Nation is one of the "nations" that will bring "revival" to America (and thus the world).

Political Economy and Instrumental Conversion

This book has been a small-scale and qualitative study of a local community. And yet, as the vignette that opens this chapter suggests, Navajo neo-Pentecostalism is part of a much bigger global religious trend. Pentecostal or charismatic faith, also called global Pentecostalism, has grown exponentially in the past few decades, particularly in the global south, leading some scholars to predict that this type of Christianity may surpass Catholicism as "the most predominant form of Christianity in the 21st century" (Casanova 2001, 435).[2] Since anthropologists and religious studies scholars have been unable to ignore this growth, they have tried out various theoretical models in attempts to explain it. The vast majority of these explanations have been grounded in what we can broadly call the "instrumentalist" reasons for conversion that are grounded theoretically in a political-economic view of the world. That is, people convert to global Pentecostalism in order to gain power or economic benefits. Without doubt, global Pentecostal Christianity has spread most aggressively in precisely the places in the world where people are poorest, usually displaced rural populations most disenfranchised by the neo-liberal capitalist order. Because global Pentecostalism often takes root where economic disparities are so strikingly obvious, these political-economic models make a lot of sense. However, to rely on instrumentalist reasons alone is not enough to explain the growth of global Pentecostalism. Recent scholars have begun to look closely at the role of social networks in influencing conversion to neo-Pentecostalism. In Native North America, in particular, a long history of religious revival movements spread through intertribal social networks indicates the power of these networks in promoting religious change.

Without doubt, the dramatic spread of global Pentecostalism over the past few decades calls for explanation. What many scholars refer to as global Pentecostalism has roots in the American "Holiness" movement of the late nineteenth century, was galvanized to global mission by the Azusa Street Revival between 1906 and 1910 (Robeck 2007), and was institutionalized through the formation of Pentecostal denominations (such as the Assemblies of God). This spirit-filled form of worship quickly grew beyond Pentecostal denominational boundaries, however, infusing both Catholicism and mainline Protestantism and becoming what is called the charismatic movement. It also grew beyond denominationalism itself, becoming the exponentially multiplying neo-Pentecostal movement (also sometimes called charismatics). Because of the theological basis in spirit-derived leadership rather than centralized denominational control, these unaffiliated, decentralized neo-Pentecostal churches spread rapidly in the southern hemisphere and areas outside the West, including Africa, Latin America, Oceania, and Asia. A 2006 study by the Pew Forum on Religion and Public Life illustrated the extent and importance of this movement. According to this study, of the world's two billion Christians, around 500 million (one quarter of the total) are now Pentecostals or charismatics. More than half of those who identify as Pentecostal or charismatic live in the global south, particularly in Latin America and Africa.[3] This study also showed that in several of the nations surveyed, Pentecostals or charismatics account for more than a quarter of the population.[4] In general, this movement is distinct from other forms of global Christianity because of its emphasis on mysticism, Puritanism, belief in prophecy, faith healing, exorcism, and dream-visions (Jenkins 2002; Anderson 2004).[5]

As noted, scholars encountering the proliferation of global Pentecostalism have relied to a large extent on political-economic theories to explain its growth. Andrew Chestnut's landmark study *Born Again in Brazil* (1997) is representative of this trend. In this book, Chestnut argues that the rise of Pentecostalism in Brazil is rooted in its ability to address what he calls the "pathogens of poverty": both physical disease and the social and psychological stresses that accompany it (such as depression, domestic violence, drugs, and alcohol). In Latin America in particular, scholars have emphasized the way in which Pentecostalism provides a safety net for those most at risk in the face of neo-liberal privatization (see, for instance, Kevin O'Neill's *City of God*, 2010) as well as other political realities (Freston 2001; Löwy 1996; Smith 1998; Steigenga 2001; Stoll 1990).

In many ways these political-economic theories of conversion globally carry forward the "deprivation" explanations developed by early anthropologists in response to the new religious movements across Native North America. Deprivation theory was introduced by James Mooney in an 1896 Bureau of American Ethnology report on the growing Ghost Dance religious movement, wherein he argued that the external material pressures of American expansion had so overturned the social worlds of Native people that they followed the universal human tendency to adopt ecstatic religious practice and charismatic leadership in order to cope with a material reality that was not of their making (Smoak 2006, 199). Other applications of deprivation theory continued throughout the twentieth century, including Anthony F. C. Wallace's (1969) discussion of the role of deprivation in encouraging revitalization movements (such as the Handsome Lake Religion among the Seneca), and David Aberle's (1991) conclusion that the spread of the Native American (Peyote) Church was rooted in what he called "relative deprivation."[6] As I have stated in the present work, new religious movements in Native North America (and the Navajo Nation) have often been framed as responses to the deprivations in material conditions present in Native American lives, up to the present. Neo-Pentecostalism is no exception.

Without doubt, Oodlání lives are filled with many of the "pathogens of poverty" mentioned by Chestnut (1997): depression, domestic abuse, substance abuse, unstable home lives, childhood abuse, chronic disease, and high infant mortality. All these pathogens are directly traceable to the trauma of settler-colonialism (boarding schools, livestock reduction, unregulated uranium mining, unhealthy commodity foods, etc.). So I certainly do not dismiss political-economic explanations for why any person in these conditions would look for hope wherever it could be found. However, in searching for the indigenous *agency* in these situations, I join a growing body of scholars writing about global Pentecostalism who seek to expand on materialism and look for the appeal of Pentecostalism from cultural, ritual, or social perspectives. As Susan Harding (2000, 36) has pointed out, instrumentalist explanations for conversion are incomplete because they do not explain why many people in similar circumstances choose other paths. Joel Robbins has also asked for more nuance, claiming that materialist explanations are often tautological: "Making the fact of conversion the proof of prior experiences of deprivation or anomie" (2004b, 124). Thomas Csordas has encouraged us to look at the nature of Pentecostalism itself as an ideally portable religious practice with a highly transposable message, making it well suited for global spread (2009, 4–5). And as Gregory Smoak has written, materialist explanations are found wanting because they tend to emphasize external motivation and cultural trauma. Thus, "What could be read as a tale of hope and survival has usually been cast as one of despair and death" (Smoak 2006, 199). And as the detailed ethnography of this book makes clear, materialist frameworks cannot explain why, in practicing their faith, Navajo neo-Pentecostals continue to traverse the dangerously ambiguous ground of resonant rupture. For those choices to make sense, we need to turn to the role of social networks in spreading global Pentecostalism.

Networks of Navajo Missionaries

In February 2008 I got a call from Pastor Wallace asking if I knew anything about Africa. He had been invited to accompany a mission trip to Benin, West Africa, and needed some information to start raising funds for a plane ticket to New York. Over the following month I assisted him in making the arrangements necessary for this (his first) international travel: researching and facilitating travel vaccinations, obtaining his passport, and arranging airline reservations for him. While in Benin, Pastor Wallace and the mission team met with local traditional rulers, visited orphanages, and held tent meetings. In sermons after returning to Shiprock, Pastor Wallace framed his experience as both culturally disorienting and crucially urgent. He was adamant about the calling of Navajos like himself to spread the Pentecostal faith. In a letter from Benin, he stated, "These people really do need our prayers. They really need to hear the Gospel, the good news. And . . . I thank God for bringing me here, you know? And I don't know why He's brought me here but to experience this—to see these people. But . . . I thank Him for bringing me out here."[7]

Religious ideas do not spread themselves. They are spread by people: often by individuals who feel it is their calling or duty to share their faith. For centuries, religious ideas have accompanied the colonial forces of Western Europe, and global missionary dynamics have typically involved European or American missionaries preaching a foreign faith among indigenous peoples. Over the past few decades, this dynamic has been changing. Because neo-Pentecostalism's spirit-driven theology does not require formal education or certification to legitimate preachers or evangelists, it has allowed indigenous actors to take control of the faith quite rapidly, fueling its exponential growth. But the influx of spirit-driven preachers has also altered the missionary dynamic, transforming indigenous actors into evangelists for a faith they no longer view as foreign. Pastor Wallace's Navajo church saw themselves not as a "missionized" people but as a "missionizing" people. This change in dynamic is absolutely crucial to understanding the spread of global Pentecostalism.

For Pastor Wallace, born and raised in a small, rural community in the middle of the Navajo Nation, sixty miles from the closest off-reservation town, serving as a short-term missionary to Benin was both disorienting and faith affirming. All his observations of life in Benin, from the poverty and smells of the market place, to the hospitality of local hereditary royals to the reasons for the large number of orphans they met at a local orphanage, he interpreted within a totalizing Pentecostalist framework. In this framework, God is daily engaged in battles with demonkind, a drama played out among the lives of individual humans, whose only real hope is to hear the gospel message from a missionary like Pastor Wallace, accept the narrative, and therefore align themselves with the power of God and receive His blessings.

It is not simply the theology of neo-Pentecostalism that transforms men like Pastor Wallace into global evangelizers. It is also the structure of this movement: facilitated through reciprocal visiting at revivals and the social connections that visiting creates. Increasingly, the importance of personal connections is being recognized in processes of religious change (Blumhofer 1993; Synan 1997; Coleman 2000).[8] Pastor Wallace's path to Africa reveals the importance of these social connections. He was invited to accompany the mission team to West Africa by Negiel Bigpond, a Yuchi evangelist from Oklahoma who has been visiting Navajo revivals for decades. Pastor Wallace has participated as an evangelist in these networks as well, traveling as a visiting preacher at Apache, Hopi, Ute, and Crow revivals. This cross-visiting fits into a long-established pattern among Native Christians in the Southwest. As Spicer relates of early twentieth-century Native preachers of independent, nonaffiliated churches: "Each church usually had a [Native] minister who was widely known as an effective preacher who visited frequently the other independent churches to preach and hold revival meetings" (Spicer 1962, 522). There is little doubt that this early cross-visiting laid the groundwork for the spread of neo-Pentecostalism throughout Native communities in the Southwest.[9]

Appreciating the role of networks in Native Pentecostalism also encourages us to think broadly about how we define "indigenous" Christianity.[10] *Oodlání* churches are undoubtedly autonomous and self-governing, but certainly arose from outside missionary activity, both Native and non-Native. These non-Navajo influences, however, are only one part of a dynamic and interdependent network in which Navajos are not simply passive receivers of religious messages. In many ways, this relationship mirrors contemporary theories on interdependent indigenous sovereignty. Seen in this light, resonant rupture itself represents an assertion of a type of cultural sovereignty.

Interdependent Sovereignty

Sovereignty is typically interpreted as a type of political autonomy, linked to Western concepts of kingship, the right to governance without interference, and of supreme authority over a polity. In Indigenous Studies, however, scholars have recently demonstrated the Western-centric bias of this definition of sovereignty, proposing alternative indigenously based definitions that do not emphasize autonomy (a fictional concept anyway) but instead value interdependence and responsibility to a collective whole (Alfred 2002, 460). Furthermore, many within Indigenous Studies have encouraged us to attend to ways in which Native sovereignty is exerted in the nonpolitical realm. Indigenous sovereignty, then, can be asserted in literature (Womack 1999), history (Denetdale 2007), architecture (Cattelino 2008), and in overall epistemologies—ways of knowing the world (Warrior 1994; Lee 2014a). In this spirit, I argue that we can see the interconnected networks in global Pentecostalism as a pathway through which Oodlání exert a type of Navajo sovereignty.

Sovereignty is a wide-ranging concept, with implications well beyond the political realm. Most often, sovereignty in Native North America is interpreted to mean the government-to-government relationships that exist among tribes and between tribes and the U.S. federal government (see Wilkins and Lomawaima 2001).

And without doubt tribes have been working steadily for the past several decades to increase this type of sovereign authority and the contingent right to govern their own citizens and territories. Recent work in Indigenous Studies, however, has begun to emphasize that Native American sovereignty should not be limited to political autonomy. Native American literature, for instance, can represent an exercise in sovereignty, since as Craig Womack (Creek, Cherokee) argues, "A key component of nationhood is a people's idea of themselves, their imaginings of who they are. The ongoing expression of a tribal voice, through imagination, language, and literature, contributes to keeping sovereignty alive" (Womack 1999, 14). Sovereignty can also be exercised in valuing alternative epistemologies (ways of knowing). Jennifer Denetale (Navajo) drives home this point particularly well in her biting criticism of Western historical narratives. She argues that a Navajo-centric historical epistemology privileges oral histories in ways that benefit local communities. Finally, sovereignty can be viewed in the multitude of daily assertions that create the minutiae of details that fill ethnographies of contemporary Native American life. For example, in her study of the Seminole high-stakes gaming industry, Jessica Cattelino utilizes a definition of sovereignty that includes "Seminoles' collective assertions, everyday enactments, and lived experiences of political distinctiveness" (2008, 15). Sovereignty, then, is not a simple political concept related to governance, but a multivalent one that can apply to any daily assertion of a distinct Native American autonomy.

Another way that indigenous definitions of sovereignty differ from Western-centric notions is that they emphasize not autonomy but interdependency; not domination but collective good. As Alfred has pointed out, when applied to Native Americans, sovereignty is too often measured along a flat continuum that tallies only degrees of autonomy or dependency (Alfred 2002, 460). However, as Amanda Cobb (2005) has pointed out, there is no modern sovereign nation in the world that exercises complete autonomy. Rather, modern sovereigns are *interdependent*: economically, militarily, and legally. According to Cattelino's reading, Seminole interactions with the other sovereigns that surround them (city governments, state governments, the federal government, and international governments) represent precisely this kind of sovereign interdependence. By this reading, Seminoles exert sovereignty not through complete autonomy but through engaging in "intersovereign relations" (Cattelino 2008, 163) with other tribes—such as venture capital and lending, social events, and emergency relief (2008, 165–66); with surrounding cities—revenue sharing, philanthropy (2008, 172–73)), and with the state of Florida—contributing to political campaigns, lobbying for political causes, and revenue sharing (2008, 167–68). Comments Cattelino, "Negotiating government-to-government memoranda of understanding . . . while neither especially glamorous nor highly visible, is the everyday work of local sovereign interdependence" (Cattelino 2008, 172).

Navajo missionaries engage in precisely the same kind of sovereign interdependence when they both receive outside evangelists to their camp meetings and travel as missionaries across Indian country, America, and internationally. Several scholars of global Pentecostalism have commented about the central value of evangelization to this religious movement (d'Epinay 1969, 55; Blumhofer 1993, 208–9), and the rapid transformation of recent converts to evangelists spreading the faith is very well established in the literature. As I have mentioned, the theological basis for this evangelistic push is closely tied to the spirit-filled nature of the movement. As evangelist Don Stewart put it, the Oodlání movement among Navajos "was built more on, 'These signs shall follow them that believe,' 'If you're a believer, go heal the sick.' [Laughs] You know? Very simple" (Stewart 2008). This "very simple" concept of decentralized spirit-filled leadership is actually built into the structure of global Pentecostalism and creates a web of interdependent connections between evangelists.[11]

Just as with interdependent sovereignties outlined by Cattelino, interdependent relations between traveling global Pentecostal evangelists should not be interpreted through "an equalizing frame"; that is, we cannot ignore the unequal power relations that exist between different autonomous actors (Cattelino 2008,

163). Just as interdependent relationships between nation-states are characterized by unequal power relations (think of international debt relations), interactions between different actors in the global Pentecostal missionary network are also unequal. Globe-trotting Anglo evangelists, arriving in Navajo country via private jet, continue to fill big tents on the Navajo Nation with promises of miracle blessings and healing, transmitted through white hands. However, as this ethnography has shown, the cross-visiting of any inspired convert that is built into global Pentecostalism allows Navajo actors significantly greater autonomy in asserting themselves as participating partners in a global project to "bring revival" to "the nations."

Resonant Rupture as Sovereignty

There is a photo that Pastor Wallace brought back from his mission trip to Africa and regularly showed in slideshows to Navajo supporters. It shows him shaking hands with an "African king" in a long white tunic, large beaded necklace, and red velvet-and-silk cap. In the picture Pastor Wallace is wearing a maroon velveteen shirt with a woven sash-belt over one shoulder. His jewelry is elaborate and fine: heavy turquoise and coral necklaces and a turquoise drop earring in each ear. Tied around his head is a maroon silk headband. It is the most traditionally Navajo dress I ever saw Pastor Wallace don. In another (more blurry) picture, Pastor Wallace sits on a couch with this king. Negiel Bigpond (Yuchi) sits next to them in a ribbon-work white Yuchi jacket and a plains-style feathered warbonnet headdress with blue and red beadwork trim.[12] The fact that Pastor Wallace packed this Navajo outfit specifically for his trip to Benin is significant (as is the additional luggage space that must have been reserved by Bigpond for his elaborate headdress!). In a global Pentecostal landscape filled with multicultural variety, "culture" and cultural distinctiveness continue to matter.

As I have shown in this book, resonant rupture makes productive use of the ambiguity of expressive forms, allowing Oodláni to retain a sense of Navajoness, while simultaneously denying the validity of traditional meanings of Navajoness. The meaning of religious practice is amplified by the similarities, without actu-

FIG. 18. Pastor Wallace in Benin. Photo by Negiel Bigpond.

ally syncretizing or forging continuity with past practice. So to return to the orienting question for this conclusion: if resonant rupture can be mistaken for continuity (and often is, by outsiders), why not simply abandon these ambiguous forms altogether? Why continue to practice a form of Pentecostalism both marked as Navajo and decidedly opposed to Navajo traditionalism? Oodlání do not use Navajo terms for God or Jesus, so why do they continue to call the Holy Spirit *Niłch'i Diyini?* I contend that resonant rupture continues to be practiced because it allows Oodlání to exercise sovereign autonomy, as Navajos, on the global Pentecostal stage.

Resonant rupture, then, allows Oodlání to practice a distinctly Navajo "flavor" of Pentecostalism. This Navajo character is evidenced in all the expressive forms explored in this book: ritual, poetic language, music, dance, and healing rituals. Oodlání tent revivals are the Christian worship style that most resembles important Navajo ceremonials (such as the Enemy Way). Poetic language at revivals reflects stable Navajo-inflected performative language ideologies. Music at Oodlání revivals reflects the broader popularity of Navajo cowboy culture. Movement at tent revivals reflects a distinctly Navajo take on interactions with non-human actors. And health and healing, paramount concerns in Navajo culture, are also central to Pentecostalism, as practiced by Oodlání. This community practices a markedly Navajo form of Pentecostalism, one that is unique within global Pentecostalism and celebrated for its distinctiveness.

For example, on a number of occasions Pastor Wallace preached about the connections of Navajos gathered in various Oodlání churches and tents to the ultimate projected domination of global Pentecostalism. He would shout: "Billy Graham has prophesied! He told us that our Native people are a sleeping giant starting to wake up. He said the tribes could be the evangelists who will be the key to winning America for Christ!" So Navajo Pentecostalism is not only celebrated for its uniqueness within global Pentecostal evangelical networks; as in Billy Graham's prophecy it is often portrayed as *uniquely* positioned in God's global plan. Negiel Bigpond (Yuchi) has several times emphasized at Oodlání revivals the special role that Native Americans have in the global Pentecostal revival, because as "tribal" people, they are specially connected to the "tribal" people of the Bible.[13] Andrea Smith has noted this undercurrent of sovereignty discourse undergirding Bigpond's preaching as well and interpreted it as positive movement toward indigenous political sovereignty (Smith 2008, 100).

But the concept of resonant rupture as I have developed it in this book through careful ethnographic work with one Native neo-Pentecostal community does not project the same kind of optimism for the role of Native neo-Pentecostalism in promoting projects of Native American political sovereignty. At its root, resonant rupture is a move away from the foundational philosophies of traditional Native American culture and, instead, a move of spiritual warfare against those foundational philosophies.[14] Oodláni no longer walk the sunwise path. While the ambiguity of certain expressive forms allows Oodláni to assert Navajo distinctiveness in the global multicultural Pentecostal landscape, the meaning of these forms still represents for them a clear break with the past.

I have demonstrated this fundamental rupture through all the expressive forms assessed in this book. The apparent continuity of the tent revival ritual actually pairs with private rituals (like *jish* burning) that are deliberately anti-traditional. Language ideologies may remain stable, but new compositions cannot cross the line into anything resembling medicine man chant. Discourses of exclusion in music make sure that the Navajo-inflected country image does not actually cross the boundary into Oodláni musicians playing for country dances, thus polluting their ability to communicate the anointing. And Oodláni view the continuity of involved nonhuman actors as potentially threatening, since many nonhuman actors are demonic. This very Pentecostal theology of a cosmic battle between God and the Devil is reflected in changes to Oodláni healing etiology as well, so that when one carefully attends to what they are doing, one can observe that Navajo neo-Pentecostals are no longer searching for harmony but for "prosperity." All of this is to say that even though they enter the global Pentecostal landscape as distinctly marked Navajos,

Oodlání have fundamentally reinterpreted what it means to be Navajo. Their worldview is, fundamentally, Pentecostal.

Participants in the Oodlání movement continue to value their Navajo cultural identity, but they do so without compromising their religious conviction that the religion of their ancestors is a tool of the Devil. They will tell you, in Navajo, that they seek holiness, not *hózhǫ́*. This book has emphasized the importance of expressive culture in explaining how a coherent worldview can be forged out of perspectives seemingly so at odds, fundamentally changing the path of some Navajos.

Introduction

1. Diné is the name Navajo people call themselves. In contemporary usage, it has political connotations related to the assertion of sovereignty. While I respect this move for sovereignty, the community I worked with used the name Navajo, and so I continue to use this term when referring to Oodlání but use Diné when referring to scholars more consciously engaged in the academic work of sovereignty. The revival where Ma Beverly Joe described her skinwalker encounter was in 2014.

2. The most accurate estimation of the size of the Oodlání movement comes from demographic data collected by Derek Milne. Milne's data were gathered in 2000, during a random-sample and Navajo Nation–wide survey about an unrelated topic. His demographic data are especially important because as a researcher familiar with Navajo Pentecostalism he did not elide important distinctions between forms of Navajo Christianity, as other researchers have done. Milne reports that Pentecostalism was the most popular form of exclusive Christianity, followed by Mormonism and Catholicism, and that these three accounted for almost 90 percent of the Christian total (Milne 2011, 527).

3. All of these stances are, of course, oversimplistic constructions.

4. For more on religion as reality structures and "religious worlds," see Paden (1988).

5. There is a longstanding Navajo belief that the successful curing of a witchcraft curse will cause harm to the witch (Kluckhohn and Leighton 1946, 189).

6. Tinker (1993, 6–8) argues that each of these aspects constitutes genocide and that Christianity has had a hand in each of these aspects of assimilation. Politically, the "Civilization" Act of 1819 co-opted missionaries for political ends, as did the "Grant Peace Policy" (see also Prucha 1962; 1976). Economically, missionaries helped settle Native people on reservations, which allowed for the exploitation of natural resources and land. Religiously, missionaries played a large role in lobbying for the passage of the 1890 legislation restricting the religious freedom of Native People (including banning the Sun Dance). And socially, missionaries were quite invested in reordering Native collectivist ideals because salvation, after all, is not a team sport.

7. See especially Brugge 2010, 111–15, and Spicer 1962, 28–30, 158–59, 346–53, 411.

8. For more on Pratt's school and philosophy of Indian education, see Prucha (1976), Fear-Segal (2007), and Pfister (2004).

9. See Adams (1995), Trafzer et al. (2006), Szasz (1999), and Szasz and Ryan (1988).

10. This is according to Iverson (2002, 124).

11. In addition to these studies, see the recent ethnohistorical work of Morrison (2002), McLoughlin (1994), and Harkin (1993).

12. These studies follow the insight of Jean and John Comaroff (1991, 25–27) that Christian hegemony is always imperfect and unstable. Multivocality is a technique successfully employed in the collections of James Treat (1996), Christopher Vecsey (1997), and Jace Weaver (1998), providing multiple, nearly unmediated perspectives on being Native and Christian.

13. As Jackson points out, this view is most often expressed in public discourses such as the inaugural exhibition of the National Museum of the American Indian, titled *All Roads Are Good* (Jackson 2004, 192).

14. See, for instance, Pavlik (1997, 50). Smith also claims that any anti-traditional sentiment on the part of Native Christians must be a way to "appeal to white Christians for inclusion" (2008, 82). My ethnographic data contradict this assumption (and that of Pavlik) rather sharply.

15. To be clear, viewing the devil as an active agent in daily life is not entirely new in the Southwest. As Daniel Reff has argued (2005), the Jesuit missionaries to Mexican territory in the 1600s also brought with them a "foot firmly planted in the Middle Ages" (27), viewing Satan not as a symbol or metaphor for evil but as an evil being "capable of almost anything" (2005, 230). Beliefs about what Reff calls an "activist" God (and, therefore Devil) continued sporadically throughout the intervening centuries, particularly in folk Catholicism as it was interpreted by Indigenous Christians (Kozak and Lopez 1999; Spicer 1962). However, both the Protestant Reformation and the broader Enlightenment in Europe changed the tenor of Christianity. In what Webb Keane has called the "moral narrative of modernity," Christianity became grounded in the idea that fetishisms undermine freedom of choice (necessary for salvation), so that for Protestants and Catholics, mission became not about engaging in spiritual warfare but about eliminating distracting superstitions (Keane 2007, 5). As Reff puts it, "The Jesuits and Indians no longer were in agreement about what previously had united them: the immediate reality of an invisible world" (Reff 2005, 241). Neo-Pentecostalism of the mid-twentieth century is different from the mission efforts of the past three centuries because it reinvests the world with an activist God (and Devil; see Behar 1987, 44-45). This rejection of modernist and Enlightenment principles in favor of an active host of supernatural actors (which I take up in chapter 4), has contributed to neo-Pentecostalism's success (Jenkins 2002; Marshall 2015b). For more on the history and theology of spiritual warfare, see McAlister 2016.

16. In some ways this argument is used in support of the outmoded scholarly trope of Navajos as the "perennial incorporators," which Denetdale criticizes (2007, 92–95).

17. Certainly the spectrum of continuity and rupture has varied by denomination and through time. I am inclined to believe that many of these studies (particularly the ethnographic work of Reichard, Aberle, Blanchard, and Hodge) accurately described particular Navajo Christian communities of the past. However, the analysis of these scholars does tend to conform to the anthropological trope that Robbins (2003b) has called "continuity thinking."

18. Fieldnotes, May 14, 2008.

19. For more on the Diné Philosophy of Learning (DPL), see Aronilth (1994).

20. According to Turino's interpretation of Peirce's semiotic framework, feelingful connections emphasize the pre-rational meaning communicated by iconic and indexical signs (Turino 2008, 12–16).

21. Boas's *Primitive Art* was first published by Harvard University Press in 1927.

22. According to Bourdieu's theory of practice, learned values attached to "perceptions, appreciations, and actions" are precisely what makes them "lasting, transposable dispositions" at the core of cultural stability (*habitus*; Bourdieu 1977, 82–83).

23. Often the "transportable dispositions" that make up *habitus* are embodied ways of being in the world: something that was not lost on Bourdiu, who drew inspiration from Marcel Mauss's article "Body Techniques" (2006).

24. In discussing the punlike nature of expressive forms I am building on a strong contribution from the Southwesternist literature, especially as developed by Samuels (2004) and Bahr (2001). Because of the active denial of continuity present in rupture, I feel punning (Samuels 2004) is a more apt description of the situation than parody (Bahr 2001). Parodies, as described by Bahr, are an affectionate way of making fun of preexisting forms (in his case, mythologies), while also remaining silent about the other's existence (Bahr 2001, 588). Oodlání articulation against preexisting traditional practice is neither silent nor affectionate. My thanks to one of the anonymous reviewers of the present work for encouraging me to develop this connection further.

25. Brass instruments are where I have the majority of my musical training and have shaped my thinking about resonance.

26. Myers calls this resonant alignment a "co-operative regime" (1997, 21).

27. This is the meaning of resonance that has recently been used as well to describe an empathetic orientation toward those with whom anthropologists conduct fieldwork. See Paerregaard 2002 and Unni Wikan's 2013 book *Resonance: Beyond the Words*. My use of the term tends to emphasize the more technical definition, the sense of something amplifying something else that is similar but ultimately different.

28. As mentioned, the Protestant Reformation and the broader Enlightenment in Europe changed Christian mission. For more see Keane (2007, 5), Reff

(2005, 241), or Behar (1987, 44–45). While recognizing this "paradox" of what Casanova has called "an uprooted local culture engaged in spiritual warfare with its own roots" (Casanova 2001, 437–38), some scholars have mistaken this situation for continuity (Smith 2008, 84).

29. As M. E. Nevins has pointed out, "the continuity asserted by Traditionalists and the disruption asserted by AIC are just that: assertions" (Nevins 2010, 29).

30. Points of resonance are the expressive dimension of Smilde's concept of "imaginative rationality." According to Smilde, the Venezuelan Pentecostals he worked with ascribed meanings to the things around them "by attaching images from a relatively better known domain (source domain or vehicle)" (Smilde 2007, 215). Furthermore, and drawing upon the work of Paul Friedrich, Smilde argues that to be "potent," a concept "must be sufficiently different from the inchoate subject matter that it actually provides new meaning, yet not so different as to be irrelevant to the task of understanding" (Smilde 2007, 215). The similarity between the two domains is important, but they should not be mistaken for "replacement." Resonant rupture builds on this idea by focusing on how this transfer of meaning progresses in aesthetically charged expressive practices.

31. According to the Indian Health Service report, the rate per 100,000 for diabetes deaths was 63.8 for Navajos versus 25.2 for U.S. all races. The rate per 100,000 for alcohol-related deaths was 45.7 for Navajos versus 6.9 for U.S. all races. The rate per 100,000 for injury and poisoning deaths was 111.1 for Navajos versus 24.6 for U.S. all races (Indian Health Service 2003, 56–63).

32. This is a major difference between my study and Aberle's seminal study of another new religious movement among Navajos: the Native American Church. I generally agree with Aberle's framework (outlined in 1966, sharpened in 1982, republished in 1991) that Navajo religious change is driven by "a negative discrepancy between legitimate expectation and actuality" (Aberle 1991, 323), particularly in regard to power. But the NAC is still actively operating among Navajos and in general has a much more positive relationship with Navajo traditionalism than does neo-Pentecostalism. A driving question of my study, then: given that there are other, less cognitively dissonant options for regaining supernatural power, why do so many Navajos choose neo-Pentecostalism?

33. On "taking seriously," see Robbins (2003b, 230).

1. The Oodlání Movement

1. Elaine Lawless calls this a "greeting ceremony" preceding the service (1988a, 60).

2. As Aberle noted about another new religious movement among Navajos, tears accompanying prayer are "absolutely atypical for traditional Navaho" (Aberle 1991, 156) and are considered astonishing, surprising, and somewhat unmanly by nonmembers. Although public crying has probably become more

common among Navajos since Aberle's study in the 1950s, crying is still a marked and unusual activity (see, for instance, Schwarz 2001, 134-51).

3. Fieldnotes, June 13, 2014.

4. Fieldnotes, May 20, 2007.

5. Much like the southern Indiana Pentecostals in the work of Lawless, Oodlání regularly expressed the need to surrender to the will of the Holy Spirit, and sometimes Pastor Wallace would forgo the sermon entirely in order to "let God have His will" (Fieldnotes, June 1, 2008). However, in spite of the knowledge that the format may be overridden by the Holy Spirit at any time, there is a "discernible order to the events that occur" (Lawless 1988a, 59) in an Oodlání revival service, and the Holy Spirit is "consciously wooed only at certain points and in particular ways" (Lawless 1988a, 60).

6. See Turino (2008, 51-53) for more on the formal characteristics of presentational music making.

7. It is likely that the order of people giving an offering is structured by social posturing (those who want to be seen giving money will eagerly go first), centrality in the community (regular participants will proceed confidently forward), sheer location of seating (those in the back will take longer to wend their way through the crowd than those in the front), and other types of social constraints. I only mean to indicate that there is no pre-set order (row by row, men first, etc.).

8. For instance, the first type might be a sermon about how to be a good husband or wife. The preacher would then use biblical passages to support an argument for a biblical model about being a good spouse (e.g., Proverbs 31:10-31, Ephesians 5:33, Mark 10:6-9, James 1:19, and I Peter 3:7). The second type might be a sermon discussing a longer biblical story, such as the parable of the prodigal son (Luke 15:11-32), and how despite their past mistakes, listeners should understand this as a story about God's unwavering love.

9. The hours I spent listening to rambling, stream-of-consciousness sermons were the times I enjoyed my fieldwork the least. In my defense, Oodlání did not typically like listening to these kinds of sermons either. My discussions with them about "the Word" made it clear that they genuinely liked learning new things about the Bible and thinking about new ways to apply its teachings to their daily lives. Pastor Wallace was particularly good at engaging listeners intellectually in this way, to which several members attributed his success.

10. This transition is discussed in chapter 5. See also Titon (1978; 1988) and Lawless (1988a) for details on the altar call in Pentecostal contexts.

11. In evangelical (non-Pentecostal) contexts, the altar call serves as the invitation for unsaved participants to come and publicly dedicate their lives to Christ. In denominational Pentecostal contexts, this altar call provides an opportunity for attendees to come forward to pray for the baptism of the Holy Spirit, expressed in the speaking of tongues (Titon 1978; Lawless 1988a, 66).

12. At this point in the revival, the musical form more closely resembles what Turino (2008, 26-38) has called *participatory*.

13. Throughout this work, pastors and evangelists are addressed as they are locally, with the respectful title of "Pastor" followed by their first name. Thus throughout this work I refer to "Wallace Begay" as "Pastor Wallace."

14. In this work I use the term *Anglo* as it is used locally: to describe any person who is non-Native and "European" in appearance. Locally, this term applies to all "white"-looking persons, regardless of whether they are actually of English descent, but not generally to anyone of Mexican or Spanish heritage.

15. Being "slain in the spirit" is a charismatic practice whereby the supplicant loses consciousness and falls to the ground.

16. See Peterson (2006, 118) for the distinction between border communities and border towns.

17. This combination of networks (both the pastor's family and the family of the original pastor) is not too unusual, particularly around major Navajo towns, although familial affiliation to the pastor typically determines attendance in smaller Navajo communities.

18. As a caveat, Kluckhohn and Leighton's 1946 ethnography was not written with Navajo audiences in mind.

19. Pastor Wallace and his mother Beverly Joe were of the *Tódích'íi'nii* (Bitter Water) clan and very quickly adopted me into this clan as well. From then on Pastor Wallace would commonly refer to me as *Asdzą́ą́ Tódích'íi'nii* (Bitter Water Woman), in a teasing manner. Frankly, it was the teasing that made me feel accepted, more than the clan designation.

20. The title "Ma" has double meaning, since the Navajo word for "mother" is *Shimá*, literally "shi-" (my) and "má" (mother).

21. I really enjoyed working with these women, and I hope I was of help.

22. For more on the interaction between Shiprock Oodlání and A. A. Allen, see Marshall (2015a).

23. Mr. Joe and his wonderful family welcomed me into their home, and I enjoyed our many chats under the shade trees in his yard. He also bestowed adopted clan membership on me, what I consider to be my "paternal" clan: *Bit'ahnii*.

24. See, for example, Aberle (1982); Csordas (2000, 2004); Frisbie (1992); Milne (2011). It is important to note that while all these scholars discuss a strong and growing movement of "evangelical Christianity" among Navajos that is native-led and independently operating, and some of them mention the Pentecostal/charismatic nature of much of this movement, none of these scholars identifies this group as Oodlání.

25. At this time government boarding schools were church run because of the Grant Peace Policy (a government program that turned over the administration of Indian affairs to churches). They remained church run after the repeal of the Grant Peace Policy due to chronic federal underfunding of local secular alternatives (Iverson 2002, 82).

26. See also Warner (1973); Adams (1995); Szasz (1999); Stout (2012).

27. Although, as Spicer points out, Protestant missionaries used tents for evangelization as well (1962, 522).

28. The more formal Navajo term is *Éé'neishoodii be'éé' danineezígíí*. This is a name that descriptively references the long robes of the Franciscan fathers. The more formal Navajo term is *Éé'neishoodii be'éé' Éé' ádaałts' íísígíí* in reference to the short coats of the Protestant missionaries.

29. The *Gáamalii* ("Mormons," or members of the Church of Jesus Christ of Latter Day Saints) form yet another group with a distinct history among Navajos.

30. Both Schwarz (2008, 74) and Milne (2011, 340–41) also note this preference in self-identification.

31. The heterogeneity of Oodlání church names has thrown off many observers. In practice, however, this idiosyncratic naming is rather unimportant, since Oodlání refer to the various churches not by the name on the sign but by the name of the pastor.

32. As Diné scholar Vincent Werito has pointed out (2014, 27), these behavioral guidelines are grounded in the Navajo orienting philosophy of *Sa'ąh Naagháí Bik'eh Hózhǫ́ǫ́n* (SNBH). Other scholars have observed the implications of this principle for cooperative behavior (Lamphere 1977), healthcare (Epple et al. 1997), and balancing of kinship obligations (Shepardson and Hammond 1970).

33. I am a practicing Presbyterian (PCUSA), and a few of my recent ancestors were Presbyterian ministers. Being able to identify as a Christian may have influenced my access to the Oodlání community, regardless of the vast differences in our theological orientations. However, I made it very clear on multiple occasions that I was not in Shiprock as a missionary; that I came to learn, not to teach. As a fieldworker, I strove at all times to maintain a neutral position of empathetic objectivity. I attempt to communicate this position of empathetic neutrality in my writing as well.

34. As developed by Boas (1887) and refined by Boas's students (Robert H. Lowie and others).

35. Other scholars within the growing anthropology of Christianity have frequently commented on the difficulty of maintaining relativism but also objective credibility among anthropologists.

36. And vice versa.

37. See also Milne (2011).

38. I occasionally use the phrase "The Diné" or "The Oodlání" because in the Navajo language plurality is attached to the verb, not the noun. Both these are intended in the plural form.

39. For more on the interaction between verbal framing and identity congealed in the concept of "Narratives of Navajoness," see Webster (2009, 152–81).

40. See, for instance, Briggs's (1996) critique of Handler and Linnekin (1984).

41. See L. Lee (2014a) and Werito (2014) for SNBH as it is experienced. Also see the work of Witherspoon (1977) and Farella (1984).

42. As I reiterate several times in this book, new research into the Navajo traditional ceremonial complex by outsiders is strongly discouraged by the Navajo Nation, so all my original research focused solely on Navajo Christianity. All information on the Navajo ceremonial complex comes from well-known published sources such as Haile 1938; Kluckhohn and Wyman 1940; Reichard 1963; Gill 1981; Werner et al. 1983; Wyman 1983; Frisbie 1987; and Vecsey 1991. I took very seriously the writing and perspectives of Navajo scholars on this topic as well, such as Aronilth 1994, Faris and Walters 1990, and Lee 2014a.

43. See Lawless (1992).

2. Under the Tent

1. Charismatic tent evangelists from the outside have always employed Navajos to translate their preaching into the Navajo language. Some of these translators have become famous Navajo evangelists.

2. Again, it is more accurately seen as a total lifeway. In particular, see Kidwell et al. (2001), McNally (2000b), Morrison (2002), and Shorter (2009).

3. Talal Asad (1993) has written extensively about the cross-cultural problem of belief, though his response is largely in answer to the work of Geertz. An early anthropologist to note the problems with belief is Rodney Needham (1972). See also a good summative discussion of this issue in Bielo (2015, 18–19).

4. Shorter calls for a focus on Indigenous religions as "epistemologically actualizing." That is, indigenous rituals are epistemological "because they make knowledge and set the standards for what counts as truth," and they are actualizing because they have real effects in the world: they are "active, effective, and internally logical" (Shorter 2009, 18).

5. See also McNally (2000b, 849).

6. Robert Young and William Morgan cross-reference *nahaghá* with *nahasłá* "to perform a ceremony, to go through a religious ritual. Literally, to cause things to go, move things about" (1980, 531).

7. This gloss is supported linguistically. Werner, Manning, and Begishe elicited the phrase *(Diné) Binahagha'* as a subset of *Diné yee hináanii,* "that by means of which Navajos live" (1983, 589).

8. Milne has explored this contemporary construction of "traditional religion" in more detail, calling it the "orthodoxy" of the "ideology of traditionalism" (Milne 2011, 513). He finds that rather than thinking about spirituality as part of a holistic Navajo lifeway, many contemporary Navajo (both neo-Pentecostal and "traditional") participate in a constructed "ideology" of traditional religion. For supporters, he finds this ideology has strong overtones of nostalgia (2011, 570). For neo-Pentecostals, this ideology has strong overtones of witchcraft (2011, 605).

9. In fact, the assertion of many Oodláni that they are culturally Navajo (just not *religiously* Navajo) implies a colonial framework for viewing cultures, what Philip Scher (drawing from Wilk 1995) has called "structures of common difference." This food-court mentality organizes diversity "through

mutually recognizable classification" (Scher 2002, 460), so that languages, material cultures, foodways, and religions of all the cultures in the world can be mixed and matched to suit the desires of the individual. Through colonial institutions, many generations of Navajos have been indoctrinated into this view of religious diversity that Sher calls "hegemony as taxonomy" (Scher 2002, 460).

10. In discussing how religion is transposed into locally meaningful practice, McNally comments: "People make practices their own not simply by assigning them their own inner meanings but by performing them in ways that render the practices relevant and coherent (and perhaps beautiful) to them. But again, coherence here has less to do with the consistency of meaning interior to the practices as with a kind of formal coherence. Here the logic of practice allows for the suspension of contradictions or inconsistencies that might obtain if one were to spell out theologically what the meanings of their practices are for them" (McNally 2000b, 852).

11. As one woman told him, "I don't just like to sit all the time and listen to the some old preacher stand up and talk to me. I like to take part in what's going on" (Blanchard 1977, 210).

12. See Dolaghan and Scates (1978, 41–42).

13. "Mission compounds" refer to strategies of missionization from the early twentieth century and before. This mission strategy was based on the development of a separated (and often walled off) mission station that included a church but also several support buildings. These buildings could include housing for the missionary or missionaries, a school, a dormitory for school children, a kitchen, storehouses, housing for domestic workers, or a hospital/clinic. The idea was to provide a total Christian existence separate from the cultural context that surrounded the mission.

14. This revival movement, while widely recognized in charismatic circles, is not typically discussed by secular or mainstream Christian historians. Ethnographic data led me to investigate these evangelists, including published literature from within the movement (see Stewart 1999; Liardon 2011). My primary scholarly source on this revival is historian David Harrell (1975).

15. See Robbins 2004b, 119–22, for an excellent overview of the historical roots of charismatic and Pentecostal churches.

16. For more on William Branham's life and ministry, see Harrell 1975, 29–38. For more on Oral Roberts's life and ministry, see Harrell 1975, 45–48. Branham and Roberts inspired the ministry of many other evangelists, including Jack Coe, T. L. Osborn, Velmer Gardner, and David Nunn, all popularized by Gordan Lindsay in his magazine The Voice of Healing (Harrell 1975, 54).

17. For more on A. A. Allen and his connection to the nascent Oodláni movement, see Marshall 2015a.

18. Spicer describes the historical precedent of cross-visiting independent ministers set by Natives who had broken off from denominational churches among the Hopi, Pima, San Carlos Apache, and Mohave (Spicer 1962, 522).

Charismatically inspired "anointed" Native evangelists built on these established cross-visiting patterns.

19. Negiel Bigpond, personal communication, December 3, 2012.

20. Most private rituals are performed for the benefit of an individual and "are therefore a private family affair" (Haile 1938, 23). As I mentioned in the introduction, new research on Navajo traditional religion by outsiders is strongly discouraged by the Navajo Nation, and I conducted none. In this section my discussions of Navajo traditional ceremonialism rely solely on already published sources, especially Reichard 1949, McAllester 1954, Gill 1987, Frisbie 1980 and 1987, and Aberle 1991. Other public ceremonials might include the Night Way (with its public Ye'ii bichii dancing) or the Mountain Way. On the Night Way, see Faris (1990) and Francis (1996). Frisbie points out that contemporary Enemy Ways and Night Ways are marked by the presence of vendors and "the use of tribal police to maintain order" (Frisbie 1992, 480–81).

21. For a more contemporary account of the Enemy Way, and its contemporary articulation among Navajos who undergo surgery, see Schwarz 2008, 310–20.

22. When McAllester wrote, the preferred nomenclature of the Navajo Nation was to write Navaho (with an "h") rather than Navajo (with a "j"). McAllester is, therefore, following the current practice at the time of his writing.

23. The actual Navajo phrase is *"ahizhdi áhai* ('two come together') songs" (McAllester 1954, 19).

24. These include competitive singing of "sway dance" and "circle dance" songs (McAllester 1954).

25. This comment is embedded in McAllester's larger account of a visiting group critical of the drinking that had marred this particular dance (1954, 13). McAllester makes several references to alcohol and Enemy Way dances, including widespread drunkenness and the chastising by elders that this kind of behavior should not be tolerated. McAllester observed Enemy Way ceremonies in the 1950s, precisely the same period in which tent revivals were gaining popularity. It is speculative, but not outside the realm of possibility, to imagine that increasing alcohol use at Enemy Way dances may have led some Navajo families to spend their summer evenings under a Pentecostal tent instead.

26. As we examine in chapter 2, the aesthetic classification of *nizhóni* indicates an aesthetic dimension (beautiful) a moral dimension (good), and a spiritual dimension (holy). Thus all good music is, in some senses, also holy music (McAllester 1954, 63).

27. Frisbie (1987, xxiii) expands on the implications of this taxonomy.

28. For a fuller discussion of traditional Navajo prayers, see Reichard (1966).

29. An early source on Navajo prayer is Washington Matthews's "The Prayer of a Navajo Shaman" (1888). A few of the most comprehensive studies of Navajo prayer include Gladys Reichard's *Prayer: The Compulsive Word* (1966) and Sam Gill's *Sacred Words* (1981).

30. Both Gill (1974, 171-74) and Reichard (1966, 13) recognize the existence of individualistic prayer within traditional Navajo ceremonialism, although both question the degree to which these prayers are really extemporaneous. Reichard sees them as "cast in a formal mode" (1966, 13), and Gill identifies this formal mode as "Unit V" form, where the basic unit of desire for blessing (using a formulaic phrase like "may it be happy") can be applied to whatever the speaker desires (Gill 1974, 184-88). For an extended discussion of this distinction as well as examples of each kind of prayer in the context of the *Hooghan Da'ashdlisígíí* (House Blessing ceremony), see Frisbie 1980, 180-87.

31. For more on power and Oodlání healing, see chapter 5.

32. McAllester also noted the role of kin-based reciprocity in "compelling" (as framed in Reichard 1966) the cooperation of the *Diyin Diné'é*. He quotes the third stanza of the Snake Offering Prayer by way of example:

Your offering I have made, for you I have made it
Today I am your child, today I am your grandchild . . .

And later from the fifth stanza:

Whatever I say to you, you will do it,
Whatever you say to me, I will do it. (McAllester 1980, 232)

33. For further discussion of *yeel* (particularly in reference to the payment made to singers), see Aberle (1967). In this work, Aberle writes the term *gheel*.

34. Traditional prayer, as already discussed, reminds them of this obligation.

35. As many scholars have noted, traditionally Navajo relationships entail continuous reciprocity, to the degree that the phrase "thank you" was not traditionally part of Navajo vocabulary. As Aberle put it, "Since relationships involve continuous reciprocity, thanks are unnecessary: there will later be a return for any favor, voluntary or sought" (Aberle 1991, 195-96).

36. And indeed, the incident that Dombrowski describes was instigated at a revival led by a traveling Tlingit evangelist, Flo Ellers.

37. When the motivations of indigenous converts who have burned sacred paraphernalia are carefully investigated (as in Whiteley 1992), the act of burning is often viewed as a way of neutralizing persistent (negative) power. However, prior to the 1950s these fears were also often mixed by converts with a modernizing discourse that claimed sacred paraphernalia was non-agentive (merely "made of wood" as one convert put it in Whiteley (1992, 64)). In contrast, the contemporary neo-Pentecostal movement often emphasizes the very real supernatural threat of these items.

38. As I have throughout the book, I maintain a neutral tone in this passage. My main goal here is to describe these controversial acts as Oodlání see them, not to suggest how readers should think about them.

39. Frisbie also notes that the practice goes beyond these two cases. By 1977 she had collected allegations of "conversion-inspired destruction" from "Window Rock, Ganado, Greasewood, Piñon, Rough Rock, Leupp, Crownpoint, Tohatchi, Newcomb, Chinle, Rock Point, Shiprock, and Many Farms"

(Frisbie 1987, 196). Several of her collaborators also reported witnessing such destruction (Frisbie 1987, 207).

40. This approach to mission, what Webb Keane has called the "moral narrative of modernity," is grounded in the idea that "modernity is, or ought to be, a story of human liberation from a host of false beliefs and fetishisms that undermine freedom" (2007, 5). See Introduction, note 15, in this work for more detail on how these ideas of mission and modernity play out in the U.S. Southwest.

41. Whiteley's discussion in "Burning Culture: Auto-da-fé at Orayvi" (1992) shows these complexities as well.

42. In part, the theological ontology of the anointing undergirds the apprenticeship-style training of pastors as well. As one Anglo evangelist (Don Stewart) told me, the early Navajo translators of the 1950s were not just picking up the vocal patterns and biblical knowledge of the traveling tent evangelists; they were also being affected by the strong anointing of the main evangelist. He stated, "You get in an atmosphere that's anointed . . . it's kind of like the measles . . . you catch it, you know?" (Stewart 2008). According to Stewart, it was this "exposure" to the anointing that allowed Navajo translators to begin their own effective ministries.

43. Fred Yazzie, personal communication, June 18, 2000.

44. For example, Negiel Bigpond, a Yuchi neo-Pentecostal leader with longstanding ties to Pastor Wallace's church, runs a military-style training camp in Bixby, Oklahoma, for the purposes of training Native pastors and others to "deal with occult and territorial enemy strongholds on the reservations" (Smith 2008, 86). For more on the specific theologies of spiritual warfare, and the ways in which Native neo-Pentecostals are trained as spiritual "warriors," see McAlister 2016.

45. These ontological sentiments of "spiritual warfare" reinforce why the approaches toward sanctification (Jacobs 1996, 188) or cultural contextualization (Alexander 2012) that are suggested by other Christian Native Americans (including Navajos) are regarded with suspicion by the neo-Pentecostal Oodlání. Other works on contemporary Native American evangelical Christianity sometimes miss this nuance.

3. Háálá Ayóo Diyin

1. Fieldnotes, July 1, 2006.

2. Silverstein (1979); Schieffelin et al. (1998); Kroskrity (2000); Field and Kroskrity (2009).

3. David Samuels notes this problem with "Medicine Man Talk" among San Carlos Apache as well (2006, 533).

4. Fieldnotes, August 10, 2007. The interplay of Christian and pre-Christian musical aesthetic systems has been of interest to other ethnomusicologists as well. See, for instance, the 2005 *World of Music* special issue: Musical Reverberation from the Encounter of Local and Global Belief Systems, 47(1). See especially Scruggs (2005) and Sherinian (2005).

5. This linguistic situation parallels other Native American linguistic landscapes such as San Carlos Apaches (Samuels 2006) and the Eastern and Oklahoma Cherokees (Bender 2009), where the heritage language is associated with both traditionalists and Native Christians.

6. There are many different aspects of the Navajo language ideology—or many language ideologies, as some have put it (Field 2009). Either way, there is good reason to emphasize the heterogeneity of Navajo language ideology, since (as illustrated by Peterson and Webster 2013) some Navajo beliefs and feelings about the Navajo language contradict one another.

7. Of course, ideologies do not exist on their own but are enacted in what Peterson and Webster (2013) have called "fleeting, spontaneous, and context-dependent practices" that bring together individual agency, creativity, and language ideologies in the performative moment (94).

8. According to Jacobsen, their cognitive abilities might be questioned as well, and older fluent speakers may address them in louder-than-normal voices (2012, 281).

9. This aspect of the Navajo language ideology has been much discussed by linguists because it proves a significant roadblock to the continuing health of the Navajo language (see House 2002; Webster 2009; and Jacobsen 2012).

10. Fluency in the Navajo language is a criterion for Navajo Nation president, as stipulated in the Navajo legal code. In a referendum held on July 21, 2014, members of the Navajo Nation narrowly voted to loosen this requirement, allowing fluency in Navajo to be determined by voters rather than in courts.

11. See, for instance, Landry (2014).

12. Fieldnotes, December 15, 2007.

13. Fieldnotes, July 16, 2006.

14. See Lassiter et al. (2002) for a contrasting case of hymn singing among Kiowa Christians. Hymns also play a large part in Ojibwe Christianity (McNally 2000a).

15. The Reverend L. P. Brink was a Christian Reformed missionary who began translating hymns into Navajo in the early twentieth century. For more information on Brink, see Dolaghan and Scates (1978, 35).

16. The tendency to favor orally transmitted praise songs or popular contemporary Christian songs over group hymn singing is relatively typical for neo-Pentecostal song practice globally.

17. According to Peterson and Webster (2013) other aspects of Navajo language ideologies include ideas that the Navajo language is "variously whole, sacred, healing, descriptive, difficult, adaptable, disappearing, individualistic, iconic of identity, ripe for humor, accepting of variation, and incommensurate with English" (99).

18. Fieldnotes, October 6, 2007.

19. Religious pluralism has long been viewed as the common practice of most Navajo (Wood 1982; Lewton and Bydone 2000).

20. Meyer (1998), Casanova (2001), Robbins (2003a), Daswani (2013). As Joel Robbins succinctly put it, global Pentecostalism often accepts local ontol-

ogies (spirits, witchcraft, etc.), but because it takes these forces as "paramount among the forces it struggles against," it does not seek to "forge any continuity with them" (Robbins 2003b, 223).

21. Beverly Joe interview, July 6, 2008; Fred Yazzie, personal communication, June 18, 2000; Megan Martin, personal communication, May 26, 2000. As Elizabeth McAlister comments, "People who subscribe to this idea understand the whole of human history as a consequence of the cosmic batter of Satan against God" (2016, 2).

22. "Navaho" was the commonly accepted spelling when McAllester wrote.

23. The enclitic -jí is typically attached to the Navajo word for the ceremony's purpose (Frisbie 1992, 461).

24. To reiterate, I conducted no new research on traditional Navajo ceremonialism, as this kind of research by outsiders is discouraged by the Navajo Nation. All information on traditional ceremonialism comes from well-known published sources.

25. Nasal tones appear to be unaccounted for in this system.

26. As Baldridge reports, "Smiley's ideas have met with considerable opposition, and so he is reluctant to try out some of his concepts for fear of retaliation . . . other area pastors tell people not to attend his church—he is considered extreme and radical" (Baldridge 2000, 89).

27. Minnie Wood, personal communication, June 1, 2000.

28. It is interesting to note that the concept of exclusivity is part of Navajo language ideologies as well. See Webster (2009, 99–121).

29. Admittedly, Austin's framing of "performative" language does fit better within the Western rational framework that regards language as ultimately a referential system, not a performative one. Silverstein (1979) takes up this point in more detail, as do Field and Kroskrity (2009).

30. Interestingly, many of my informants have directly contradicted the claims of Baldridge and Stoner, claiming that they can understand the Navajo words in hymns even without the high and low tones.

31. Fieldnotes, June 8, 2012.

32. Kinlichini is a Navajo clan name.

33. Because of his involvement in the public sphere, I have used a pseudonym to identify this individual.

34. Meyer (1998) worked with neo-Pentecostals in Ghana. Robbins, who has also noted this focus on rupture within the Urapmin Pentecostal community of the Western Sepik region of New Guinea, explains this focus through the "Pauline" model of conversion promoted by Pentecostalism (Robbins 2010).

35. See Corten (1997); Casanova (2001, 437–38); Robbins (2003b, 223); Engelke (2010); and Daswani (2013).

36. As stated in Peterson and Webster (2013), this is one of many ideologies about the Navajo language.

37. See Haile (1938), Reichard (1966), Wyman (1975), Gill (1981), Matthews (1995), and most important, Field and Blackhorse (2002).

4. "God Never Listened to Country"

1. Concerts and booking information for these bands can be accessed on the internet clearing site rezbandz.com (Jacobsen 2009, 449).

2. These include *The Grand Old Opry, Hee Haw,* and *Red Foley's Ozark Jubilee.*

3. These include Hank Williams's *I Saw the Light* (1954, MGM); George Jones's *Country Church Time* (1959, Mercury), *Homecoming in Heaven* (1962, United Artists), and *In a Gospel Way* (1973, Epic); Loretta Lynn's *Hymns* (1965, Decca), *Who Says God Is Dead!* (1968, Decca), and *God Bless America Again* (1972 Decca); Willie Nelson's *Family Bible* (1980, Songbird); Dolly Parton's *Golden Streets of Glory* (1971, RCA); and numerous albums by Johnny Cash, including *The Holy Land* (1969, Columbia) and *The Gospel Road* (1973, Columbia).

4. According to the KOMA radio website, "Throughout the 60s and 70s, KOMA was the favorite of teens all across the western US. With the big 50,000-watt signal and the relatively few rock-n-roll radio stations across the plains, KOMA was the main station for the hits.... Often teens in New Mexico, Arizona, Wyoming, Kansas, Colorado, Nebraska, and other western states would eagerly await sunset when the mighty 1520 would come booming through with the newest hits of the day. They would sit in their cars on hilltops, turn it up at parties, or fall asleep with the radio next to their beds as they listened to Chuck Berry, the Supremes, Paul Revere and the Raiders, and the Beatles" (http://www.komaradio.com/komainfo.aspx).

5. As Samuels has pointed out, "The rise of rock bands in San Carlos and Bylas during the 1950s and 1960s was predicated on this sort of active participatory experience of the radio and records, and on the way the play of imagination mobilized local identities as a response to the flow of musical expressions in the community" (Samuels 2004, 109).

6. See Jacobsen 2009 for the significance of this mono ("rez") sound.

7. According to Jacobsen, this strong duple beat is called the chapter house beat or more poetically "jung jigga jung." David McAllester also identified a proclivity for chapter house bands to use "certain melodic and rhythmic shortcuts" (McAllester 2002, 76), a pattern common in Oodlání revival music as well.

8. For more on the contemporary Navajo secular country music scene, see Jacobsen 2009 and Jacobsen 2012.

9. Emerson appears on the second album of the Chinle Galileans.

10. According to Jacobsen (2009, 458), these associations include the linking of the Navajo Sundowners with Waylon Jennings's "Pickin' White Gold" (1972), the Navajo artist Jimmy King Jr. with Jimmy "Cajun" Newman's "The Alligator Man" (1962), and the chapter house band Aces Wild with Cher and Sonny Bono's "Baby Don't Go" (1965).

11. McAllester calls this selection "Navajo Hymn Music," but the influential style of the Chinle Galileans was much more country gospel than "hymn" singing. This important local distinction is reflected in the title of the LP that

Worlds of Music used to source the Chinle Galilean's song: *Navajo Country Gospel* LPS 909.

12. For example, see Travis Friday's album *Gospel Songs: Be with Me,* or Harvest Glory's album *Volume 3.* "House of Gold" also appeared on recordings by the Chinle Galileans.

13. The use of country western symbolism appears most prominently on Travis Friday's 2005 album *Gospel Songs: Be with Me.* But as I discuss later, Friday presents a special case. My point here is that rural symbolism is widespread, even among non-crossover country gospel bands.

14. Fox paraphrases these grammars and poetics as "assholes talking shit" (Fox 2004, 41).

15. In fact, the economic benefits of Christianity constituted the primary lens through which Navajo conversion was explained until very recently (Blanchard 1977; Hodge 1964; Pavlik 1997).

16. I use here Peterson's distinction between "border communities" and "border towns." In contrast to border towns like Farmington and Gallup in New Mexico or Page and Flagstaff in Arizona, which are off the reservation, border communities like Shiprock, Window Rock, and Fort Defiance are on the reservation but close enough to the border to have incorporated significant Anglo influence, including housing styles and technological diffusion (electricity, plumbing, cell phones; Peterson 2006, 118).

17. Kelly's story appears in detail in chapter 6.

18. Also like the term *redneck,* many people find this nickname irredeemably offensive. As Navajo educator Wilson Aronilth Jr. cautions, "Sometimes we are called a 'Jaan.' Occasionally we even call each other, 'Hey, you Jaan!' To call each other a Jaan is very insulting to our older people, so please do not use this term. To be called a 'Navajo' is okay" (Aronilth 1994, 57).

19. This pattern of country music and class holds true for the patrons of East Texas honky-tonk culture documented by Fox (2004), and the first and second generation migrants to urban areas in south-central Brazil documented by Dent (2009).

20. I should note that Ma Beverly's portrait of chapter house dances is in direct contrast to the descriptions of Jacobsen, who conducted extensive fieldwork at chapter house dances by playing with a chapter house band. Jacobsen's descriptions paint a rather wholesome and family-friendly portrait of these gatherings (Jacobsen 2009, 454).

21. This transcript is set to emphasize the dialogic nature of this exchange.

22. Unlike Ma Beverly, Layne Joe had actually attended chapter house dances with friends as a teenager. However, as she got older and dedicated her life to being Oodlání, she now felt that the threat of demon attack made these dances too dangerous.

23. Since I had heard about similar Oodlání cosmologies of evil ("demon") spirits hanging around traditional sings, I asked her to clarify if she meant

"evil spirits" metaphorically or literally. She confirmed that she meant it literally (L. Joe 2014).

24. This pattern of alternating allegiance throughout a lifetime is fairly common for non-musician Oodlání as well.

25. Talent, of course, has a double meaning, which they recognized. Fieldnotes, July 6, 2008.

26. See Kluckhohn and Leighton (1946, 122, 252) for a discussion of the social uses of Navajo gossip.

27. Focus group, July 20, 2008.

5. Dancing in the Spirit

1. As mentioned in previous chapters, both the Protestant Reformation and the broader Enlightenment in Europe changed the tenor of Christianity, tying it to modernist discourse about freedom from superstition as a crucial element the free choice necessary for salvation (Keane 2007, 5; Reff 2005, 241; Behar 1987, 44-45). Neo-Pentecostalism rejects this intellectualism in favor of an embodied relationship with supernatural forces.

2. Fieldnotes, September 13, 2007.

3. Described in English.

4. As Hamera reminds us, these aesthetic systems of valuation are never agentless but always entangled in relations of power, questions of "who gets to create, to consume, to judge, and the social contingencies undergirding all these privileges" (Hamera 2007, 3).

5. Anthropologists have long been interested in the training of bodies as an important aspect of socialization. See Mauss (2006), "Techniques of the Body," an essay that fueled Bourdieu's revolutionary concept of *habitus* (Bourdieu 1977).

6. Other landmark studies of embodied culture include Desjarlais' (1992) concept of the "aesthetics of experience," Geertz's description of Balinese embodied aesthetics (1973), and Royce's writing about the "aesthetics of the ordinary" (2011).

7. According to Reed (1998, 504) early anthropologists mentioning dance included Tylor, Boas, Malinowski, Radcliffe-Brown, and Evans-Pritchard.

8. Other important contributions to growing the field of cultural dance scholarship include Joann Kealiinohomoku's 1969 essay "An Anthropologist Looks at Ballet as a Form of Ethnic Dance" (reprint 1983), and the 1972 meeting of the Conference on Research in Dance (CORD) held in Tucson, Arizona (Shay 2008, 93).

9. Others have also found the boundaries of dance too constraining when viewed cross-culturally and have advocated for a shift in focus from "dance" to "motion" (Kaeppler 1985; Lewis 1995).

10. Royce then arrives at a definition that dance should be understood as "patterned movement performed as an end in itself" (1977, 8).

11. For an overview of the current state of the field of cross-cultural dance scholarship, see Royce 2008.

12. These studies are Adrienne Kaeppler's dissertation for the University of Hawaii, "The Structure of Tongan Dance" (1967), and György Martin and Ernö Pésovar's 1961 article "A Structural Analysis of Hungarian Folk Dance," in *Acta Ethnografica Academiae Scientiarum Hungaricae* 10.

13. This is one interpretation of why spirit-filled dancing conforms to a certain technique. Another interpretation that Oodlání themselves would privilege is that spirit-filled dancing takes this form because that is what it looks like when the Holy Spirit fills someone.

14. Interestingly, the movement of teenagers is typically more athletic and marked than that of older believers.

15. I am not the first anthropologist to note that spirit possession conforms to rules of technique. As early as 1950 Melville Herskovits commented, "In some cultures the patterns underlying the forms of possession are difficult to discern.... However, on closer acquaintance, the patterned regularities which underlie the individual expression" become apparent (Herskovits 1950, 881).

16. Sign language may provide a complicating case for this framework.

17. Some scholars have suggested that persisting in using the prefix "ethno-" continues to perpetuate a ghettoization of these non-Western aesthetic spectrums (see Coote 1995, 615). While I agree that the term "aesthetics" should encompass more than it does, the reality of the Western hegemonic control (particularly in the arts) necessitates, I feel, the continued distinction.

18. Cynthia Jean Cohen Bull also published under the name Cynthia Novack.

19. Here Myers is presumably referencing the work of Malinowski. In his review of *Looking High and Low: Art and Cultural Identity,* edited by Brenda Jo Bright and Liza Bakewell (1995), Myers also suggests that we should consider the productivity of ethno-aesthetics not just in what the West has overlooked as beautiful but also in what these boundaries of exclusion might tell us (F. Myers 1997, 166).

20. In yet another point of resonant rupture, the elision of aesthetic and theological systems is a long-held principle of the Navajo Way as well (McAllester 1954; Witherspoon 1977).

21. Again, by Pentecostal I mean to indicate that the Oodlání derive their theology from the same charismatic revivals that led to the founding of denominational Pentecostalism (such as the Assemblies of God). Like other decentralized churches within global neo-Pentecostalism, the Oodlání movement is not formally Pentecostal in the sense that they are not bound to any kind of centrally organized or denominational Pentecostalism.

22. This "yielding" is much the same as described for musicians in the previous chapter.

23. Early Franciscan missionaries attempted to codify the Navajo term for the Judeo-Christian God as "*Diyin 'Ayói 'Át'éii*" (*diyin*, "holy"; *'ayói*, "exceedingly"; *'át'éii*, "that which is"), in consultation with local Navajos (Bodo 1998, 4).

This term does not seem to have been adopted by contemporary Oodlání. Neither are the terms for God mentioned by Aberle in the Native American Church context (*nítchi diyiní*, "Holy Spirit"; *diyin aláájí*, "first holy one"; or *diyin binant'a'í*, "boss holy one"; Aberle 1991, 153).

24. Although I do not have space to develop this argument in full, I feel that this "letting go of control" is different from the transparency of artistry discussed by Royce (2004).

25. The use of aesthetic forms (such as testimony narration) in determining the authenticity of a spirit-filled experience has also been discussed by Lawless (1988b).

26. For foundational writing on the indigenous category of nonhuman actors, see the work of Irving Hallowell, especially "Ojibwa Ontology, Behavior, and Worldview" (1975).

27. As mentioned in previous chapters, new research on Navajo traditional religion by outsiders is strongly discouraged by the Navajo Nation and I conducted none. All information on Navajo traditional religion in this chapter comes from well-known published sources such as Haile 1938; Kluckhohn and Wyman 1940; Reichard 1963; Gill 1981; Werner et al. 1983; Wyman 1983; Frisbie 1987; and Vecsey 1991. The perspectives of Navajo scholars, such as Aronilth 1994, Faris and Walters 1990, and Lee 2014, are included as well.

28. Reichard states: "[The deities] brought them into being and designated, through long suffering and teaching of one object lesson after another, the control man should exert over himself and his natural surroundings. Through them he learned what was good and what was harmful, and how evils and dangers could be converted to good" (1963, 49).

29. In describing the complex world of supernatural beings among traditional Navajos, Reichard identifies three main categories of deities: *yé'ii, haashch'éé*, and *diyinii*. Among the *diyinii* are beings such as Changing Woman, Sun, Talking God, Monster Slayer, Thunders and Winds (Reichard 1963, 51). Aronilth emphasizes Changing Woman, Talking God, divine nature, and the 12 Holy People (1994, 92) as the *Diyin Diné'é* who guide the people but also mentions that Holy People encompass "Forty-eight Holy People, Six Sacred Mountains, Four Directions of Life, [and] Four Divine Elements" (Aronilth 1994, 14).

30. For details on how Holy People are persuaded, see the discussion of prayer and offerings in chapter 2.

31. According to Frisbie, "Only those who die of old age and those infants who die before using their voices are not credited with *ch'įįdiii*" (Frisbie 1978, 304).

32. Reichard states: "The dead body, the house where the person dies, things in contact with the body are *ch'įįdii*—that is, full of dreaded power, potentiality for evil" (1963, 48–49).

33. This "ghost fear" was such an integral part of traditional Navajo worldview that Reichard named it a "tribal phobia" (1949, 67).

34. Fieldnotes, June 2, 2008.

35. Fieldnotes, June 9, 2007.

36. Fieldnotes, June 9, 2007.

37. Fieldnotes, June 4, 2008.

38. A possible exception to this generalization may lie in the role of the Navajo diagnostician, called a "hand-trembler," who may use shamanic-style practices to divine the source of illnesses. See Milne and Howard (2000).

39. For details on this reciprocal obligation, see chapter 2.

40. As a vast literature in New World devil studies has shown, it is important to look carefully at the way supernatural actors, such as demons or the Devil, are conceived by indigenous actors instead of assuming a Western European image of the Devil. Sometimes, as in Kozak and Lopez (1999), they appear as "phantasms to humans—as wealthy cattlemen or ranchers—but they also appear as ordinary cowboys" (7). See also Taussig's landmark work (1980) and other literature that expands on Taussig's materialist approach to devil lore (Harris 1982; Ingham 1986; Behar 1987; Silverblatt 1987; Crain 1991; Edelman 1994).

41. Although not specifically discussing charismatic Christians, Reichard first made this distinction between the non-personified *ch'įįdii* of traditional Navajo religion and the personified "ghost" or "devil" English-language gloss (1963, 48).

42. Helpers are always on hand at tent revivals to help ease the dancers to the ground and to cover them with red cloths to protect their modesty while they lie sprawled on the ground. Helpers can also help to make sure that dancers who have been slain are not stepped on by dancers who are still filled with the spirit and oblivious to their surroundings. In a really large service with a good evangelist this can be quite a task, requiring many hands.

6. Embodying Healing

1. See also Lamphere (1977), Witherspoon (1977), Farella (1984), and Levy (1998).

2. Sometimes these chants are accompanied by a rattle or small drum. But they are sonically quite different from Native American Church songs.

3. Steven Feld has called this sensual and bodily way of knowing through the experiencing of sound *acoustemology* (Feld 1994, 11).

4. In the late 1990s the contemporary interactions among these three modes of religious healing (traditional ceremonial, NAC, and "Christian") were investigated by a team of researchers led by anthropologist Thomas Csordas, called the "Navajo Healing Project." This team consisted of ethnographers, paired with Navajo partners, dispersed to the four corners of the Navajo Nation to conduct team-based research on the cultural system of healing utilized by contemporary Navajos (Csordas 2000, 466). In part, this project was important for emphasizing the centrality of faith healing in explaining the spread of Christianity among Navajos, a connection that Csordas points out had been "virtually neglected" (Csordas 2000, 466). The proj-

ect yielded several impressive results, including establishing the simultaneous co-utilization of several healing systems by most Navajos (Lamphere 2000). But despite good intentions, and partly due to its vast scope, the project continued to emphasize traditional and NAC modes of healing to the exclusion of Christianity (see, for example, Milne and Howard 2000), or to elide differences between different forms of Christianity.

5. As introduced in previous chapters, resonant rupture explains how the anti-traditional breaks inherent in conversion to Pentecostalism can be enriched by "feelingfully" familiar aesthetic or cultural forms.

6. See also Garrity (2000, 533).

7. In using the term *matrix* (rather than *philosophy* or *worldview*), I draw upon Lloyd Lee (2014a, 3) and Cordova (2007).

8. They assert that this continuity of SNBH through the restoration of relationships holds for NAC healing as well.

9. The concept of SNBH has been explored by numerous scholars, both Navajo and non-Navajo. See, for instance, Haile 1943, Reichard 1963, Witherspoon 1974, Wyman 1975, Farella 1984, Lewton and Bydone 2000, and L. Lee 2014a.

10. An etiology is a theory of causation, an explanation for why things happen. In medical anthropology, etiology refers specifically to the factors that are believed to cause illness. Understanding why people think they get sick is important when studying why they believe certain curing practices to be efficacious.

11. Due to modesty concerns both Navajo and Pentecostal, a male usher in this role would have been improper.

12. Lewton and Bydone do recognize the role of congregants as vessels in the healing process (2000, 489).

13. See SNBH as discussed earlier by Lewton and Bydone (2000).

14. See also Schwarz (2008, 10) and Aberle (1982, 219).

15. According to Navajo linguist Lorraine Begay Manave, the phrase *Shi'doolzii'* uses a form of the verb *yisį́į'* and can mean "I was blessed," specifically by having paraphernalia pressed against one (letter to author, November 9, 2010).

16. Fieldnotes, February 10, 2008.

17. Alternately, it is known as *Diyingo ak'ah* (*Diyin,* "holy"; *ak'ah,* "oil"), or holy oil.

18. Corn pollen does have a wider range of symbolic associations, including the personification as *Tádídíín Ashkii,* "Pollen Boy," one of the twelve divinities who can aid Diné (Wyman 1975, 31; Aronilth 1994). According to Aronilth, Corn Pollen Boy represents Diné mental ability (1994, 9).

19. There may be, in practice, some variation in how clearly this distinction is understood among Oodlání.

20. Corn pollen (like the "drums" and "feathers" mentioned in previous chapters) appears to be a material substance, the meaning of which is not ambig-

uous enough to allow for the attachment of new meanings. Distinctions like this highlight how discursively created these "assertions" are (Nevins 2010).

21. Fieldnotes, August 12, 2007.

22. This massive production of discourse surrounding illness and healing found in testimony is in direct contrast to traditionally held Navajo beliefs about the power and efficacy of language. Because of the strong connections between thought, speech, and effect (explored in chapter 2), traditionally oriented Navajos engage in talk about illness cautiously. As one hand-trembler (diagnostician) told Milne and Howard, she was reluctant to discuss the health problems of her patients because, they report, this talk "could undo the healing and have a deleterious effect on the patient" (2000, 564). Milne and Howard point out that narration of the underlying causes of the illness could also (along this same principle) have efficacy in healing. But Oodlání do not just "narrativize" the underlying causes in order to change their thinking (at the root of traditional healing etiologies; Milne and Howard 2000, 565). Oodlání testimonies "narrativize" the illness as well.

23. This structure of verbal improvisation is common to many forms of oral literature, referred to by folklorists as "oral-formulaic" composition (Lord 1960; Foley 1995).

24. This movement, which grew out of the teaching of healing evangelists like Oral Roberts, William Branham, and A. A. Allen, has been popularized by Kenneth Hagin and Kenneth Copeland (see Anderson 2004, 220–24).

25. These phrases are taken not from an interview but directly from a field recording of the public testimony given by Billie Yazzie. Although this testimony was given in public and I had the permission of the pastor to be recording the service, I have used a pseudonym in order to protect this person's identity. Her testimony, full of hesitations and false starts, is typical of the hundreds of other healing testimonies I observed and the dozens I recorded during my research. She makes particularly high use of common stock phrases.

26. According to Harding, this is the linguistic aspect of what fundamentalist Christians call "coming under conviction" (Harding 2000, 34).

27. For the full testimony, see Marshall (2011a, 205–11). Structurally, the testimony emphasizes stock phrases over plot. Passage one suggests that something miraculous has happened, which passage two elaborates slightly. But then passage three diverges from the storyline, and passages four through eight become simply affirmations of the power of God. The details of the actual event are slow to emerge, and even the crux of the story (being in the hospital in Phoenix) in passages eight through eleven is scattered through with phrases of affirmation, rather than plot.

28. Oodlání do recognize natural causes for disease as well (i.e., smoking causes lung cancer). But for non-natural illness, their etiology is quite different from other religious healing etiologies among Navajos.

29. Another possible category of stock phrases deals with the theme of the appropriate orientation of the believer, given this experience with heal-

ing. This category includes phrases like "I'm not ashamed of my God," and "I'm an example for God" as well as suggestions that one should witness about these things.

30. The following story is paraphrased from Kelly (2008), quotation being Lynda's own words.

31. Fieldnotes, April 27, 2008. Clearly there are resonant connections as well to the "philosophy of obstacles" that Csordas mentions is central to traditional Navajo healing etiology. However, while an Oodlání healer can point out things that are "blocking up" a person's healing, the etiology ultimately remains unchanged. For Ooldání healing ultimately comes from God, who can overcome any demonic obstacle.

Conclusion

1. Fieldnotes, June 7, 2012.

2. A brief note on terms: global Pentecostalism as I (and others) use it includes three main branches. These are classical Pentecostal denominations (Assemblies of God, Church of God in Christ, or Brazil-based Universal Church of the Kingdom of God); charismatic movements within Catholicism or mainline Protestantism; and those I have referred to throughout this book as neo-Pentecostals—people who practice charismatic gifts but do not identify with any centralized denomination (including Pentecostalism). Many studies treat these populations together, because they seem to reflect a fairly coherent religious view and the lines between them are not always clear (they all attend one another's revivals, after all). For instance, the 2006 study of Pentecostalism in ten countries conducted by the Pew Forum on Religion and Public Life grouped all these global Pentecostal believers together as "Renewalists."

3. For ethnographies documenting Pentecostalism in Africa, see Kiernan (1992), Meyer (1998), van Dijk (1998), and Kalu (2008). For ethnographies documenting Pentecostalism in Central and South America, see Berger (1990), Martin (1990), Stoll (1990), Bowen (1996), Löwy (1996), Chestnut (1997), Cleary and Stewart-Gambino (1997), Smith (1998), Freston (2001), and Steigenga (2001).

4. These nations included Brazil (49 percent), Chile (30 percent), Guatemala (60 percent), Kenya (56 percent), Nigeria (26 percent), South Africa (34 percent), and the Philippines (44 percent).

5. East and Southeast Asia, as well as Oceania, represent other areas where a robust ethnographic literature on global Pentecostalism exists. See, for example, Mark Mullins's (1994) description of Pentecostalism in Korea, Katharine Wiegele's (2005) description of charismatic Catholicism in the Philippines, and the work of Joel Robbins (2004a) and Courtney Handman (2010) in Papua New Guinea.

6. For Aberle, relative deprivation represented a mismatch between expected status and actual status (1991, 323).

7. From Pastor Wallace's Africa journal.

8. See Robbins (2004b, 123–27) for an excellent overview of this shift in scholarly orientation toward conversion.

9. Native evangelist cross-visiting also likely facilitated the spread of neo-Pentecostalism across Indian country. Several scholars have begun exploring the history and contemporary ethnography of these Native American neo-Pentecostal communities. See Clint Westman's work among Cree Pentecostal communities in Alberta (2010a; 2013); M. Eleanor Nevins's linguistic anthropological work among what she calls "Apache Independent Christians" (2010, and with T. J. Nevins 2009); and Robert Burkinshaw's work with Native Pentecostalism in British Columbia (2009). Both T. Eric Bates and Mark Clatterbuck have been conducting recent work with Blackfeet and Crow Pentecostals (unpublished). Many of these scholars were involved in a panel that I and Westman organized for the 2013 meeting of the American Anthropological Association.

10. Many scholars and missionaries have grappled with the proper criteria for defining "indigenous" Christianity, as reflected by the many Native voices represented in James Treat's (1996) collection. See also the work of Kidwell et al. (2001) and Tarango (2014).

11. According to Gerlach and Hine (1970), global Pentecostalism is decentralized, segmentary, and reticulate. It is "characterized both by a lack of centralized authority able to question the propriety of local evangelical efforts and by a web-like structure of personal connections that allows members to easily find support in new locales" (in Robbins 2004b, 125).

12. Although Bigpond's shirt is traditionally Yuchi (Jackson 2013, 126–28), his tribe is not a group that would traditionally have worn a plains-style headdress. Bigpond is here either indexing an Oklahoma identity (where Yuchi/Creek people were relocated during the Removal Era) or referencing a generalized pan-Indian plains identity popularized through Hollywood images. Pastor Wallace's outfit, however, is clearly marked as distinctly Navajo.

13. This connection to the "tribal" people of the Bible is often further interpreted by Bigpond (and Pastor Wallace) as an explicit connection to the modern nation of Israel. For more on the relationship between the "territorial dominion" of Native People and their efficacy as spiritual warriors through this theology, see McAlister 2016.

14. As McAlister puts it, "The fact that tribal groups join white evangelicals in recasting ancestral spirits as demonic, only to take up leadership in that project . . . is also a symptom of profound dispossession" (McAlister 2016, 15).

REFERENCES

Aberle, David F. 1967. "The Navajo Singer's Fee: Payment or Prestation." In *Studies in Southwestern Ethnolinguistics: Meaning and History in the Languages of the American Southwest*, ed. Dell Hymes, 15–32. Paris: Mouton and Company.

———. 1982. "The Future of Navajo Religion." In *Navajo Religion and Culture: Selected Views*, ed. David M. Brugge and Charlotte J. Frisbie, 219–31. Santa Fe: Museum of New Mexico.

———. (1966) 1991. *The Peyote Religion among the Navaho*. Norman: University of Oklahoma Press.

Adams, David W. 1995. *Education for Extinction: American Indians and the Boarding School Experience, 1875–1928*. Lawrence: University Press of Kansas.

Alexander, Corky. 2012. *Native American Pentecost: Praxis, Contextualization, Transformation*. Cleveland TN: Cherohala Press.

Alfred, Taiaiake. 2002. "Sovereignty." In *A Companion to American Indian History*, ed. P. J. Deloria and N. Salisbury, 460–74. Malden MA: Blackwell.

Amster, Matthew H. 2009. "Portable Potency: Christianity, Mobility and Spiritual Landscapes among the Kelabit." *Anthropological Forum* 19(3): 307–22.

Anderson, Allan. 2004. *An Introduction to Pentecostalism: Global Charismatic Christianity*. New York: Cambridge University Press.

Aronilth, Wilson Jr. 1994. *Diné Bi Bee Óhoo'aah Bá Silá: An Introduction to Navajo Philosophy*. Tsaile: Center for Diné Studies.

Asad, Talal. 1993. *Genealogies of Religion: Discipline and Reasons of Power in Christianity and Islam*. Baltimore MD: John Hopkins University Press.

Austin, J. L. 1970. *Philosophical Papers*. 2nd edition. Oxford: Oxford University Press.

Baldridge, Terry. 2000. "Navajo Christian Worship and Music: The Struggle for Cultural Relevance." Master's thesis, Crown College.

Bastian, Jean Pierre. 1993. "The Metamorphosis of Latin American Protestant Groups: A Sociohistorical Perspective." *Latin American Research Review* 28: 33–61.

Bauman, Richard. 1975. "Verbal Art as Performance." *American Anthropologist* 77(2): 290–311.

——. 2004. *A World of Other's Words: Cross-Cultural Perspectives on Intertextuality.* Malden MA: Wiley-Blackwell.

Begay, Fred. 2008. Interview with Kimberly J. Marshall. July 20.

Begay, Wallace. 2008a. Interview with Kimberly J. Marshall. June 25.

——. 2008b. Interview with Kimberly J. Marshall. July 17.

——. 2008c. Sermon. July 20.

——. 2012. Interview with Kimberly J. Marshall. June 25.

Bahr, Donald. 2001. "Bad News: The Predicament of Native American Mythology." *Ethnohistory* 48(4): 587–612.

Behar, Ruth. 1987. "Sex and Sin, Witchcraft and the Devil in Late-Colonial Mexico." *American Ethnologist* 14(1): 34–54.

Bender, Margaret. 2009. "Visibility, Authenticity, and Insiderness in Cherokee Language Ideologies." In *Native American Language Ideologies: Beliefs, Practices, and Struggles in Indian Country* ed. Paul V. Kroskrity and Margaret C. Field, 123–47. Tucson: University of Arizona Press.

Berger, Peter. 1990. Forward. In *Tongues of Fire: The Explosion of Protestantism in Latin America,* by David Martin. Oxford: Basil Blackwell.

Bernard, H. Russell. 1994. *Research Methods in Cultural Anthropology.* 2nd edition. Newbury Park CA: Sage Publications.

Bielo, James. 2011. *Emerging Evangelicals: Faith, Modernity, and Authenticity.* New York: NYU Press.

——. 2015. *Anthropology of Religion: The Basics.* New York: Routledge.

Blanchard, Kendall. 1977. *The Economics of Sainthood: Religious Change among the Rimrock Navajos.* Rutherford NJ: Fairleigh Dickinson University Press.

Blumhofer, Edith. 1993. *Aimee Semple McPherson: Everybody's Sister.* Grand Rapids MI: Eardmans.

Boas, Franz. 1887. "Museums of Ethnology and Their Classification." *Science* 9:589.

——. 1955. *Primitive Art.* New York: Dover Publications.

Bodo, Fr. Murray. 1998. *Tales of an Endishodi: Father Berard Haile and the Navajos, 1900–1960s.* Albuquerque: University of New Mexico Press.

Bowen, Kurt Derek. 1996. *Evangelism and Apostasy: The Evolution and Impact of Evangelicals in Modern Mexico.* McGill-Queen's Studies in the History of Religion 23. Montréal: McGill-Queen's University Press.

Bourdieu, Pierre. 1977. *Outline of a Theory of Practice.* Trans. Richard Nice. Cambridge: Cambridge University Press.

Briggs, Charles L. 1996. "The Politics of Discursive Authority in Research on the 'Invention of Tradition.'" *Cultural Anthropology* 11(4): 435–69.

Browning, Barbara. 1995. *Samba: Resistance in Motion.* Bloomington: Indiana University Press.

Brugge, David M. 2010. *Navajos in the Catholic Church Records of New Mexico, 1694–1875.* Santa Fe: School for Advanced Research Press.

Bryant, Elizabeth. 2008. Interview with Kimberly J. Marshall. July 12.

Bull, Cynthia Jean Cohen. 1997. "Sense, Meaning, and Perception in Three

Dance Cultures." In *Meaning in Motion: New Cultural Studies of Dance*, ed. Jane C. Desmond, 269–87. Durham NC: Duke University Press.

Burkinshaw, Robert K. 2009. "Native Pentecostalism in British Columbia." In *Canadian Pentecostalism: Transition and Transformation* ed. Michael Wilkinson, 142–70. Montreal: McGill-Queen's University Press.

Burnim, Mellonee. 2006. "The Gospel Music Industry." In *African American Music: An Introduction*, ed. Mellonee Burnim and Portia Maultsby, 416–26. New York: Routledge.

Cajete, Gregory. 2014. Foreword. In *Diné Perspectives: Revitalizing and Reclaiming Navajo Thought*, ed. Lloyd L. Lee, ix–xi. Tucson: University of Arizona Press.

Casanova, José. 2001. "Religion, the New Millennium, and Globalization." *Sociology of Religion* 62(4): 415–41.

Cattelino, Jessica R. 2008. *High Stakes: Florida Seminole Gaming and Sovereignty*. Durham NC: Duke University Press.

Chesnut, R. Andrew. 1997. *Born Again in Brazil: The Pentecostal Boom and the Pathogens of Poverty*. New Brunswick NJ: Rutgers University Press.

Chua, Liana. 2012. "Conversion, Continuity, and Moral Dilemmas among Christian Bidayuhs in Malaysian Borneo." *American Ethnologist* 39(3): 511–26.

Cleary, Edward L., and Hannah W. Stewart-Gambino. 1997. *Power, Politics, and Pentecostals in Latin America*. Boulder CO: Westview Press.

Cobb, Amanda. 2005. "Understanding Tribal Sovereignty: Definitions, Conceptualizations, and Interpretations." Special issue: Indigeneity at the Crossroads of American Studies, *American Studies* 46(3–4): 115–32; co-published as joint issue with *Indigenous Studies Today*, no.1 (2005–6).

Coleman, Simon. 2000. *The Globalisation of Charismatic Christianity: Spreading the Gospel of Prosperity*. Cambridge: Cambridge University Press.

Comaroff, Jean, and John Comaroff. 1991. *Of Revelation and Revolution: Christianity, Colonialism, and Consciousness in South Africa*. Chicago: University of Chicago Press.

Coote, Jeremy. 1995. "Indiscipline and Indigestion: A Reply to Whitten and Whitten." *American Ethnologist* 22(3): 615–16.

Coplan, David B. 1988. "Musical Understanding: The Ethnoaesthetics of Migrant Workers' Poetic Song in Lesotho." *Ethnomusicology* 32(3): 337–68.

Cordova, Viola F. 2007. *How It Is: The Native American Philosophy of V. F. Cordova*. Tucson: University of Arizona Press.

Corten, André. 1997. "The Growth of the Literature on Afro-American, Latin American and African Pentecostalism." *Journal of Contemporary Religion* 12: 311–34.

Crain, Mary M. 1991. "Poetics and Politics in the Ecuadorean Andes: Women's Narratives of Death and Devil Possession." *American Ethnologist* 18(1): 67–89.

Csordas, Thomas. 1999. "Ritual Healing and the Politics of Identity in Contemporary Navajo Society." *American Ethnologist* 26(1): 3–23.

———. 2000. "The Navajo Healing Project." *Medical Anthropology Quarterly* 14(4): 463-75.

———. 2002. *Body/Meaning/Healing*. New York: Palgrave Macmillan.

———. 2004. "Healing and the Human Condition: Scenes from the Present Movement at Navajo Land." *Medicine and Psychiatry* 28: 1-14.

———. 2009. "Introduction: Modalities of Transnational Transcendence." In *Transnational Transcendence: Essays on Religion and Globalization*, ed. Thomas Csordas, 1-29. Berkeley: University of California Press.

D'Epinay, Christian. 1969. *Haven of the Masses: A Study of the Pentecostal Movement in Chile*. London: Lutterworth.

Daswani, Girish. 2013 "On Christianity and Ethics: Rupture as Ethical Practice in Ghanaian Pentecostalism." *American Ethnologist* 40(3): 467-79.

Denetdale, Jennifer Nez. 2007. *Reclaiming Diné History: The Legacies of Navajo Chief Manuelito and Juanita*. Tucson: University of Arizona Press.

———. 2014. "The Value of Oral History on the Path to Diné/Navajo Sovereignty." In *Diné Perspectives: Revitalizing and Reclaiming Navajo Thought*, ed. Lloyd L. Lee, 68-82. Tucson: University of Arizona Press.

Dent, Alexander. 2009. *River of Tears: Country Music, Memory, and Modernity in Brazil*. Durham NC: Duke University Press.

Desjarlais, Robert. 1992. *Body and Emotion: The Aesthetics of Illness and Healing in the Nepal Himalayas*. Philadelphia: University of Pennsylvania Press.

DiBernardi, Jean. 1999. "Spiritual Warfare and Territorial Spirits: The Globalization and Localization of a 'Practical Theology.'" *Religious Studies and Theology* 18(2): 66-96.

Dijk, Rijk van. 1998. "Pentecostalism, Cultural Memory, and the State: Contested Representations of Time in Pentecostal Malawi." In *Memory and the Postcolony: African Anthropology and the Critique of Power*, ed. R. Werbner, 155-81. London: Zed Books.

Dolaghan, Thomas, and David Scates. 1978. *The Navajos Are Coming to Jesus*. Pasadena: William Carey Library.

Dombrowski, Kirk. 2001. *Against Culture: Development, Politics, and Religion in Indian Alaska*. Fourth World Rising. Lincoln: University of Nebraska Press.

Domingo, Jerry. 2012. Interview with Kimberly J. Marshall. June 7.

Donovan, Bill. 2011. "Census: Navajo Enrollment Tops 300,000." *Navajo Times*, July 7.

Edelman, Marc. 1994. "Landlords and the Devil: Class, Ethnic, and Gender Dimensions of Central American Peasant Narratives." *Cultural Anthropology* 9(1): 58-93.

Emerson, Larry. 2008. Interview with Kimberly J. Marshall. June 7.

———. 2014. "Diné Culture, Decolonization, and the Politics of Hózhǫ́." In *Diné Perspectives: Revitalizing and Reclaiming Navajo Thought*, ed. Lloyd L. Lee, 49-67. Tucson: University of Arizona Press.

Engelke, Matthew. 2007. *A Problem of Presence: Beyond Scripture in an Afri-*

can Church. The Anthropology of Christianity. Berkeley: University of California Press.

———. 2010. "Past Pentecostalism: Notes on Rupture, Realignment, and Everyday Life in Pentecostal and African Independent Churches." *Africa* 80(2): 177–99.

Epple, Carolyn, Frank Morgan, and Mark Bauer. 1997. Implications of *Tad ho djit'eego* for Navajo Diabetics. Paper presented to the American Anthropological Association meetings, Washington DC.

Farella, John R. 1984. *The Main Stalk: A Synthesis of Navajo Philosophy*. Tucson: University of Arizona Press.

Faris, James C. 1990. *The Nightway: A History and a History of Documentation of a Navajo Ceremonial*. Albuquerque: University of New Mexico Press.

Faris, James, and Harry Walters. 1990. "Navajo History: Some Implications of Contrasts of Navajo Ceremonial Discourse." *History and Anthropology* 5: 1–18.

Fear-Segal, Jacqueline. 2007. *White Man's Club: Schools, Race, and the Struggle of Indian Acculturation*. Lincoln: University of Nebraska Press.

Feld, Steven. 1994. "From Ethnomusicology to Echo-Muse-Ecology: Reading R. Murray Schafer in the Papua New Guinea Rainforest." *Soundscape Newsletter* (8): 9–13. June.

Field, Margaret C. 2009. "Changing Navajo Language Ideologies and Changing Language Use." In *Native American Language Ideologies: Beliefs, Practices, and Struggles in Indian Country*, ed. Paul V. Kroskrity and Margaret C. Field, 31–47. Tucson: University of Arizona Press.

Field, Margaret, and Taft Blackhorse Jr. 2002. "The Dual Role of Metonymy in Navajo Prayer." *Anthropological Linguistics* 44(3): 217–30.

Field, Margaret C., and Paul V. Kroskrity. 2009. "Introduction: Revealing Native American Language Ideologies." In *Native American Language Ideologies: Beliefs, Practices, and Struggles in Indian Country* ed. Paul V. Kroskrity and Margaret C. Field, 3–30. Tucson: University of Arizona Press.

Foley, John Miles. 1995. *The Singer of Tales in Performance*. Bloomington: Indiana University Press.

Fox, Aaron. 2004. *Real Country: Music and Language in Working Class Culture*. Durham NC: Duke University Press

Francis, Sandra Toni. 1996. "The Ye'ii Bicheii Dancing of the Nightway: An Examination of the Role of Dance in a Navajo Healing Ceremony." PhD diss., Ohio State University.

Freston, Paul. 2001. *Evangelicals and Politics in Asia, Africa, and Latin America*. New York: Cambridge University Press.

Frisbie, Charlotte J. 1978. "Introduction: A Special Symposium Issue on Navajo Mortuary Practices and Beliefs." *American Indian Quarterly* 4(4): 303–8.

———. 1980. "Ritual Drama in the Navajo House Blessing Ceremony." In

Southwestern Indian Ritual Drama, ed. Charlotte Frisbie, 161–98. School of American Research Book. Albuquerque: University of New Mexico Press.

———. 1987. *Navajo Medicine Bundles or Jish: Acquisition, Transmission, and Disposition in the Past and Present*. Albuquerque: University of New Mexico Press.

———. 1992. "Temporal Change in Navajo Religion: 1868-1990." *Journal of the Southwest* 34(4): 457–514.

Garrity, John F. 2000. "Jesus, Peyote, and the Holy People: Alcohol Abuse and the Ethos of Power in Navajo Healing." Theme issue: Ritual Healing in Navajo Society. *Medical Anthropology Quarterly* 14(4): 521–42.

Geertz, Clifford. 1973. *The Interpretation of Cultures: Selected Essays*. New York: Basic Books.

Gelo, Daniel. 2005. "Powwow Patter: Indian Emcee Discourse on Power and Identity." In *Powwow*, ed. Clyde Ellis, Luke Eric Lassiter, and Gary H. Dunham, 130–51. Lincoln: University of Nebraska Press.

Gerlach, Luther, and Virginia Hine. 1970. *People, Power, Change: Movements of Social Transformation*. Indianapolis: Bobbs-Merrill.

Gill, Sam D. 1974. "A Theory of Navajo Prayer Acts: A Study in Ritual Symbolism." PhD diss., University of Chicago Divinity School.

———. 1981. *Sacred Words: A Study of Navajo Religion and Prayer*. Westport CT: Greenwood Press.

———. 1987. *Native American Religious Action: A Performance Approach to Religion*. Columbia: University of South Carolina Press.

Glassie, Henry. 1986. "The Idea of Folk Art." In *Folk Art and Art Worlds*, ed. John M. Vlach and Simon J. Bronner, 269–74. Ann Arbor MI: UMI Research Press.

Goldstein, Kenneth. 1991. "Notes toward a European-American Folk Aesthetic: Lessons Learned from Singers and Storytellers I Have Known." *Journal of American Folklore* 104(412): 164–78.

Haile, Berard. 1938. *Origin Legends of the Navajo Enemy Way*. Yale University Publications in Anthropology 17. New Haven: Yale University Press.

———. 1943. "Soul Concepts of the Navajo." *Annali Lateranensi* 7: 59–94.

Hallowell, A. Irving. 1975. "Ojibwa Ontology, Behavior, and Worldview." In *Teachings from the American Earth: Indian Religion and Philosophy*, ed. Dennis Tedlock and Barbara Tedlock, 141–78. New York: Liveright.

Hamera, Judith. 2007. *Dancing Communities: Performance, Difference and Connection in the Global City*. New York: Palgrave Macmillan.

Handelman, Don. 2007. "Bureaucratic Logic, Bureaucratic Aesthetics: The Opening Event of Holocaust Martyrs and Heroes Remembrance Day in Israel." In *Aesthetics in Performance: Formations of Symbolic Construction and Experience*, ed. Angela Hobart and Bruce Kapferer, 196–15. New York: Berghahn Books.

Handler, Richard, and Jocelyn Linnekin. 1984. "Tradition: Genuine or Spurious." *Journal of American Folklore* 97(385): 273–90.

Handman, Courtney. 2010. "Events of Translation: Intertextuality and Christian Ethno-Theologies of Change among Guhu-Samane, Papua New Guinea." *American Anthropologist* 112(4): 576–88.

Harding, Susan Friend. 2000. *The Book of Jerry Falwell: Fundamentalist Language and Politics.* Princeton NJ: Princeton University Press.

Harkin, Michael. 1993. "Power and Progress: The Evangelic Dialogue among the Heiltsuk." *Ethnohistory* 40(1): 1–33.

———. 2004. "Introduction: Revitalization as History and Theory." *Reassessing Revitalization Movements: Perspectives from North America and the Pacific Islands,* ed. Michael E. Harkin, xv–xxxvi. Lincoln: University of Nebraska Press.

Harrell, David Edwin. 1975. *All Things Are Possible: The Healing and Charismatic Revivals in Modern America.* Bloomington: Indiana University Press.

Harris, Olivia. 1982. "The Dead and the Devils among the Bolivian Laymi." In *Death and the Regeneration of Life,* ed. Maurice Bloch and Jonathan Parry, 45–73. Cambridge: Cambridge University Press.

Herskovits, Melville. 1950. "Possession." In *Funk and Wagnalls Standard Dictionary of Folklore, Mythology, and Legend,* ed. Maria Leach and Jerome Fried, 881–82. New York: Funk and Wagnalls.

Hodge, William. 1964. "Navaho Pentecostalism." *Anthropological Quarterly* 37(3): 73–93.

House, Deborah. 2002. *Language Shift among the Navajos: Identity Politics and Cultural Continuity.* Tucson: University of Arizona Press.

Hymes, Dell. 1981. *In Vain I Tried to Tell You.* Philadelphia: University of Pennsylvania Press.

Indian Health Service. 2003. *Regional Differences in Indian Health, 2002-2003 Edition.* Washington DC: U.S. Department of Health and Human Services.

Ingalls, Monique, and Amos Yong, eds. 2015. *In the Spirit of Praise: Music and Worship in Global Pentecostal-Charismatic Christianity.* University Park PA: Penn State University Press.

Ingham, John M. 1986. *Mary, Michael, and Lucifer: Folk Catholicism in Central Mexico.* Austin: University of Texas Press.

Iverson, Peter. 2002. *Diné: A History of the Navajos.* Albuquerque: University of New Mexico Press.

Jackson, Jason Baird. 2004. "Recontextualizing Revitalization: Cosmology and Cultural Stability in the Adoption of Peyotism among the Yuchi." In *Reassessing Revitalization Movements,* ed. Michael Harkin, 183–205. Lincoln: University of Nebraska Press.

———. 2013. *Yuchi Folklore: Cultural Expression in a Southeastern Native American Community.* Norman: University of Oklahoma Press.

Jacobs, Adrian. 1996. "The Meeting of the Two Ways." In *Native and Christian: Indigenous Voices on Religious Identity in the United States and Canada,* ed. James Treat, 184–90. New York: Routledge.

Jacobsen, Kristina. 2009. "Rita(hhh): Placemaking and Country Music on the Navajo Nation." *Ethnomusicology* 53 (3): 449–77.

———. 2012. "Navajo Voices: Country Music and the Politics of Language and Belonging." PhD diss., Duke University.

Jacobsen Bia, Kristina. Forthcoming. *Indian Cowboy: Country Music and the Politics of Indigenous Belonging.* Chapel Hill: University of North Carolina Press.

Jenkins, Philip. 2002. *The Next Christendom: The Coming of Global Christianity.* Oxford: Oxford University Press.

Joe, Beverly. 2008. Interview with Kimberly J. Marshall. July 6.

Joe, Eugene. 2008. Interview with Kimberly J. Marshall. May 7.

Joe, Layne. 2014. Interview with Kimberly J. Marshall. June 12.

Joe, Naomi. 2008. Interview with Kimberly J. Marshall. April 16.

Jones, Michael Owen. 1987. *Exploring Folk Art.* Logan: Utah State University Press.

Kaeppler, Adrienne L. 1967. "The Structure of Tongan Dance." PhD diss., University of Hawaii.

———. 1985. "Structured Movement Systems in Tonga." In *Society and the Dance: The Social Anthropology of Process and Performance,* ed. Paul Spencer, 92–118. Cambridge: Cambridge University Press.

Kalu, Ogbu. 2008. *African Pentecostalism: An Introduction.* Oxford: Oxford University Press.

Kan, Sergei. 1999. *Memory Eternal: Tlingit Culture and Russian Orthodox Christianity through Two Centuries.* Seattle: University of Washington Press.

Kealiinohomoku, Joann. (1969) 1983. "An Anthropologist Looks at Ballet as a Form of Ethnic Dance." In *What Is Dance? Readings in Theory and Criticism,* ed. Roger Copeland and Marshall Cohen, 533–49. Oxford: Oxford University Press.

Keane, Webb. 2007. *Christian Moderns: Freedom and Fetish in the Mission Encounter.* Berkeley: University of California Press.

Kelly, Lynda. 2008. Interview with Kimberly J. Marshall. June 27.

Kidwell, Clara Sue. 1997. *Choctaws and Missionaries in Mississippi: 1818–1918.* Norman: University of Oklahoma Press.

Kidwell, Clara Sue, Homer Noley, and George Tinker. 2001. *A Native American Theology.* Maryknoll NY: Orbis Books.

Kiernan, Jim. 1992. "The Herder and the Rustler: Deciphering the Affinity between Zulu Diviner and Zionist Prophet." *African Studies* 51: 231–42.

———. 1994. "Variation on a Christian Theme: The Healing Synthesis of Zulu Zionism." In *Syncretism/Anti-Syncretism: The Politics of Religious Synthesis,* ed. Charles Stewart and Rosalind Shaw, 69–84. London: Routledge.

King, Larry. 2008. Interview with Kimberly J. Marshall. June 16.

Kluckhohn, Clyde, and Dorothea Leighton. 1946. *The Navaho.* London: Harvard University Press.

Kluckhohn, Clyde, and Leland C. Wyman. 1940. *An Introduction to Navajo Chant Practice.* Menasha WI: American Anthropological Association Memoirs 53.

Kozak, David L., and David I. Lopez. 1999. *Devil Sickness and Devil Songs: Tohono O'odham Poetics*. Washington: Smithsonian Institution Press.

Kroskrity, Paul V. 2000. *Regimes of Language: Ideologies, Politics and Identities*. Santa Fe NM: School of American Research Press.

Kuntz, Richard. 2008. Interview with Kimberly J. Marshall. July 12.

Kurath, Gertrude P. 1960. "A Panorama of Dance Ethnology." *Current Anthropology* 1(3): 233–54.

Lampe Frederick P. 2010 "The Anthropology of Christianity: Context, Contestation, Rupture, and Continuity." *Reviews in Anthropology* 39: 66–88.

Lamphere, Louise. 1977. *To Run after Them: Cultural and Social Bases of Cooperation in a Navajo Community*. Tucson: University of Arizona Press.

——. 2000. "Comments on the Navajo Healing Project." Theme issue: Ritual Healing in Navajo Society. *Medical Anthropology Quarterly* 14(4): 598–602.

Landry, Alysa. 2014. Navajo Fluency Could Change Landscape of Navajo Election, Deschene Out? Indian Country Today Media Network. October 13.

Lange, Barbara R. 1996. "Gender Politics and Musical Performers in the Isten Gyülekezet: A Fieldwork Account." *Journal of American Folklore* 109(431): 60–76.

Lassiter, Luke E., Clyde Ellis, and Ralph Kotay. 2002. *The Jesus Road: Kiowas, Christianity, and Indian Hymns*. Lincoln: University of Nebraska Press.

Laugrand, Frederic, and Jarich Oosten. 2009. *Inuit Shamanism and Christianity: Transitions and Transformations in the Twentieth Century*. Montreal: McGill-Queens University Press.

Lawless, Elaine. 1988a. *God's Peculiar People: Women's Voices and Folk Tradition in a Pentecostal Church*. Lexington: Kentucky University Press.

——. 1988b. "'The Night I Got the Holy Ghost . . .': Holy Ghost Narratives and the Pentecostal Conversion Process." *Western Folklore* 47(1): 1–20.

——. 1992. "'I Was Afraid Someone Like You . . . An Outsider . . . Would Misunderstand': Negotiating Interpretive Differences between Ethnographers and Subjects." *Journal of American Folklore* 105(417): 302–14.

Lee, Lloyd. 2014a. Introduction. In *Diné Perspectives: Revitalizing and Reclaiming Navajo Thought*, ed. Lloyd L. Lee, 3–13. Tucson: University of Arizona Press.

——. 2014b. "The Navajo Nation and the Declaration of the Rights of Indigenous Peoples." In *Diné Perspectives: Revitalizing and Reclaiming Navajo Thought*, ed. Lloyd L. Lee, 170–86. Tucson: University of Arizona Press.

Lee, Tiffany S. 2014. "'If I Could Speak Navajo, I'd Definitely Speak It 24/7': Diné Youth Language Consciousness, Activism, and Reclamation of Diné Identity." In *Diné Perspectives: Revitalizing and Reclaiming Navajo Thought*, ed. Lloyd L. Lee, 158–70. Tucson: University of Arizona Press.

Levy, Jerrold. 1998. *In the Beginning: The Navajo Genesis*. Berkeley: University of California Press.

Lewis, Bonnie Sue. 2003. *Creating Christian Indians: Native Clergy in the Presbyterian Church*. Norman: University of Oklahoma Press.

Lewis, J. Lowell. 1995. "Genre and Embodiment: From Brazilian Capoeira to the Ethnology of Human Movement." *Cultural Anthropology* 10(2): 221-43.

Lewton, Elizabeth L., and Victoria Bydone. 2000. "Identity and Healing in Three Navajo Religious Traditions: *Są'ah Naaghá Bik'eh Hózhǫ́.*" *Medical Anthropology Quarterly* 14(4): 476-97.

Liardon, Roberts. 2011. *God's Generals: The Healing Evangelists.* New Kensington PA: Whitaker House.

Lord, Albert B. 1960. *The Singer of Tales.* Cambridge: Harvard University Press.

Löwy, Michael. 1996. *The War of Gods: Religion and Politics in Latin America.* New York: Verso.

Luhrman, Tanya. 2012. *When God Talks Back: Understanding the American Evangelical Relationship with God.* New York: Vintage Books.

Mack, Bill. 2004. *Bill Mack's Memories from the Trenches of Broadcasting.* Fort Worth TX: Unit II.

Mann, Darrell. 2008. Interview with Kimberly J. Marshall. July 20.

Manning, Frank E. 1980. "Pentecostalism: Christianity and Reputation." In *Perspectives on Pentecostalism: Case Studies from the Caribbean and Latin America,* ed. Stephen D. Glazier, 177-87. Lanham MD: University Press of America.

Marshall, Kimberly. 2011a. "Performing Conversion among the Diné Oodlání (Navajo Believers)." PhD diss., Indiana University.

———. 2011b. "Performing Christianity with Navajo 'Believers.'" *Anthropology News:* Society for North American Anthropology 51(8): 49-50.

———. 2015a. "'Navajo Reservation Camp Meeting A Great Success!': The Advent of *Diné* Pentecostalism after 1950." *Ethnohistory* 62: 1.

———. 2015b. "Non-Human Agency and Experiential Faith among *Diné Oodlání* ('Navajo Believers')." *Anthropologica* 57(2): 397-409.

Martin, David. 1990. *Tongues of Fire: The Explosion of Protestantism in Latin America.* Cambridge: Blackwell Press.

Martin, György, and Ernö Pésovar. 1961. "A Structural Analysis of Hungarian Folk Dance." *Acta Ethnografica Academiae Scientiarum Hungaricae* 10.

Matthews, Washington. 1888. "The Prayer of a Navajo Shaman." *American Anthropologist* 1(2): 149-71.

———. (1902) 1995. *The Night Chant.* Salt Lake City: University of Utah Press.

Mauss, Marcel. (1935) 2006. "Techniques of the Body." In Marcel Mauss, *Techniques, Technology, and Civilization,* ed. Nathan Schlanger 77-96. Oxford: Berghahn.

McAlister, Elizabeth. 2016. "The Militarization of Prayer in America: White and Native American Spiritual Warfare." *Journal of Religious and Political Practice* 2(1): 114-30.

McAllester, David P. 1954. *Enemy Way Music: A Study of Social and Esthetic Values as Seen in Navaho Music.* New Haven CT: Peabody Museum.

———. 1979. "The Astonished Ethno-Muse." *Ethnomusicology* 23(2): 179-89.

———. 1980. "Shootingway, an Epic Drama of the Navajos." In *Southwestern Indian Ritual Drama*, ed. Charlotte Frisbie, 199–238. School of American Research Book. Albuquerque: University of New Mexico Press.

———. 2002. "North America/Native America." In *Worlds of Music: An Introduction to the Music of the World's Peoples*, ed. Jeff Todd Titon, 33–82. Belmont CA: Schirmer/Thomson Learning.

McCleary, Timothy P. 2000. "An Ethnohistory of Pentecostalism among the Crow Indians of Montana." *Wicazo Ša Review* 15(1): 117–35.

McElwain, Thomas. 1990. "'The Rainbow Will Carry Me': The Langauge of Seneca Christianity as Reflected in Hymns." In *Religion in Native North America*, ed. Christopher Vecsey, 83–103. Moscow: University of Idaho Press.

McLoughlin, William G. 1994. The Cherokees and Christianity, 1794–1870: *Essays on Acculturation and Cultural Persistence*, ed. Walter H. Conser. Athens: University of Georgia Press.

McNally, Michael David. 2000a. *Ojibwe Singers: Hymns, Grief, and a Native Culture in Motion*. Religion in America. New York: Oxford University Press.

———. 2000b. "The Practice of Native American Christianity." *Church History* 69(4): 834–59.

McNeley, James K. 1981. *Holy Wind in Navajo Philosophy*. Tucson: University of Arizona Press.

Meyer, Birgit. 1998. "'Make a Complete Break with the Past': Memory and Post-Colonial Modernity in Ghanaian Pentecostalist Discourse." *Journal of Religion in Africa* 28(3): 316–49.

Milne, Derek. 2011. "Diyin God Bizaad: Tradition, Change and Pentecostal Christianity among the Navajo." PhD diss., University of California, Los Angeles.

Milne, Derek, and Wilson Howard. 2000. "Rethinking the Role of Diagnosis in Navajo Religious Healing." Theme issue: Ritual Healing in Navajo Society. *Medical Anthropology Quarterly* 14(4): 543–70.

Morrison, Kenneth. 2002. *The Solidarity of Kin: Ethnohistory, Religious Studies, and the Algonkian-French Religious Encounter*. Albany: State University of New York Press.

Mullins, Mark. 1994. "The Empire Strikes Back: Korean Pentecostal Mission to Japan." In *Charismatic Christianity as Global Culture*, ed. Karla Poewe. Columbia: University of South Carolina Press.

Murphy, Clifford R. 2014. *Yankee Twang: Country and Western Music in New England*. Urbana: University of Illinois Press.

Myers, Arnold. 1997. "How Brass Instruments Work." In *The Cambridge Companion to Brass Instruments*, ed. Trevor Herbert and John Wallace, 19–23. New York: Cambridge University Press.

Myers, Fred R. 1997. "Moving the New Anthropology of Art Beyond the Museum." Review of *Looking High and Low: Art and Cultural Identity* by Brenda Jo Bright and Liza Bakewell. *American Anthropologist* 99(1): 166–67.

Navajo Nation. 2010. *2009–2010: Comprehensive Economic Development Strategy Report*. Window Rock A Z: Division of Economic Development of the Navajo Nation.

Needham, Rodney. 1972. *Belief, Language, and Experience*. Chicago: University of Chicago Press.

Ness, Sally Ann. 1992. *Body, Movement, and Culture: Kinesthetic and Visual Symbolism in a Philippine Community*. Philadelphia: University of Pennsylvania Press.

Nevins, M. Eleanor. 2010. "The Bible in Two Keys: Traditionalism and Evangelical Christianity on the Fort Apache Reservation." *Language and Communication* 30: 19–32.

Nevins, T. J., and M. Eleanor Nevins. 2009. "We Have Always Had the Bible: Christianity and the Composition of White Mountain Apache Heritage." *Heritage Management* 2(1): 11–34.

Norton, Alice. 2012. Interview with Kimberly J. Marshall. June 15.

O'Neill, Kevin. 2010. *City of God: Christian Citizenship in Postwar Guatemala*. Berkeley: University of California Press.

Paden, William. 1988. *Religious Worlds: The Comparative Study of Religion*. Boston: Beacon Press.

Paerregaard, Karsten. 2002. "The Resonance of Fieldwork: Ethnographers, Informants and the Creation of Anthropological Knowledge." *Social Anthropology* 10(3): 319–34.

Patterson, Jan-Mikael. 2009. "Playing for Family: Fans Keep Coming for Stateline's Special Flavor." *Navajo Times*, January 29.

Pavlik, Steve. 1997. "Navajo Christianity: Historical Origins and Modern Trends." *Wicazo Ša Review* 12(2): 43–58.

Peterson, Leighton. 2006. "Technology, Ideology, and Emergent Communicative Practices among the Navajo." PhD diss., University of Texas at Austin.

Peterson, Leighton C., and Anthony K. Webster. 2013. "Speech Play and Language Ideologies in Navajo Terminology Development." *Pragmatics* 23(1): 93–116.

Pew Forum on Religion and Public Life. 2006. Spirit and Power—A 10-Country Survey of Pentecostals. Pew Research Center for Religion and Public Life, http://www.pewforum.org/2006/10/05/spirit-and-power/.

Pfister, Joel. 2004. *Individually Incorporated: Indians and the Multicultural Modern*. Durham N C: Duke University Press.

Platero, Paul R. 1992. *Navajo Head Start Language Study*. Window Rock A Z: Navajo Division of Education.

Porcello, Thomas, Louise Meintjes, Ana Maria Ochoa, and David W. Samuels. 2010. "The Reorganization of the Sensory World." *Annual Review of Anthropology* 39: 51–66.

Prucha, Francis Paul. 1962. *American Indian Policy in the Formative Years: The Indian Trade and Intercourse Acts, 1780–1834*. Cambridge: Harvard University Press.

———. 1976. *American Indian Policy in Crisis: Christian Reformers and the Indian, 1865–1900*. Norman: University of Oklahoma Press.

Rappoport, Dana. 2004. "Ritual Music and Christianization in the Toraja Highlands, Sulawesi." *Ethnomusicology* 48(3): 378–404.

Reed, Susan A. 1998. "The Politics and Poetics of Dance." Annual Review of Anthropology 27: 503–32.

Reff, Daniel T. 2005. *Plagues, Priests, and Demons: Sacred Narratives and the Rise of Christianity in the Old World and the New*. Cambridge: Cambridge University Press.

Reichard, Gladys. (1944) 1966. *Prayer: The Compulsive Word*. Seattle: University of Washington Press.

———. 1949. "The Navaho and Christianity." *American Anthropologist* 51(1): 66–71.

———. (1950) 1963. *Navaho Religion: A Study of Symbolism*. Bollingen Series. New York: Pantheon Books.

Robbins, Joel. 2003a. "What Is a Christian? Notes toward an Anthropology of Christianity." *Religion* 33(3): 191–99.

———. 2003b. "On the Paradoxes of Global Pentecostalism and the Perils of Continuity Thinking." *Religion* 33(3): 221–31.

———. 2004a. *Becoming Sinners: Christianity and Moral Torment in a Papua New Guinea Society*. Ethnographic Studies in Subjectivity. Berkeley: University of California Press.

———. 2004b. "The Globalization of Pentecostal and Charismatic Christianity." *Annual Review of Anthropology* 33: 117–43.

———. 2007. "Continuity Thinking and the Problem of Christian Culture: Belief, Time, and the Anthropology of Christianity." *Current Anthropology* 48(1): 5–38.

———. 2010. "Anthropology, Pentecostalism, and the New Paul: Conversion, Event, and Social Transformation." *South Atlantic Quarterly* 109(4): 633–52.

Robeck, Cecil M. 2007. "Pentecostalism and Mission: From Azusa Street to the Ends of the Earth." *Missiology: An International Review* 35(1): 75–92.

Royce, Anya Peterson. 1977. *The Anthropology of Dance*. Bloomington: Indiana University Press.

———. 2004. *Anthropology of the Performing Arts: Artistry, Virtuosity, and Interpretation in a Cross-Cultural Perspective*. Walnut Creek CA: AltaMira Press.

———. 2008. "Dance." In *International Encyclopedia of the Social Sciences*, 2nd edition, ed. William A. Darity Jr. London: Macmillan.

———. 2011. *Becoming an Ancestor: The Isthmus Zapotec Way of Death*. Albany: State University of New York Press.

Samuels, David. 2004. *Putting a Song on Top of It: Expression and Identity on the San Carlos Apache Reservation*. Tucson: University of Arizona Press.

———. 2006. "Bible Translation and Medicine Man Talk: Missionaries, Indexicality, and the 'Language Expert' on the San Carlos Apache Reservation." *Language in Society* 35: 529–57.

Scher, Philip. 2002. "Copyright Heritage: Preservation, Carnival and the State in Trinidad." *Anthropological Quarterly* 75(3): 453–84.

Schieffelin, Bambi, Kathryn Woolard, and Paul V. Kroskrity. 1998. *Language Ideologies: Practice and Theory*. New York: Oxford University Press.

Schwarz, Maureen Trudelle. 2001. *Navajo Lifeways: Contemporary Issues, Ancestral Knowledge*. Norman: University of Oklahoma Press.

———. 2008. *"I Choose Life": Contemporary Medical and Religious Practices in the Navajo World*. Norman: University of Oklahoma Press.

Schultz, Jack. 1999. *The Seminole Baptist Churches of Oklahoma: Maintaining a Traditional Community*. Norman: University of Oklahoma Press.

Scruggs, T.M. 2005. "(Re)Indigenization?: Post-Vatican II Catholic Ritual and 'Folk Masses' in Nicaragua." *World of Music* 47(1): 91–123.

Shay, Anthony. 2008. *Dancing across Borders: The American Fascination with Exotic Dance Forms*. Jefferson NC: McFarland and Company.

Sheets-Johnstone, Maxine. 2000. "Kinetic Tactile-Kinesthetic Bodies: Ontogenetical Foundations of Apprenticeship Learning." *Human Studies* 23: 343–70.

Shepardson, Mary. 1982. "Changing Attitudes toward Navajo Religion." In *Navajo Religion and Culture: Selected Views*. Museum of New Mexico Papers in Anthropology 17. Papers in Honor of Leland C. Wyman, ed. David M. Brugge and Charlotte J. Frisbie, 198–208. Santa Fe: Museum of New Mexico.

Shepardson, Mary, and Blodwen Hammond. 1970. *The Navajo Mountain Community: Social Organization and Kinship Terminology*. Berkeley: University of California Press.

Sherinian, Zoe. 2005. "The Indigenization of Tamil Christian Music: Musical Style and Liberation Theology." *World of Music* 47(1): 125–65.

Shorter, David Delgado. 2009. *We Will Dance Our Truth: Yaqui History in Yoeme Performances*. Lincoln: University of Nebraska Press.

Silverblatt, Irene. 1987. *Moon, Sun, and Witches: Gender Ideologies and Class in Inca and Colonial Peru*. Princeton: Princeton University Press.

Silverstein, Michael. 1979. "Language Structure and Linguistic Ideology." In *The Elements: A Parasession on Linguistic Units and Levels*, ed. Paul Clyne, William Hanks, and Carol Hofbauer, 193–247. Chicago: Chicago Linguistic Society.

Sims, Patsy. 1988. *Can Somebody Shout Amen!: Inside the Tents and Tabernacles of American Revivalists*. New York: St. Martin's Press.

Singer, Milton B. 1972. *When a Great Tradition Modernizes: An Anthropological Approach to Indian Civilization*. New York: Praeger Publishers.

Smilde, David. 2007. *Reason to Believe: Cultural Agency in Latin American Evangelicalism*. The Anthropology of Christianity. Berkeley: University of California Press.

Smith, Brian H. 1998. *Religious Politics in Latin America, Pentecostal vs. Catholic*. Titles from the Helen Kellogg Institute for International Studies. Notre Dame IN: University of Notre Dame Press.

Smith, Andrea. 2008. *Native Americans and the Christian Right: The Gendered Politics of Unlikely Alliances.* Durham NC: Duke University Press.

Smith, Linda Tuhiwai. 1999. *Decolonizing Methodologies: Research and Indigenous Peoples.* New York: Zed Books.

Smoak, Gregory. 2006. *Ghost Dances and Identity: Prophetic Religion and American Indian Ethnogenesis in the Nineteenth Century.* Berkeley: University of California Press.

Spicer, Edward. 1962. *Cycles of Conquest: The Impact of Spain, Mexico, and the United States on the Indians of the Southwest, 1533-1960.* Tucson: University of Arizona Press.

Steigenga, Timothy J. 2001. *The Politics of the Spirit: The Political Implications of Pentecostalized Religion in Costa Rica and Guatemala.* Lanham MD: Lexington Books.

Stewart, Don. 1999. *Only Believe: An Eyewitness Account of the Great Healing Revivals of the 20th Century.* Shippensburg PA: Revival Press.

———. 2008. Interview with Kimberly J. Marshall. May 15.

Stoll, David. 1990. *Is Latin America Turning Protestant?: The Politics of Evangelical Growth.* Berkeley: University of California Press.

Stoller, Paul. 1997. *Sensuous Scholarship.* Philadelphia: University of Pennsylvania Press.

Stout, Mary. 2012. *Native American Boarding Schools.* Santa Barbara: Greenwood.

Synan, Vinson. 1997. *The Holiness-Pentecostal Tradition: Charismatic Movements in the Twentieth Century.* Grand Rapids MI: Eardmans.

Szasz, Margaret C. 1999. *Education and the American Indian.* Albuquerque: University of New Mexico Press.

Szasz, Margaret C., and Carmelita Ryan. 1988. "American Indian Education." In *Handbook of North American Indians*, vol. 4: *History of Indian-White Relations*, ed.Wilcomb E. Washburn, 284-300. Washington DC: Smithsonian Institution Press.

Tapahonso, Luci. 1993. *Sáanii Dahataał: The Women Are Singing.* Tucson: University of Arizona Press.

———. 1997. *Blue Horses Rush In: Poems and Stories.* Tucson: University of Arizona Press.

Tarango, Angela. 2014. *Choosing the Jesus Way: American Indian Pentecostals and the Fight for the Indigenous Principle.* Chapel Hill: University of North Carolina Press.

Taussig, Michael. 1980. *The Devil and Commodity Fetishism in Latin America.* Chapel Hill: University of North Carolina Press.

Tedlock, Dennis. 1983. *The Spoken Word and the Work of Interpretation.* Philadelphia: University of Pennsylvania Press.

Tinker, George E. 1993. *Missionary Conquest: The Gospel and Native American Cultural Genocide.* Minneapolis: Fortress Press.

Titon, Jeff T. 1978. "Some Recent Pentecostal Revivals: A Report in Words and Photographs." *Georgia Review* 32(3): 579-606.

———.1988. *Powerhouse for God: Speech, Chant, and Song in an Appalachian Baptist Church*. Austin: University of Texas Press.

Trafzer, Clifford E., Jean A. Keller, and Lorene Sisquoc. 2006. *Boarding School Blues: Revisiting American Indian Educational Experiences*. Lincoln: University of Nebraska Press.

Treat, James. 1996. *Native and Christian: Indigenous Voices on Religious Identity in the United States and Canada*. New York: Routledge.

Turino, Thomas. 2008. *Music as Social Life: The Politics of Participation*. Chicago Studies in Ethnomusicology. Chicago: University of Chicago Press.

Vecsey, Christopher. 1990. *Religion in Native North America*. Moscow: University of Idaho Press.

———. 1991. *Imagine Ourselves Richly: Mythic Narratives of North American Indians*. New York: Harper Collins.

———. 1997. *The Paths of Kateri's Kin*. Notre Dame IN: University of Notre Dame Press.

Wagner, Mariah. 2008. Interview with Kimberly J. Marshall. June 6.

Wallace, Anthony F. C. 1969. *The Death and Rebirth of the Seneca*. New York: Random House.

Warner, Michael J. 1973. "The Fertile Ground: The Beginnings of Protestant Missionary Work with the Navajos, 1852–1890." In *Changing Ways of Southwestern Indians, ed.* Albert H. Schroeder, 189–202. Glorieta NM: Rio Grande Press.

Warrington, Keith. 2008. *Pentecostal Theology: A Theology of Encounter*. New York: T & T Clark.

Warrior, Robert Allen. 1994. *Tribal Secrets: Recovering American Indian Intellectual Traditions*. Minneapolis: University of Minnesota Press.

Weaver, Jace. 1998. *Native American Religious Identity: Unforgotten Gods*. New York: Orbis Books.

Webster, Anthony K. 2009. *Explorations in Navajo Poetry and Poetics*. Albuquerque: University of New Mexico Press.

Werito, Vincent. 2014. "Understanding Hózhǫ́ to Achieve Critical Consciousness: A Contemporary Diné Interpretation of the Philosophical Principles of Hózhǫ́." In *Diné Perspectives: Revitalizing and Reclaiming Navajo Thought*, ed. Lloyd L. Lee, 25–38. Tucson: University of Arizona Press.

Werner, Oswald, Allen Manning, and Kenneth Begishe. 1983. "A Taconomic View of the Traditional Navajo Universe." In *Handbook of North American Indians*, vol. 10: *Southwest*, ed. Alfonso Ortiz, 579–91. Washington DC: Smithsonian Institution Press.

Westman, Clinton. 2010a. "Pentecostalism among Canadian Aboriginal People: A Political Movement?" In *A Liberating Spirit: Pentecostals and Social Action in North America*, ed. Michael Wilkinson and Steven Studebaker, 85–112. Eugene OR: Pickwick Publications.

———. 2010b. Cree Christian Culture: Pentecostalism and Culture in Northern Alberta. Unpublished conference paper, American Anthropological

Association, discussant S. Poirier, Département d'anthropologie, Université Laval.

———. 2013. "Pentecostalism and Indigenous Culture in Northern North America." *Anthropologica* (55):141–56.

Whiteley, Peter Michael. 1992. "Burning Culture: Auto-da-fé at Orayvi." *History and Anthropology* 6(1):46–85.

Wiegele, Katharine. 2005. *Investing in Miracles: El Shaddai and the Transformation of Popular Catholicism in the Philippines*. Honolulu: University of Hawaii Press.

Wikan, Unni. 2013. *Resonance: Beyond the Words*. Chicago: University of Chicago Press.

Wilk, Richard. 1995. "Learning to Be Local in Belize: Global Systems of Common Difference." In *Worlds Apart: Modernity through the Prism of the Local*, ed. Daniel Miller, 110–33. New York: Routledge.

Wilkins, David E., and K. Tsianina Lomawaima. 2001. *Uneven Ground: American Indian Sovereignty and Federal Law*. Norman: University of Oklahoma Press.

Witherspoon, Gary. 1974. "The Central Concepts in Navajo World View (I)." *Linguistics* H9: 41–59.

———. 1977. *Language and Art in the Navajo Universe*. Ann Arbor: University of Michigan Press.

Womack, Craig. 1999. *Red on Red: Native American Literary Separatism*. Minneapolis: University of Minnesota Press.

Wood, John. 1982. "Western Navajo Religious Affiliations." In *Navajo Religion and Culture: Selected Views*. Museum of New Mexico Papers in Anthropology 17. Papers in Honor of Leland C. Wyman, ed. David M. Brugge and Charlotte J. Frisbie, 176–86. Santa Fe: Museum of New Mexico.

Wyman, Leland. 1970. *Blessingway*. Tucson: University of Arizona Press.

———. 1975. *The Mountainway of the Navajo*. Tucson: University of Arizona Press.

———. 1983. "Navajo Ceremonial System." In *Handbook of North American Indians*, vol. 10: *Southwest*, ed. A. Ortiz, 536–57. Washington DC: Smithsonian Institution Press.

Yazzie, Alfred W. 1984. *Navajo Oral Tradition*, vol. 3. Rough Rock AZ: Rough Rock Demonstration School.

Yazzie, Amanda. 2008. Interview with Kimberly J. Marshall. July 14.

Yazzie, Raymond. 2008. Interview by Kimberly J. Marshall. July 3.

Yazzie, Rose. 2008. Interview with Kimberly J. Marshall. June 27.

Young, Robert W. 1948. "What's in a Name?" *El Palacio* 55(3): 86–88.

———. 1961. *The Navajo Yearbook: 1951–1961, A Decade of Progress*. Window Rock AZ: Navajo Agency.

Young, Robert, and William Morgan. 1980. *The Navajo Language: A Grammar and Colloquial Dictionary*. Albuquerque: University of New Mexico Press.

Zolbrod, Paul G. 1984. *Diné Bahane': The Navajo Creation Story*. Albuquerque: University of New Mexico Press.

assimilation: by Christian conversion, 3–6, 42–46, 59, 113, 129, 197n6, 205n11; by language, 85; by music, 103; and resonant rupture, 15. *See also* colonialism

Austin, J. L., 90, 210n29

autonomy. *See* sovereignty

Azusa Street Revival, 184

Bahr, Donald, 199n24

Baldridge, Terry, 92, 210n26, 210n30

baptism, 76, 201n11

Baptists, 27, 93–94

Bates, T. Eric, 220n9

Bauman, Richard, 13, 94

béeso naa'ii nííh. See offerings

Begay, Andrew, 90

Begay, Wallace, *33*, *52*; on anointing, 75–76, 79, 162–67; on biblical tribes, 220n13; charisma of, 32–33, 201n9; clothing of, 192, 220n12; and dance, 134–35; family of, 36, 202n19; on global Pentecostalism, 194; on Holy Spirit, 138, 139, 161–62; and jish burning, 72; languages of, 83, 85, 86; location of church of, 112; as missionary, 187, 188, 192, *193*; and music, 63, 102, 114–25, 138; and Negiel Bigpond, 208n44; as pastor, 2, 202n13; on radio, 31; research at church of, 33–41, 51–53, 92–93; at tent revivals, 27, 131, 145–47, 176–78, 181, 182, 201n5

Benin, West Africa, 187, 188, 192, *193*

Bible: on anointing, 138, 167; at boarding schools, 4; on evil spirits, 1, 78; in healing, 171–73; and music, 89, 115, 126; in Navajo language, 83; in Oodlání movement, 2, 187, 188, 208n42; reading of, 34, 92; sermons on, 29, 201nn8–9; story of Pentecost in, 162–63; on talents, 124, 213n25; tribes of, 195, 220n13

Bigpond, Negiel (Yuchi), 29, 63, 188, 192, 194–95, 208n44, 220nn12–13

bikéé anáshdááh, 104–5, 203n32

biyee, 66. *See also* offerings; *yeel*

Blackfeet (people), 63, 220n9

Blackhorse, Taft, Jr., 97

blacks, 103, 116, 129

Blanca Peak, 9, 47. *See also* four sacred mountains

Blanchard, Kendall, 60, 199n17, 205n12

blessings, 67, 69, 70, 164, 165, 167, 207n30, 217n15

Blessingway ceremony, 47

boarding schools: assimilation through, 3–4, 43, 44, 46, 202n25, 205n11; avoidance of, 111–12; and influence on Oodlání, 50, 58; socioeconomic effects of, 186

Boas, Franz, 12, 16, 213n7

bodies: contact with dead, 215n32; and healing, 155–62, 178, 216n3; techniques of, 133, 199n23, 213nn5–6

Bourdieu, Pierre, 110, 199nn22–23, 213n5

Branham, William, 62, 205n16, 218n24

Brazil, 185, 212n19, 219n2, 219n4

Brethren of Christ, 89

Briggs, Charles, 203n40

Brink, Rev. L. P., 209n15

Brugge, David, 198n7

Bryant, Elizabeth, 127

Bull, Cynthia, 137

Bureau of Indian Affairs, 39

Burkinshaw, Robert, 220n9

Bydone, Victoria, 157, 158, 161, 167, 217n12

Bylas AZ, 211n5

camp meetings, 34, 53, 92–93. *See also* tent revivals

Canyon Records, 105

Carlisle Indian Industrial School, 4

Casanova, José, 78, 199–200n28

Catholicism: and charismatic worship, 61, 219n2, 219n5; conversions to, 42; devil in, 198n15; Oodlání view of, 44, 203n28; popularity of, 183, 184, 197n2; prayer in, 67. *See also* Franciscans; Jesuits

Cattelino, Jessica, 190–91

ceremonial practitioners: ceremonies of, 88, 148, 155, 216n2; and Christianity, 7, 39, 129, 195; diagnostics in, 216n38, 218n22; and social class, 110, 113

ceremonies: and dancing in the spirit, 130, 144–45, 150; joy of Native, 59, 60,

64–66; knowledge of, 110; language of, 82–83, 90–92, 97–98; music at, 87–89; Navajo word for, 88, 210n23; offerings in, 70; philosophy of, 47–49, 142–43, 148; prayer in, 66–68, 206n29, 207n30; rejection of Navajo, 77; study of, 47, 155, 204n42, 206n20, 210n24; suppression of Native, 43. See also *Diné Binahagha'*; ritual; singing; traditionalism

Changing Woman, 142, 148, 169, 215n29

chants. *See* ceremonies

chapter house bands: formation of, 105, 128; performances of, 105-7, 114–16, 212n20, 212n22; sound of, 106, 113, 211n7, 211n10; symbolism of, 109–10. *See also* musicians

charismatic worship: and anointing, 75–76, 138, 140, 208n42; at church services, 34, 202n15; and deprivation theory, 185–86; history of, 43–44, 61–63, 205n14, 205–6n18; in Pentecostalism, 2, 49, 138, 163, 184–85, 202n24, 214n21, 219n2, 219n5. *See also* dancing in the spirit; tent revivals

Cherokee (people), 209n5

Chestnut, Andrew, 185, 186

ch'įįdii, 143–49, 215nn31–32, 216n41. *See also* ghosts

children, 43, 146–47, 215n31. *See also* girls

Chilkat dancing, 71

Chinle AZ, 107, 207–8n39

Chinle Galileans, 101, 105-9, 127–28, 211–12n11, 212n12

Christianity: and anointing, 75–76, 138; assimilation through, 3–6, 42–46, 59, 129, 197n6, 205n11; criticism of American, 181; and destruction of sacred objects, 71, 74; healing in, 155, 158, 163–66, 169–74, 177, 178, 201n11, 216–17n4; and language ideologies, 83, 173, 209n5, 218n26; music of, 82–83, 86, 90, 98–99, 103-9, 114–17, 122, 127–28, 208n4, 209nn15–16; Natives' adaptation of, 4–9, 16–18, 44, 56–64, 86–88, 130, 145–49, 155, 188–89, 198n12, 198nn14–15, 199n16, 209n14,

213n1, 216–17n4, 220nn9–10; in Oodláni movement, 2–3, 46–56, 145, 197n2, 202n24; prayer in, 67, 70; in Shiprock, 39; socioeconomic effects of, 16–17, 111–13, 183–84, 212n15; spiritual warfare in, 77–78, 87, 96, 116, 145, 171–73, 198n15, 199–200n28, 208nn44–45, 212–13nn22–23; study of, 2–6, 41, 45, 57–61, 184–85, 197n2, 198n12, 199n17, 199–200n28, 202n24, 203n33, 203n35, 204n3, 205n14; trinity in, 140. *See also specific denominations*

Christian Reformed Church, 44, 76, 209n15

church(es): of A. A. Allen, 62–63; anointing oil in, 165; Christian assimilation through, 3, 43, 202n25; in Christian network, 111; as family, 156–62, 170; fund-raising for, 36, 66; musicians at, 116–17, 122–24, 126; and Oodláni movement, 2, 44, 50, 58–64, 79, 156–57, 203n31, 205n12, 205–6n18; of Pastor Wallace, 33–41, 51–53, 92–93, 112, 115, 146–47, 176–77. *See also* ministries

Church of God in Christ, 27, 219n2

Church of Jesus Christ of Latter Day Saints. *See* Mormons

church services: Holy Spirit at, 76; language of, 83, 86; music at, 93–94, 107; offerings during, 69; participation in, 60, 205n12; of Pastor Wallace, 33–41

Chuska Mountains, 34

"Civilization" Act (1819), 197n6

clans, 36, 50, 111, 202n19, 202n23, 210n32. *See also* kinship structures

Clatterbuck, Mark, 220n9

"Clingin' to a Savin' Hand," 101, 107, 109, 211–12n11

clothing, 43, 46, 48, 109, 150, 192–94, 220n12

Cobb, Amanda, 190

Coe, Jack, 205n16

colonialism: and destruction of sacred objects, 71; and history of Christianity, 42–46, 49; in music, 104; and religious movements, 58, 187, 204–5n9; researchers' sensitivity to, 42, 50; and

colonialism (*continued*)
SNBH, 47–48; socioeconomic effects of, 16–17, 186. *See also* assimilation

Colorado, 81, 111–12, 211n4

Comaroff, Jean and John, 198n12

communities: "border," 35, 112, 212n16; dance in, 131–32, 136–39, 214n19; and healing rituals, 158–64, 173–77, 217n12; networks of Navajo, 35, 202n17; participant observers in, 23, 42, 50–53; public rituals of, 64–66, 88

community identity: in cultural practices, 11–14, 46–49; in music, 93, 104–6, 211n5; in Native Christianity, 4, 170; in Oodlání movement, 56, 122, 127; and Pentecostalism, 7, 182, 184, 187–89, 220n11; researchers' sensitivity to, 42, 50; in social class, 110–11; sovereignty through, 189–92; at tent revivals, 28, 78–79, 201n7. *See also* kinship structures

continuity: of country music, 102–5, 127–28; and dance, 129–30; and language ideologies, 83, 84; in Oodlání movement, 2–6, 144–49, 182, 192–96, 209–10n20; of rituals, 57–60, 65–79, 155–56, 163–67, 171, 177–79; and rupture with culture, 6–9, 13–20, 96, 99–100, 195, 199nn16–17, 199n24, 199–200n28, 200n29; of tent revivals, 55–56, 59, 79. *See also* resonant rupture

conversion: as cultural betrayal, 46; and healing, 154, 170–77; and jish burning, 74, 207n37, 207–8n39; reasons for, 16–18, 44–45, 113, 183–87, 191, 192; rebirth through, 2, 9; and rupture with culture, 6–8, 19, 71–72, 87, 96–99, 111–12, 130, 150, 155, 207n37, 210n34, 212n15, 217n5; "soft," 2–3

Coplan, David, 137

corn pollen, 142. See also *tádídíín*

"corn-pollen path." See *Sa'ąh Naagháí Bik'eh Hózhǫ́ǫ́n* (SNBH); sunwise path teachings; *tádídíín*

cowboy culture, 102–6, 109, 115, 122, 127–28, 194, 212n13

Cree (people), 7, 99, 220n9

Creek (people), 220n12

Crow (people), 188, 220n9

Crownpoint NM, 207–8n39

crying, 26, 30, 39, 64, 126, 200–201n2

Csordas, Thomas, 46, 154, 169–71, 175, 186, 216–17n4, 219n31

cultural genocide, 3–4, 197n6

cultural revitalization. *See* traditionalism: turn toward

culture: boundaries of, 77–78, 114–15, 122, 127; and Christianity, 4–9, 59, 130, 182–83, 205n11; suppression of Native, 43; expressive forms of, 9–15, 18, 96–100, 103, 133–37, 151, 177–79, 192–95; knowledge of, 58, 157, 179, 204–5nn8–9; and language, 83–90. *See also* traditionalism

Current Anthropology, 133

dancing: at church services, 34, 81; to country music, 102, 106, 114–16, 124, 127, 128, 212n20; and *Háálá Ayóo Diyin*, 94; in Pentecostalism, 2, 19–20; in public ceremonies, 64–65, 79, 87, 206n20, 206n25; regalia of Chilkat, 71, 207n36; scholarship on, 133–36, 213nn7–10, 214n12; at tent revivals, 13, 22, 26–32, 30, 64, 77, 79. *See also* anointing; expressive forms

dancing in the spirit: aesthetics of, 131–41, 215n25; continuity of, 146, 151; description of, 129–30; mocking of, 117; power of, 75, 130, 138, 161–62; protection while, 150, 156, 160, 161, 216n42; resonant rupture of, 147–50; technique of, 134–37, 214nn13–15. *See also* charismatic worship; slain in the spirit

day, parts of, 47. *See also* sunwise path teachings

death, 17, 62, 143, 149, 174, 186, 200n31, 215nn31–32. *See also* funerary practices

deities: categories of Navajo, 215n29; communication with, 92, 130; gifts to, 69–70; lessons from, 142, 215n28; as part of religion, 49. *See also* nonhuman actors

demons: and dance, 130, 141; exorcism

Goldstein, Kenneth, 137
gourd rattles, 155, 178
Graham, Billy, 194
Grant Peace Policy, 197n6, 202n25

Háálá Ayóo Diyin: composition of, 93–94; history of, 81–83; performance of, 92–94; popularity of, 19, 83, 93, 98–99; in public ceremony, 87; and resonant rupture, 93–100. *See also* singing
habitus, 199n22, 213n5
Haida (people), 6, 71
Haile, Berard, 204n42, 206n20, 210n37, 215n27, 217n9
Hallowell, Irving, 57, 215n26
Hamera, Judith, 132, 133, 213n4
Handman, Courtney, 219n5
Handsome Lake Religion, 185–86
Harding, Susan, 17, 173, 186, 218n26
Harkin, Michael, 17, 198n11
Harrell, David, 61–62, 205n14
Harris, Samuel (San Carlos Apache), 63
Harvest Glory, 212n12
hatáál, 66
hataałii. See ceremonial practitioners
healing: and Enemy Way ceremony, 64, 65; history of American, 60–63, 205n14; with jish bundles, 72–75; language of, 82, 91–92, 98, 159–60, 167–77, 218n22, 218n24; material culture of, 162–67, 178, 217–18n20; of Mr. Joe Sr., 39; and music, 122, 126, 127, 155, 177–78, 216n2; in Oodláni movement, 29, 154–65, 217n10, 217n12; in Pentecostalism, 2, 20, 96, 138, 148, 151, 158–61, 182, 185, 194, 195; philosophy of, 47, 48, 151; power of, 75, 87; prayer in, 66–67; study of Navajo, 46, 50, 154–58, 161, 216–17n4; at tent revivals, 13, 22, 26, 29, 29–31, 43–44, 63, 153–54, 159–62, 167–68, 192, 201n11, 217n11; in traditional culture, 88–89, 142–43, 148, 154–59, 161–71, 174, 177–78, 216–17n4, 216n38, 217n8, 218n28, 219n31. *See also* illness; patients
Healing Revival, 60–63, 205n14
healthcare, 17, 200n31, 203n32, 205n11
heaven, 14, 166

hell, 14, 45, 140, 149, 171–72. *See also* Devil
hero twins, 142
Herskovits, Melville, 214n15
Hesperus Mountain, 10. *See also* four sacred mountains
history, social: in country gospel music, 104–10; and expressive forms, 11–12, 16, 104; and language, 85–86; of Oodláni, 111–12; and resonant rupture, 18, 78–79, 96–97; sovereignty through, 189, 190; value of oral, 48
Hodge, William, 60, 199n17
hogans, 9, 88, 110, 164. *See also* homes, Diné
holiness, 50, 65, 88, 89, 165, 166, 206n26
"Holiness" movement, American, 21–22, 184
Holy People: creation myth of, 91; and dance, 87, 145; in Diné culture, 10; healing by, 98, 142–49, 158, 164, 174; as messengers, 68, 207n32; purpose of, 215n29
Holy Spirit: at church services, 34; in dance, 129, 131, 137–39, 139, 141, 148; healing by, 159, 161, 167, 178; offerings to, 70; in Oodláni movement, 2, 146–50, 194; as part of trinity, 139–40; power of, 75–76, 140; at tent revivals, 26–31, 64, 156, 201n5, 201n11. *See also* anointing; *Níłch'i Diyini*; nonhuman actors; slain in the spirit
Holy Wind. *See* Holy Spirit; *Níłch'i Diyini*
homes, Diné, 9, 11. *See also* hogans
Hopi (people), 188, 205–6n18
House, Deborah, 8, 44, 84, 209n9
Howard, Wilson, 174, 218n22
hózhó: ceremonies for, 88–92, 142, 148; and cultural identity, 49; and *Háálá Ayóo Diyin*, 98; in healing, 157, 169–70; in Oodláni movement, 20, 196
humility. *See* pride
Hwéeldí (Fort Sumner), 42–43
hymns: and country gospel music, 103, 211–12n11; Natives' singing of, 4, 86, 101; in Navajo language, 83, 86, 89, 92, 101, 209nn14–15, 210n30; at tent revivals, 27. *See also* music; singing

musicians (*continued*)
in healing rituals, 153–54; melodic
strategies of, 89–90, 99, 105, 106;
payment of, 69; status of, 75, 102, 117,
122–28; at tent revivals, 28, 63. *See also*
chapter house bands; pride; vessels
Myers, Arnold, 137, 214n19
"My God Is a Good God," 134–35
mythology, 48, 64, 66, 70, 91–92, 142–
44, 158

náá'ii niih. See offerings
Naat'áanii Nez. See Shiprock NM
nadir, 9–10, 14. *See also* directions,
cardinal
nahatá, 9, 11, 47. *See also* sunwise path
teachings
National Museum of the American
Indian, 198n13
Native American Church (NAC): "God"
in, 214–15n23; healing in, 154–58, 163,
164, 169–71, 174, 177, 178, 216n2, 216–
17n4, 217n8; music of, 122; prayer in,
70; turn toward, 17, 186, 200n32
Native Americans: agency of, 4–7, 186;
charismatic worship among, 63, 205–
6n18; as evangelists, 63, 194–95; language ideologies of, 83, 91, 209n5;
musical aesthetics of, 99; nationalism
of, 17; neo-Pentecostalism among,
188–89, 220n9; religious freedom of,
3, 197n6; scholarship of, 49, 217n9;
sovereignty of, 189–90
Native networks, 36, 47, 53, 63, 111, 184,
187–89, 192, 194, 202n17. *See also*
evangelists
natural world, 7, 47, 48, 69, 142, 143,
146–47, 215n28, 215n29
"Navaho Hymnody," 19, 89
Navajo (people): Christian history of,
42–46, 62–63; cooperation among,
104–5, 158; cross-gender socialization
of, 64–65, 114–16; cultural identity of,
46–49, 58, 82–89, 96–97, 102–13, 122,
127–28, 148, 150, 154, 157, 204–5nn8–9,
209n8, 211n5, 214n20; historical epistemology of, 58, 190, 204n8; mental
ability of, 217n18; names of, 2, 197n1;

Oodláni movement among, 2, 44–
45, 182–83, 186–89, 192–96; religious
pluralism of, 87, 128, 130, 209n19;
research on, 41, 49–53, 215n27, 218n22;
as translators, 55, 204n1, 208n42
Navajo Country Gospel (LP), 211–12n11
"Navajo Healing Project," 216–17n4
Navajo Housing Authority, 112
Navajo language: on anointing, 138,
163–66, 178, 217n15; cultural identity through, 46, 83–90, 96–97, 111,
113, 150, 209n6, 209nn8–9, 209n17;
and dance, 144–45; fluency in, 84,
209n10; God and Holy Spirit in, 140,
214–15n23; interviews in, 39–41; performative force of, 90–92; preaching
in, 2, 21, 55, 63, 117–21, 204n1; punishment for using, 43; reciprocity in,
207n35; "religion" in, 58, 204nn6–7;
revitalization of, 44, 48; and SNBH,
157; songs in, 19, 81–83, 86–93, 97–
101, 113, 209n15, 210n30; testifying in,
168. *See also* languages
Navajo Medicine Bundles or Jish (Frisbie), 73
Navajo Medicine Men's Association, 71,
73, 74
Navajo Nation: boarding schools in,
4; conducting research in, 51–52,
206n20, 210n24, 215n27, 216–17n4;
cowboy culture in, 109–10; cultural
revitalization in, 47; dancing in, 129;
description of, 34–36; language of, 84–
85, 209n10; maps of, 10, 35; minority status in, 48, 49; music in, 93–94,
101–6; outlawing of jish burning by,
19, 56, 71, 73; tent revivals in, 22–31,
63, 78–79. *See also* Navajo Reservation
Navajo Nation Office for Historic Preservation, 51
Navajo Reservation: border communities of, 35, 112, 212n16; country dances
on, 102, 106; cowboy culture on,
109; socioeconomic conditions on,
4, 16–17, 94, 110–13; tent revivals on,
63, 107, 108. *See also* Navajo Nation;
reservations
Navajo Sundowners, 211n10

Navajo Way. See *Sa'ąh Naagháí Bik'eh Hózhǫ́ǫ́n* (SNBH); sunwise path teachings

Nazarenes, Navajo, 60

Needham, Rodney, 204n3

neo-Pentecostalism: charismatic worship in, 63, 138, 214n21, 219n2; concept of God in, 198n15; in Ghana, 210n34; global network of, 182–87; growth of, 9, 55–56, 61, 184–89, 220n9; healing in, 29; prayer in, 67; as religion, 50; research on, 53, 60, 94–96, 130; supernatural powers in, 130, 213n1. See also charismatic worship; Christianity; global Pentecostalism; Oodlání movement

Nevins, M. E., 200n29, 220n9

New Mexico: border communities in, 212n16; Brethren of Christ mission in, 89; jish burning in, 207–8n39; Navajo Nation in, 34–35; Oodlání movement in, 2, 9; radio in, 211n4; revivals in, 122, 125. See also Farmington NM; Shiprock NM

Night Way, 87, 206n20

Nihookáá Dine'é. See Earth Surface People

Níłch'i Diyini, 138, 140–41, 143–50, 194. See also Holy Spirit

nitsáhákees, 9, 11, 47. See also sunwise path teachings

nizhóní, 88, 206n26. See also aesthetics

Nomee, Roger (Crow), 63

nonhuman actors: and dance, 141, 148, 161; and offerings, 69–70, 164; in Oodlání movement, 19–20, 130–31, 144–51, 194, 195; and prayer, 68, 92; in traditional religion, 1, 141–44, 148–50, 217n18. See also deities; Holy Spirit; supernatural power

north (direction), 9, 143, 149. See also directions, cardinal

Northern Cree (people), 7. See also Cree (people)

Northern Navajo Fair, 87

Norton, Alice, 92, 94, 98, 141

ntł'iz, 69

offerings: ritual of, 56, 59, 66, 68–72, 77, 92; at tent revivals, 26, 28, 59, 201n7

Ojibwe (people), 209n14

Oklahoma, 63, 104, 188, 208n44, 209n5, 220n12. See also Native networks

Oodlání movement: characteristics of, 2, 5–6, 129, 189; cultural identity in, 46–49, 58, 82–90, 96, 102, 104, 110, 113, 127–28, 148, 150; cultural rupture in, 15–20, 58, 59, 66–74, 98–102, 111–22, 128–31, 145–51, 155–56, 159, 163–67, 171, 177–79, 195–96, 199n24, 200n32, 204–5nn8–9, 207n37; growth of, 2, 44–45, 58–59, 182–89, 197n2; life within, 36–41, 83; localization of, 77–78; origins of, 43–44; research on, 45, 50–53, 203n33; sovereignty through, 50, 189; on spiritual warfare, 77, 208nn44–45. See also Christianity; neo-Pentecostalism

pan-Indian identity, 99, 158, 220n12

pastoralism, 50, 85, 86

pastors: authority of Oodlání, 2, 75, 157, 187–88, 203n31, 208n42, 208n44; and dance, 134; and destruction of sacred objects, 71–74, 78; musical talent of, 126, 127; names for, 202n13; in Native Christianity, 4, 202n17; and offerings, 69, 70; and opposition to traditionalism, 5–6, 44, 87, 90, 210n26; in Shiprock, 35, 36; at tent revivals, 21–22, 26–28, 145. See also evangelists; missionaries; preaching

patients, 64, 67, 70, 88, 142, 153–55, 158, 164, 168–71, 175, 177, 218n22. See also healing

Pavlik, Steve, 198n14

pedagogy, 47. See also education

Peirce, Charles Sanders, 199n20

Pentecost, 162. See also Bible

Pentecostal Churches: in Appalachia, 27; classical denominations of, 44, 219n2; as distinct from charismatic churches, 184, 214n21, 219n2, 219n5; as distinct from neo-Pentecostalism, 184, 214n21; history of theology

portability of, 55, 57, 186; rejection of Navajo, 45, 48, 49, 98–99; scholarship on Native, 2–8, 17, 50, 57–59, 66, 184–87, 197n2, 200n32, 204nn3–4, 204nn6–8, 205n10, 206n29, 207n30. See also *Diné Binahagha'*; sunwise path teachings; traditionalism

religious movements, Navajo, 61–63, 200–201n2

religious paraphernalia, 71–75, 207nn36–37. See also jish bundles

religious relativism, 5, 42, 45, 203n35

"Renewalists," 219n2

researchers. See ethnographic fieldwork

reservations, 104, 106, 197n6. See also Navajo Reservation

resonance, 15–16, 18, 94–96, 199n25, 199n27; in fieldwork, 199nn25, 27; points of, 16, 18, 97–99, 103, 151, 178, 200n30

resonant rupture: and dance, 130–31, 147–51; description of, 8–9, 15–18, 199n24, 199n27, 200n30, 217n5; of *Háálá Ayóo Diyin*, 93–100; knowledge of, 179; in language, 82–83, 174–77; and music, 102, 103, 124, 128; in Oodlání movement, 19–20, 78, 79, 182, 189; in rituals, 56–57, 71–72, 155–69, 177–79, 219n31; as sovereignty, 192–96. See also continuity; rupture

resurrection, 62

revivals. See camp meetings; tent revivals

"rez." See Jáán

ritual: continuity of, 57–60, 65, 66, 71, 205n10; dance in, 133; for healing, 154–55, 158, 163, 169, 177–79; for *hózhǫ́*, 88–89; joy of, 59–66; language of, 90, 91; in Oodlání movement, 22, 59, 194, 195; of prayer, 56, 59, 66–68; public vs. private, 56–57, 64–65, 72, 73, 78, 79, 206n20; rupture through, 56–59, 66–79; sacred and secular, 65–66, 70, 78–79, 88; study of, 18–19; at tent revivals, 27–30, 55–58; terminology of, 58, 204nn6–7. See also ceremonies; tent revivals; traditionalism

Robbins, Joel, 6, 56, 77–79, 186, 199n17, 209–10n20, 210n34, 219n5

Roberts, Oral, 62, 205n16, 218n24

Royce, Anya Peterson, 133, 134, 213n6, 213n10

rugs, Navajo, 52

rupture: through rituals, 56–59, 66–75, 77–79; with traditionalism, 2–9, 13–16, 87–88, 199–200n28, 200n29. See also resonant rupture

Saʼąh Naagháí Bikʼeh Hózhǫ́ǫ́n (SNBH): aesthetics in, 137, 214n20; and cardinal directions, 10; and healing, 157–59, 162, 169–71, 177, 217n8; reinterpretation of, 182, 195; and religion, 58, 142–44, 203n32; scholarship on, 47–48, 217n9; and significance to Diné, 9–11. See also *Diné Binahagha'*; everyday life

Salvation Army, 27

Samuels, David, 11–12, 13, 46, 104, 105, 199n24, 208n3, 211n5

San Carlos Apache Indians, 104, 105, 205–6n18, 208n3, 209n5, 211n5

San Francisco Peaks, 10. See also four sacred mountains

San Juan College, 9, 40–41. See also education

"Scarlet Purple Robe," 108–9

Scates, David, 60

Scher, Philip, 204–5n9

Schwartz, Maureen, 67

seasons, 47. See also sunwise path teachings

Second Great Awakening, 22

Seminole (people), 190–91

Seneca (people), 186

sermons. See preaching

shamanism: ceremonies of, 88, 148, 155, 216n2; and Christianity, 7, 39, 129, 195; diagnostics in, 216n38, 218n22; and social class, 110, 113. See also ceremonial practitioners

sheep camps, 104, 110–12. See also livestock

Shiprock Historical Society, 39

Shiprock NM: as border community,

Universal Church of the Kingdom of God, 219n2
uranium mining, 186
Urapmin Pentecostal community, 210n34
U.S. government, 3, 42–43, 58, 189, 197n6, 202n25. *See also* United States
Ute (people), 188

Vacation Bible Study, 31
Vecsey, Christopher, 198n12
vessels, 126, 127, 217n12
The Voice of Healing, 205n16

Wagner, David "Boots," 63
Wagner, Mariah, 125
Wallace, Anthony F. C., 185–86
Warrington, Keith, 140
WBAP radio, 109
Weaver, Jace, 198n12
Weber, Max, 75
Webster, Anthony K., 96, 209n7, 209n17
Werito, Vincent, 203n32
west (direction), 9, 10. *See also* directions, cardinal
Westman, Clinton, 7, 220n9
Where Is My Castle (Smith album), 109
Whiteley, Peter Michael, 74–75, 207n37
whites, 46, 192, 198n14, 202n14, 220n14. *See also* Anglos

wind. See *Nílch'i Diyini*
Window Rock AZ, 73, 105–6, 207–8n39, 212n16
Wingate Valley Boys, 105, 106
witches, 2–3, 44, 74, 96, 130, 197n5, 204n8. *See also* evil
Witherspoon, Gary, 88, 90–92, 97, 170, 203n41, 214n20, 216n1, 217n9
Womack, Craig (Creek, Cherokee), 190
women, 34, *38*, 39, 64, 146–47
"Word of Faith." *See* Prosperity Gospel
Wyman, Leland, 164, 166, 204n42, 210n37, 215n27, 217n9, 217n18

Yazzie, Amanda, 60–61, 63–64, 111–13
Yazzie, Billie, 167–68, 172–75, 218n25, 218n27, 218–19n29
Yazzie, Luke, 107
Yazzie, Raymond, 93, 94, 97, 99
Yazzie, Rose, 122, 124, 139, 151, 160
Yazzie, Russell, 94
yeel, 69–70. *See also* offerings
Ye'ii Bi Chei (Ye'ii bichii) dancing, 87, 206n20
yisjj', 164, 166, 217n15
Young, Robert, 113, 204n6

zenith, 9–10, 14, 182. *See also* directions, cardinal

CPSIA information can be obtained
at www.ICGtesting.com
Printed in the USA
LVOW10*1452100517
534021LV00006B/53/P